The Female Tragic Hero
in English Renaissance Drama

The Female Tragic Hero
in English Renaissance Drama

Edited by
Naomi Conn Liebler

palgrave

THE FEMALE TRAGIC HERO IN ENGLISH RENAISSANCE DRAMA
© Naomi Conn Liebler, 2002

First published 2002 by PALGRAVE™
175 Fifth Avenue, New York, N.Y.10010 and
Houndmills, Basingstoke, Hampshire RG21 6XS.
Companies and representatives throughout the world.

PALGRAVE is the new global publishing imprint of St. Martin's Press LLC Scholarly and Reference Division and Palgrave Publishers Ltd (formerly Macmillan Press Ltd).

ISBN 0–312–22059–6 hardback

Library of Congress Cataloging-in-Publication Data
The female tragic hero in English Renaissance drama / edited by Naomi Conn Liebler.
   p.   cm.
   Includes bibliographical references and index.
   ISBN 0–312–22059–6
   1. English drama (Tragedy)—History and criticism.   2. Heroines in literature.   3. English drama—Early modern and Elizabethan, 1500–1600—History and criticism.   4. Women and literature—England—History—16th century.   5. Women and literature—England—History—17th century.   6. English drama—17th century—History and criticism.   7. Renaissance—England.   8. Heroes in literature.   9. Women in literature.   I. Liebler, Naomi Conn, 1944-

PR658.T7 F46   2002
822'.051209352042'09031—dc21

                                                    2002019887

A catalogue record for this book is available from the British Library.

Design by Letra Libre, Inc.

First edition: April 2002
10   9   8   7   6   5   4   3   2   1

Printed in the United States of America.

*This book is dedicated to
the memory of my mother,
Anne A. Conn,
and to Rose A. Zimbardo:
my own personal heroes.
NCL*

Contents

Acknowledgments

The editor of a collaborative volume enjoys both a certain privilege and a unique burden. The privilege consists in acknowledging specifically those who have helped me bring this project to fruition. The burden (although one most happily borne) is that my debts are not only to those in that first category, named below, but even more to the nine authors whose essays comprise the book and also to those whose names and contributions, unknown to me, those authors would acknowledge, had they my privilege as editor. This volume is a collaborative work in the fullest sense: none of us works alone, and my gratitude extends to everyone implicated in the preceding sentence.

I am grateful to the Trustees of the Shakespeare Association of America for sponsoring the seminar, "Wonder Women: Female Tragic Heroes in the Plays of Shakespeare and his Contemporaries," at the 1998 meeting, which led directly to the plan for this collection; the initial contributions to that seminar, two of which appear here, helped to shape its design. Maura Burnett, then of St. Martin's Press, audited that seminar and commissioned this volume. Kristi Long, who took over the project when Maura moved on and St. Martin's established the Palgrave imprint, has been a tirelessly patient support and collaborator. I would like to thank Christy Desmet who reviewed the manuscript for the press, for her gratifyingly enthusiastic and carefully critical reading; her suggestions helped me rethink a number of issues raised in the introduction. I am deeply indebted to the indispensable and always helpful staff of the Folger Shakespeare Library Reading Room and to Richard Kuhta and Georgianna Ziegler in particular, to the Interlibrary Loan staff of the Sprague Library at Montclair State University, and to the Trustees of Montclair State for a sabbatical leave in 2000–2001 that allowed me to complete this project. I owe special thanks to my graduate student, Carole Reading, for her help in proofreading. Colleagues outside my own department have given most generously of their time and expertise: Jean Alvares of Classics and General Humanities was immensely helpful with the Greek in Robert Miola's essay; Lois Oppenheim of the Department of

French, German, and Russian and Alice Freed of the Department of Linguistics suggested important resources from their own disciplines. Michael Heller of Language Learning Technology repeatedly persuaded my computer to work the way it's supposed to do. Beyond the gates of Montclair State, Corinne Abate, John Drakakis, Bernice Kliman, and Doreen Ladinski lent unflagging support. Certainly not least, my undergraduate students in English 354 and my M.A. students in English 508, by reminding me continually of why we do what we do, provided the dual springboards of encouragement and challenge that kept the project going.

Introduction

Wonder Woman, or the Female Tragic Hero

Naomi Conn Liebler

> Where is the Antique glory now become,
> That whilome wont in women to appeare?
> Where be the braue atchieuements doen by some?
> Where be the battels, where the shield and speare,
> And all the conquests, which them high did reare?
> That matter made for famous Poets verse,
> And boastful men so oft abasht to heare?
> Bene they all dead, and laid in dolefull herse?
> Or doen they onely sleepe, and shall againe reuerse?
>
> —Edmund Spenser, *The Faerie Queene*, 3.4.1

> May that man die derided and accurs'd
> That will not follow where a woman leads.
>
> —Thomas Heywood, *The Fair Maid of the West, Part 1* (4.4.17–18)

> "I think I can—I think I can—I think I can—I think I can—I think I can—
> I think I can—I think I can—I think I can—I think I can." Up, up, up. Faster
> and faster and faster and faster the little engine climbed until at last they
> reached the top of the mountain. Down in the valley lay the city. "Hurray,
> hurray," cried the funny little clown and all the dolls and toys. "The good lit-
> tle boys and girls in the city will be happy because you helped us, kind, Little
> Blue Engine." And the Little Blue Engine smiled and seemed to say as *she*
> puffed steadily down the mountain, "I thought I could. I thought I could. I
> thought I could. I thought I could. I thought I could."
>
> —Watty Piper, *The Little Engine That Could* (emphasis added)[1]

Feminist literary criticism is a practice whose apparent familiarity tends to obscure its contested applications (Baym 154); the word "feminism" means different things to different people. That there are many different kinds of "feminism" became clear by 1991 with the publication of Robyn Warhol and Diane Price Herndl's substantial anthology, *Feminisms*, properly pluralized; now, the movement that gave its (singular) name to these varied critical and theoretical praxes is historicized into "first-wave," "second-wave," and "third-wave" feminism. Profound differences among critics who ride one or another of these "waves" have made its discourses a theoretical battlefield. It has long seemed to me that the debates of feminism too often produced radically polarized readings of female representations in early modern tragedy as either oppressed and marginalized victims or demonic (and again marginalized) bitches,[2] a binary option that left little room for alternatives. As the historian Gerda Lerner noted in the introduction to *The Creation of Patriarchy* (1986), "it is a fundamental error to try to conceptualize women primarily as victims. To do so at once obscures what must be assumed as a given of women's historical situation: Women . . . are and always have been actors and agents in history" (5). What has been missing from feminist criticism of tragedy, especially, is a reading of women as such actors and agents, as tragic heroes, protagonists positioned in their plays in precisely (or nearly so) the same ways as Hamlet, Othello, King Lear, Dr. Faustus, and Macbeth. This volume aims to supply that reading by exploring the dimensions of a feminist tragic heroic discourse. In studying the possibilities for such a discourse, I have learned a great deal from colleagues within and outside literary and specifically Shakespearean criticism—art historians, linguists, and philosophers among them; by drawing upon their work, much of which has long been engaged with the same kinds of questions we are now asking, this introduction aims to set out some theoretical parameters within which to contextualize those dimensions as well as some questions whose answers remain beyond the scope of this volume.

The "law" of tragedy (Grande 13–15) calls for a representation of the futile struggle of a protagonist within and against a specific political or social arena; that is, it is in the nature of the genre to present the agon of a protagonist who will, for a variety of reasons, be destroyed in its process. The female tragic hero engages in a struggle exactly as rigorous, exactly as dangerous, and exactly as futile as that of any of her masculine counterparts. That the space where her agon is staged is sometimes (but not always) domestic rather than public does not in any way diminish either its rigor or its social and political significance. To assume, as many critics—including many feminists—have done, that the representation of the tragic agon in a domestic or interior setting is somehow degraded or trivialized is to impose a particular set of (de)valuations on that representation. Lena Cowen Orlin has shown in *Private Matters and Public Culture* that the interpenetrations of domestic and public spaces and their often contradictory significations challenge any firm separations between the two. Moreover, as any anthropologist or sociologist can tell us, culture comprises the private as well as the political. Tragedy always tells the tale of a culture in crisis; it depends no less on what happens in domestic arenas than it does on what happens on battlefields. If the female tragic heroes of English Renaissance drama suffered in ways tailored to their domestic situations or relationships (as examined, for example, in Theresia de Vroom's, Laura Denker and Laurie Maguire's, and Linda Woodbridge's essays in this volume), their suffering, nobility, and exemplarity resonated neither more nor less than those of male tragic heroes.

Linda Bamber articulated the earlier critical situation aptly: the "nightmare female figures" of Shakespearean tragedy were seen as "threatening, unpleasant, disloyal, ugly" (3). Moreover, she argued, in any male-authored text including Shakespeare's tragedies, "the privileges of the Self are attributed to the masculine hero"; "Self" *must* be constructed as masculine and the feminine *must* be constructed as "Other" in order "to resist, challenge, lead, or assist the masculine Self" (4–6). The argument that male authorship definitively precludes female heroism or that men can only write the feminine inimically will not withstand the evidence not only of the plays under study in this volume but of a considerable number of other texts that have come down to us from Renaissance England and Europe. The idea that experience can only be known and represented from within specific sexual identity, that there are irreconcilable differences between male and female "ways of knowing," that the female characters written by Shakespeare and his contemporaries are only a male fantasy of the female and can only be represented as "Other," and moreover, that this imagining must be fundamentally and substantively different from the ways in which they would have been imagined by Shakespeare's sister, implies that women readers and audiences were not and are not likely to recognize themselves admirably in these Renaissance plays and that the plays present images of women that can only be embarrassing, or feminine behaviors that need correction. In an essay primarily concerned with the practice and representation of transvestism on the English Renaissance stage, Stephen Orgel effectively challenged this commonplace notion: "this cannot be correct: theaters are viable only insofar as they satisfy their audiences. The depictions must at the very least represent *cultural* fantasies, and women are implicated in them as well" ("Nobody's Perfect" 8). Large numbers of women of both the aristocratic and mercantile/artisan classes regularly attended the theater openly and unescorted; the success of any play required the receptiveness of women (Orgel 8; Findlay 1–10; Howard 76–80, 109; Woodbridge, *Women*, 251–52). Further, and more pointedly, Orgel adds, "it is not at all clear . . . who are 'us' and who are 'them.' . . . [There] are lots of *others* in this theater; in fact, Elizabethan drama is often dependent on otherness. Comedies are Italian, French, or provincial, tragedies Spanish or Scandinavian or ancient, pastorals take place somewhere else. Dekker, Jonson, and Middleton placing comedies in contemporary London are doing something new. The Other, for this theater, is as much foreign as female—Othello is the Other. And in the largest sense, the Other is theater itself, both a threat and a refuge" (9). In an early essay, written while he was still in his twenties, Mikhail Bakhtin offered a further point important in this context: Any artistic creation, including tragedy, requires the representation of an "other"; in fact, he argues, we can *only* experience the world as "other," and when we recognize ourselves in relation to that world, we must see ourselves as "other" to *others* in that relation. Bakhtin constructs "Otherness" as positive: "it is only the other who can be embraced, clasped all around, it is only the other's boundaries that can be touched and felt lovingly" (41). To erase or misrecognize that "otherness" by "merging" or overidentifying with, for example, the tragic hero would negate entirely the aesthetic work. Taking *Oedipus Rex* as an instance, Bakhtin explains:

> Having merged with Oedipus, having lost our own position outside him . . . we immediately lose the tragic; my being-outside will cease to be for me—as Oedipus—an adequate expression and form of the life I experience. And although it will express itself in those words and actions which Oedipus himself performs, these words and actions will be experienced by me only from within *myself,* only from the standpoint of that real meaning which they possess in the events of my *own* life—and not in the least from the standpoint of their aesthetic validity, i.e., not as a constitutive moment in the artistic whole of a tragedy. . . .
>
> As a result, tragedy is nullified. . . . If the author/contemplator were to lose his firm and active position outside each of the dramatis personae, if he were to merge with them, the artistic event and the artistic whole as such . . . would disintegrate. (71–72)

Without the "other," in other words, we have no artistic work at all; any kind of representation must, on this view, occur only in terms of an "other."

Nevertheless, the negative value of "otherness" remains important for many feminist critics. In her most recent book, *Shakespeare Without Women,* Dympna Callaghan dismisses Orgel's point while acknowledging its "crucial" contribution: "Nonetheless, the *exclusion* of women from the stage and their simultaneous *inclusion* as customers . . . does not exculpate theatre from charges of misogyny" (31), and further, "What is complex [in various representations of the female body] is the way in which apparently benign representations of women operate as regulatory fictions for the suppression, exclusion, and containment of those who, in their corporeality, lived the Renaissance condition of femininity" (47). The debate exemplified here about who, what, and how exactly Renaissance English drama signified by representation embraces large numbers of partisans on both sides among those interested in gender theory and social/literary criticism. It also crystallizes the undeniably risky venture of proposing a feminine heroic: Orgel argues that not every representation of the feminine has misogyny at its core; Callaghan's view is that misogyny in this drama (and its producing culture) is inescapable, no matter how it's dressed up, and that even heroic images of women are suspect as "fictions" designed to cover up the real, "lived" experience of "suppression, exclusion, and containment." The debate risks devolution to an "is too/is not" skirmish. I don't know how to avoid this, except to say that this volume urges a recognition of the feminine heroic as something as "real" as the masculine. A useful third position was suggested 20 years ago in Simon Shepherd's observation that it was class rather than gender that made the notable difference in matters of oppression: "There is much more likelihood of shifting attitudes than is often realised, perhaps because of the anti-women texts that have come down to us. Those texts have identifiable origins: the strictures on women often emanated from the ruling élite, the governing class and the court. . . . It may be, indeed, that . . . while wives of the upper and upper middle classes were traditionally submissive, the 'wives' (often unmarried) of artisans, tradesmen, and workers were somewhat less so" (41; see also Lerner 4–5). I suggest that what we see in the tragic drama of this period, with both male and female protagonists, is an energetic and powerful resistance to oppression, suppression, silencing, and eradication; indeed, Alison Findlay has recently advanced a well-supported claim that Revenge tragedy in particular is a "feminine genre" because, among other reasons, it violates the Law of the Father, resists the practices of patriarchy, and "promotes insubordination" even when the revenger is male (49–86). If these protagonists "fail" in that resistance, it is because they are performing in tragedies where all such resistance fails (see also Woodbridge in this volume). If we want successful protagonists, we need to look in comedy, the genre of accommodation. Foucault's rhetorical question, "What matter who's speaking?" ("What is an Author" 138), expands to an obvious corollary and equally rhetorical question: "what matter who's listening?" Female tragic heroes have been dramatized since Sophocles wrote *Antigone;* the way we "listen" to them, regrettably, has been conditioned by centuries of patriarchal instruction. In the first epigraph to this introduction, Spenser records his nostalgia for them; in the second, Heywood reminds his contemporaries that they still abound. The conditioning of centuries of patriarchy has deafened some readers, even those committed to feminist recoveries of female tragic heroes, to their voices. The third epigraph, from what was for many Americans a formative childhood text remaining in print since 1930, identifies the heroic Little Blue Engine as female, a fact of gender that certainly escaped my notice at the age of five, as it did that of many of my generation (younger colleagues assure me that they knew all along she was a "girl engine"); yet I suspect that even those of us who failed to notice her female identity nonetheless in important ways took on board her courage, her agency, and her faith in herself. We "listened" subliminally to her voice, even before we got hold of the Wonder Woman comic books whose iconic subject prompts the title of this introduction, and we knew she "could" speak for us until we could speak for ourselves.

A view of female protagonists as inevitably either demonized or victimized imputes, I think, a disturbingly narrow and reductive ideology of social and political life to both the authors and their readers/audiences. It assumes too much, or rather too little, and implies that no matter what actions or dialogue occur on the stage, they can only be one or another in-, sub-, or perversion of a lapidary construction of gendered power. But as Toril Moi pointed out in 1985, "women's relationship to power is not exclusively one of victimization. Feminism is not simply about rejecting power, but about transforming the existing power structures—and, in the process, transforming the very *concept* of power itself" (148). No one would deny antecedent claims made and amply documented by feminist critics of early modern English drama and its producing culture regarding evidence of misogyny in either the dramatic or the social/political "real-world" domains. Misogyny operated, certainly, but it did so against a competing context of admiration and even awe for women both real and imagined.[3] Just as a recognition of female tragic heroism does not erase a very real history (in theater and in life) of misogyny, neither does a recognition of that misogyny erase the equally important record (in theater again as in life) of female tragic heroes. In its representation of women on the English Renaissance stage, the genetic code of the drama is a double helix of feminist and misogynist strands. If negative representations of women are taken for its DNA, representations of the feminine heroic must likewise be recognized as its RNA. And in the interstices between the two strands, "The contradiction between the woman's two positions as both superior and inferior, ruler and ruled, creates a gap in which female self-determination can develop" (Findlay 131).

L. T. Fitz (Linda Woodbridge) perceptively demonstrated in her 1977 essay on *Antony and Cleopatra* that such categorical views reflect more of the critic's biases than they do the playwright's or his culture's (see also Dusinberre 308; Jardine 3–4). By commanding an exemplary view of Cleopatra as tragic protagonist equal to Antony in both her tragedy and her heroism, Fitz suggested that female characters do not always serve and are not always sacrificed to a masculine self, but, along with their male peers, they *do* serve and *are* sacrificed to the multigendered imperatives of the larger political and social context. While many have argued that those imperatives themselves privilege the masculine, I would argue that within the generic structures of tragedy there is no privilege at all; on the contrary, it is the very structures and imprints of privilege that are contested in tragedies, and by the ends of the plays, dismantled. Taking the example of *Antony and Cleopatra,* David Kastan identified the contested cultural imperatives as "values far removed from those of the Roman world. Power and possession give way to passion and possibility" (125). But Kastan finally resists the equation he suggests: "In the histories, women are marginal; in the tragedies they are destroyed" (119). Of course, in the tragedies men are also destroyed. These observations point to the cultural valuations that tragedy investigates. By crystallizing the prodigious conflicts of the societies of which they are at once members, representatives, and *pharmakoi,* tragic heroes also suggest alternative cultural values. Kastan's binary suggests that "power and possession" can and perhaps should "give way to passion and possibility," which are not the exclusive domains of either sex. In the action of a tragedy, all such values are questioned.

The Same, Only Different

The reductive assignment of women to the position of "Other" was challenged almost as soon as it was articulated. Bamber's book appeared in 1982; in 1984 Nina Baym argued that such a view "reproduces *to the letter* the appropriation of women's experience by men, substituting only the appropriation and naming of that experience by a subset of women: themselves. Such structural repetition undermines the feminist project" (154). In the following year, in *Feminism and Linguistic Theory,* Deborah Cameron called a profoundly limiting "false dichotomy" the view "that women in patriarchy are constructed as the Other—as whatever men are not. . . . Femininity is masculinity inverted" (57); the antonym-learning that we do as children is, of course, *learned,* inculcated often by rote, and there is nothing natural in this: "the urge to dichotomize is secondary indoctrination rather than native habit, typical not so much of ordinary talk but of the systems our societies have to teach us, of logic and dialectic" (61). In a later work, she pointed a way out of this cultural trap: "unless we are aware that the masculine/feminine dichotomy is itself to be questioned, our struggle will not get beyond the inverted sexism which comes from keeping the same old categories and merely swapping around the positions of those who occupy them" (*Feminist Critique* 127; see also Penelope 215–16). Feminist linguists are concerned primarily with modern, "real-world" practice, but Orgel makes essentially the same point regarding Elizabethan drama: "The interchangeability of the sexes is an essential assumption of this theater" because "for the Renaissance the line between the sexes was blurred, often frighteningly so. Medical and anatomical treatises from the time of Galen cited homologies in the genital structure of the sexes to show that male and female were versions of the same unitary species," and "Analogously and logically, many cases were recorded of women becoming men through the pressure of some great excitement or activity" ("Nobody's Perfect" 13).

One of the consequences of sustaining this "false dichotomy" is its tendency to make one half of the polarity the model and the other half a replica of that model, as, for example, the notion that the female object of desire in much Elizabethan love poetry was represented as "a feminized version of the male body" (Berry, *Of Chastity and Power* 138). Such a view owes much to what Moi calls Freud's "specular logic" (135), by which the visible difference between male and female (the presence or absence of a penis) makes all the difference in the world: "When he looks at the woman, Freud apparently sees nothing. The female difference is perceived as an absence or negation of the male norm" (Moi 132). "The thinking man not only projects his desire for a reproduction of himself (for his own reflection) on to the woman; he is . . . incapable of *thinking* outside this specular structure" (Moi 133).

> Caught in the specular logic of patriarchy, women can choose either to remain silent, producing incomprehensible babble . . . or to *enact* the specular representation of herself as a lesser male. The latter option, the woman as mimic, is, according to Irigaray, a form of hysteria. . . . The hysteric's dramatization (or *mise en scène*) of herself is thus a result of her exclusion from patriarchal discourse. No wonder, then, that phallocracy perceives the hysteric's symptoms as an inauthentic copy of an original drama relating to the male. . . . (Moi 135)

On such a view (which has had a long currency) it is not surprising that critics, feminist and otherwise, have refused to recognize the female tragic protagonist as heroic and have assumed that the very term "hero" is a masculine form belonging properly only to masculine representations, and, further, that a feminine "version" of that representation must be only and exactly that: a version, a poor imitation, an "inauthentic copy." To ensure that we see her as such, she has traditionally been given the diminutive suffix *-ine,* so that there could be no mistaking the derivative, diminished, and "different" ontology of the hero*ine.* From this perspective, males would own the title of "hero," and any attempt to locate a "female tragic *hero*" would be futile because such a figure could only be a naturalized or misappropriated version of a masculine status or category. In this context Orgel's citation of *actual* "cases . . . of women becoming men through the pressure of some great excitement or activity" supports the imaginative possibilities of the same thing happening in plays; what greater "pressure of some great excitement or activity" could there be than the tragic agon or the cultural crisis represented in a tragedy?

The presumption of the absolute primacy of the masculine on the English Renaissance stage, against which the feminine can only appear to be an inadequate version, is increasingly now coming into critical question. As Bruce R. Smith notes in his new book, *Shakespeare and Masculinity,*

> Only recently has masculinity been subjected to the same critical scrutiny as femininity. In every binary, one term implicitly serves as the standard that marks the other term as being different. In the binary "masculine"/"feminine" the criterion has usually been taken to be "masculine." As a result, "masculine" has managed to deflect attention from itself. It is "feminine" that is different, or so the implication goes; it is "feminine" that deserves study. "Masculinity" is, however, just as much a social construction as "femininity." (2)

Feminist linguists irritated by the assumption of a generic "masculine" in such words as "mankind" have been concerned with this matter for decades. "It is not a question of men secretly believing that masculinity is the norm. What is available to them is a discourse where gender and sexual identity appear to be absent . . . [whereas] women are constantly and inescapably constructed *as women.* There is a discourse available to men which allows them to represent themselves as people, humanity, mankind. This discourse, by its very existence, excludes and marginalizes women by making them the sex" (Black and Coward 132). Recent discussions of ideology—feminism and now masculinism in particular but also discussions of class, race, and other arenas of distinction—have opened the way for questioning, if not actually answering, the implications and revelations of such created categorical imperatives. Thus, following Judith Butler's formulation in *Gender Trouble,* Smith goes on to note that "gender is a matter of performance," and that, "Because theatre is also a matter of performance, plays provide a perfect means of investigating cultural and historical differences with respect to gender identity" (2).

It is important to remember that performance is itself a matter of imitation, that all protagonists are imitative, and that it is in the nature of the action being imitated that a protagonist is heroic or otherwise. The classic Aristotelian hallmark of tragedy is *mimesis,* the "imitation of worthy and complete action having magnitude, . . . achieving through pity and fear a catharsis of such affections. . . . [Tragedy] is imitation, not of men, but of action or life, of happiness [and misery; and happiness] and misery exist in action, and the end of life is a certain action, not a quality. It is by virtue of their characters that agents are of a certain kind, but it is by virtue of their actions that they are happy or the contrary" (*Poetics* 1449b–1450a).[4] Given our modern understanding that the Hellenic culture of which he wrote was even more misogynist than Renaissance England, we might be surprised to learn that Aristotle himself had no difficulty in recognizing female tragic heroes, citing among them Antigone (Sophocles), Clytemnestra (Aeschylus, Sophocles, and Euripides), Elektra (Sophocles and Euripides), Iphigenia (Euripides), the Phoenician Women (Euripides), the Trojan Women (Euripides), Medea (Euripides), Melanippe (Euripides), Niobe (Aeschylus and others), Tyro (Sophocles), the Daughters of Phorcis (Aeschylus), and the Phthian Women (Sophocles; lost). In offering these *exempla,* Aristotle inscribes the female tragic hero's agon as equal, and equally significant, to the male's (see also Miola in this volume).

In a remarkable and eloquent book, *Visual Analogy: Consciousness as the Art of Connecting,* the art historian Barbara Maria Stafford argued recently for the development of "a sophisticated theory and practice of resemblance rather than continuing endlessly to subdivide distinctions" (xv), and noted "a dire need—in all fields and disciplines—for ways of seeing sameness-in-difference. Indeed, it is impossible to have a sophisticated theory of difference without an equally nuanced conception of similarity" (xvi). Without such a concept of analogy, she goes on to say, "there is only the negative dialectics of difference, ending in the unbreachable impasse of pretended assimilation or the self-enclosed insistence on absolute identity with no possibility for meaningful communication" (51), which, she points out, is precisely the modern/postmodern condition. Stafford draws a distinction, crucial for the recognition of a female tragic hero, between "being antithetical and being inimical. The determinism of extreme dissent, arcing from Nietzschean nihilism to the poststructuralist and deconstructionist discourse of radical dissatisfaction, continues to fuel the impoverished contemporary concept of the similar as the empty simulacrum" (106); "In analogy, resemblance is first and foremost a matter of mimesis of clothing, rather than veiling ideas" (109).

Although she does not discuss the topic of drama, much of what Stafford has to say about analogy is keenly à propos—one might even say *analogous* to—the concerns of tragedy. "Living in a society," she writes, "means learning, largely automatically, to repeat forms of behavior that already exist. But this replication of the past . . . does not preclude innovation. A remote period in which one is always able to discover some precedent for some current action, no matter how new, can hardly be accused of being static or of merely reproducing itself stereotypically" (131). Whether that "remote period" is presented as the fictional situation of a tragic play or the arguably "factual" narrative of historiography, the praxis of analogy allows us to respect and regard the past's "repertory of rules, of connections among types of actions and types of consequences, in the form of concrete events that can be analogically related to the present," and precisely for this reason "does not replicate hallowed models but enables their comparison" (131). In these words Stafford has identified exactly what is for many audiences and readers the pleasure and profit of attending (to) tragedy. Perhaps like Eliot's Prufrock, none of us wants to *be* Prince Hamlet (though I personally would confess to occasional "immortal longings" to be Shakespeare's Cleopatra or Webster's Duchess), we might find nonetheless some cathartic utility in noticing the "simultaneously homogeneous and heterogeneous" (Stafford 122) analogues of the "actions that a man [or a woman] might play," as Hamlet puts it, or those which "might come to be, i.e., what are possible by virtue of either the likely or the necessary.... The cause of this is that whatever is possible is persuasive" (Aristotle, *Poetics* 1451b).

> How we couple representations in space is the key to understanding selfhood. The activity of linking has an emotional component, fitting our desires to an expanding universe of events in which both self and others are mutually transformed. We need, then, to recorporealize not only the visual but the mental order. Human intelligence exhibits itself in artistic inter- and intrasubjective powers for bringing worlds together. It displays itself externally in mirroring moments of extension. Single vision becomes multiplied, shattered, and reconfigured as it is dynamically relayed within an infinite network of compossible perceptions. (Stafford 141–42)

The key to grasping this construct is recognizing the equal valuation of the reciprocal images. No single image has primacy, and no one is the lesser version of the other. This is in fact how tragedy works. No tragedy would have the power to move us unless we are able to recognize an analogy—but not an identity—between ourselves and the protagonist. Analogy's kaleidoscopic refractions are infinite: "single vision becomes multiplied, shattered, and reconfigured." The function of analogy, Stafford says in a truly felicitous phrase, is "duality-exorcising"; in the Renaissance especially, it "summoned the imagination to invent reconciling images to stand in the merciful middle between the dichotomies of an argument, or . . . just generally, between apparently insuperable incongruities" (181). Its alternative, our modern "intellectual and practical emphasis on extreme otherness" (180), yields only an unproductive and unrecognizable manichean system for charting human behavior. I can think of no tragedy, ancient, early modern, or modern, that rests on such a static, artificially binary, structure.

Of course in tragedy the protagonist stands apart, isolated or tormented, in important ways differentiated from the remainder of her social context. For many female tragic heroes, that context is an interior space—a household chamber, a closet, a bedroom. One of the most important contributions Stafford has made to my understanding of the dynamic of the female tragic hero is in reminding me that the *visual* arts, the paintings of the period, quite often represented interior spaces even when their subjects were male: "Like Vermeer's complex interior scenes showing a painter at his easel or a woman and her cavalier surprised in a moment of dalliance, the architecture of consciousness in the early modern period was visualized as occurring within a symbolically outfitted chamber of being" (171). Thus the domestic space, far from being a diminished or trivialized locus, presented iconographically a tableau whose material properties "painted" symbolically the space of "action having significance." We have no difficulty recognizing the "masculine" political significance of the chamber and its trappings, for instance, in Holbein the Younger's famous anamorphic rebus, *The Ambassadors* (1533). There the interior space, with its drapery, tapestry, lute, open books sharing the room with the more "exterior" references of globes, spyglass, and navigational instruments, signifies the space where the fate of nations is negotiated.

The bivalent discourse of sameness-in-difference is crucial in understanding the dynamic exchanges of tragedy even as it is crucial in understanding any of the human institutions that tragedy imagines, and it is just as evasive of definition as those institutions. As Michel de Certeau put it in an essay titled "The Arts of Dying," "it is as difficult to discuss the sex of a discourse as it is to discuss the sex of an angel: these two apparatuses of circulation and/or drift of meaning—one linguistic, the other cosmological—constantly avoid determinations as to their place. . . . [The] practice of division gives the textual artifact the energy of what it methodically eliminates" (166–67). Elsewhere, in a discussion greatly indebted to René Girard's hypothesis of the mimetic double, I have argued that what is "methodically eliminated" is a dangerous resemblance, when sameness-in-difference seems to obscure "difference" in favor of "sameness," which in turn produces or crystallizes a cultural crisis of confused or blurred boundaries, definitions, hierarchies. Distinction and differentiation are crucial in social organizations (and nowhere more than in Renaissance England) and in the ritual practices that sustain those organizations. Ambiguity, liminality, indistinction, are intolerable for long periods of time in human organizational structures such as communities, and the cultural requirement for differentiation and distinction is what we see performed in tragedies. Protagonist and antagonist so closely resemble each other that an artificial or assigned differentiation (marginalization, misrecognition, or demonization) is required to restore a sense of order and structure (Liebler 17, 73). In that book too I argued (though with attention almost exclusively upon male protagonists) that the tragic hero serves as *pharmakos,* the sacrificial victim required by all purgative ritual, whose efficacy as sacrifice signifies above all the symbolic embodiment of whatever threatens the community in crisis. The tragic hero is the community's surrogate. She could not be its surrogate if she did not *resemble* it in critical ways. And because she stands for what must be "methodically eliminated," she must be destroyed exactly as, in a play with a male protagonist, *he* must be destroyed. If all we see in a tragedy with a female protagonist is the triumph of institutions that suppress or defeat the feminine heroic, we are looking no further than the single valence of a single characterization; we are ignoring the implications of the play's full context of representations, and specifically the lesson of the cost to a society of destroying its surrogate, in this case represented as the feminine. Moreover, the "methodical elimination" of the female hero never quite eradicates her; at the very least, we know what we have seen, what was present and is at the end of the play gone. That Renaissance dramatists saw the destruction of "energy" as itself tragic may be understood by the omnipresence of tragic heroes whose agon enacts the conflicts through which social and political institutions are tested. Such enactment, whether by masculine or feminine protagonists, is not only foundational to the genre of tragedy but is also crucial for a community's understanding of itself as represented in the play. As Pierre Bourdieu observed, "An institution, even an economy, is complete and fully viable only if it is durably objectified not only in things, that is, in the logic, transcending individual agents, of a particular field, but also in bodies, in durable dispositions to recognize and comply with the demands immanent in the field" (58). This "objectification in bodies," I would argue, is performed in the dramatic representation of any "dispositions" that matter to the viability, the survival and endurance, of a community. This, too, is how tragedy works.

What's in a Name?

The language with which we speak or write about women must be the place to begin the recovery of the female tragic hero. "Once 'women' are constituted as always and unchangingly subordinate and 'men' as unqualifiedly powerful, the language structures of these groups are perceived as rigid and unchanging" (Moi 154). Feminist linguists have been writing for the past several decades about the importance of naming, of realizing that the language we use both constructs and is constructed by the way we see the world. As Deborah Cameron observed in her introduction to *The Feminist Critique of Language*, "the names we give our world are not mere reflections of reality, nor arbitrary labels with no relation to it. Rather, names are a culture's way of fixing what will actually count in reality" (12); "If . . . we acknowledge that the conventions of representation have been historically constructed, it is evident that they can also be de- and reconstructed. . . . Feminist activity has, at the very least, sensitized speakers and writers to the non-neutral nature of representation. What was previously unnoticed and unquestioned in our usage is now the site of a struggle for meaning, in which our notions of the natural, the masculine and feminine, the elegant and the offensive, can be challenged and eventually changed" (19–20). Earlier, in *Feminism and Linguistic Theory,* she had argued a similar case: "words may be 'reclaimed' either by revaluing their connotations or reviving obsolete definitions" (76), and along with a significant number of other feminist linguists, observed that "feminizing" suffixes attached to "agent nouns" are inevitably trivializing and demeaning (73; 77; see also Spender 17–18; Penelope 202–3).

The word *heroine* has in itself taken on a pejorative coloration that bans these figures from serious and equitable consideration as tragic heroes. The title of this volume calls for dropping the gendered "-ine" suffix from "hero" just as we have dropped the "-ess" suffix from such words as "actor" and refused it altogether for such words as "doctor" and "professor." Indeed, there is no particular early modern warrant for its use; it appears to be a later emendation stemming from a *modern* repressive movement. The case against "uppity" women who thought themselves the equals of men had a strong voice in that arbiter of English grammatical correctness, W. H. Fowler; under "Feminine Designations" in his *Dictionary of Modern English Usage* (1920), he rebuked women writers for rejecting the term *authoress:* "'Their view,' he said, . . . is that the female author is to raise herself up to the level of the male author by asserting her right to his name.' But who is to say that it is his name and not hers?" (Miller and Swift 45–46).

The proprietorship of signifiers is a hot topic that has occupied feminist linguists since the early 1970s. Thus Miller and Swift, among others, point out that *actor* remained a double-gendered term until 1700 (173n16); *suffragette* was a pejorative word invented by the tabloid press in America in the early part of the twentieth century to replace (and diminish) the word *suffragist* chosen by women seeking the right to vote (65; see also Treichler 69). Especially interesting in this context is the word *virago,* which,

> like *virtue,* comes from the Latin *vir* meaning "male person," [and] was once a noble word. It usually designated a woman of exceptional strength and courage, but it was also applied to men with similar qualities. Gradually it ceased to be used of men, perhaps because it signified no more than what was expected of them. Today it is applied only to females, and courage has been almost wholly replaced by bad temper and unusually great physical strength or size. . . . When the early meaning of virago became obsolete and no alternative arose to take its place, the language lost a word that described heroic qualities in women. Even so, virago had never been a completely positive word, for in addition to meaning strong and courageous, it also meant—as is clear from its derivation—man-like. In other words, a woman was not thought of as heroic in her own right; she had to be likened to a man. (Miller and Swift 64–66)[5]

Similarly, in Old English *husbonde* meant a "peasant who owns both house and land" and "could refer to a woman or a man" (Penelope 94), just as *girle* meant a child of either sex through the end of the thirteenth century and gradually, up to around the middle of the sixteenth century, came to mean only a female child or all young unmarried women (Penelope 98). Dale Spender offers an even more interesting historical survey in *Man Made Language*. Where the older semantic binaries have survived, the "feminine" form of a pair has undergone a sea-change of pejorative implications:

> Although *Lord* still preserves its initial meaning, *Lady* has undergone a process of "democratic leveling" and is no longer reserved for a woman of high rank. . . . *Baronet* also functions in its original sense, whereas its equivalent, *Dame*, has come to be used derogatively (. . . particularly in American usage). There has been some pejoration of *governor*—in cockney usage for example—but it still serves in its original meaning whereas *governess* has come to be used almost exclusively in the context of young children and not in the context that Queen Elizabeth I used it to denote her own power and sovereignty.
>
> Little stigma seems to have become attached to *courtier*, while it is almost surprising to find that *courtesan* was once an equivalent term. . . . *Sir* is still used as a title—and as a form of respect—and, unlike *Madam*, does not refer to someone who keeps a brothel. *Master*, too, has lost little of its force whereas *Mistress* has acquired almost exclusively sexual connotation and is no longer associated with the person who accepted responsibility and exercised control over the varied and essential tasks of a household. (17–18)

Restructuring and relearning a language, even (or especially) in our own postmodern, neologistic era, requires a great deal of cooperation on the part of what linguists call the "speech community": "Meanings are produced and reproduced within the political structures that condition discourse" (McConnell-Ginet 50). Resistance to understanding a female subject in such terms as doctor, surgeon, magistrate, or hero, or marking the terms as feminine by the addition of "woman," "lady," or -*ess*, makes the term "a new and lesser noun" (Treichler 70; see also Jespersen 232). As early as 1924, Jespersen attributed such perceived distinctions, even for terms of general reference or common nouns, to a pervasive social stereotyping that assigned professions to one sex or another (e.g., "*minister, bishop, lawyer, baker, shoemaker*, and many others on the one hand, *nurse, dressmaker, milliner* on the other") and went on to observe that common-sex words seemed to assume lesser importance when marked as feminine by a suffix (-*ess*, -*ine*) or prefix (she-, woman-, or lady-): "it is higher praise to say that Mrs. Browning was a great poet, than to call her a great poetess" (232).

A significant part of the problem of what to call the female protagonist of a tragedy is the convention in English as well as in German and the Romance languages that nouns indicating socially important agency are assumed to be masculine in form and/or reference because such agents are normally men. The English language, of course, is generally less concerned with gendered nouns than German or the Romance languages. French-speaking linguists in particular have waged a vigorous debate on this matter. At the end of her essay, "Aspects of the Evolution of Feminine Titles in French," Marie E. Surridge appends a comprehensive list of terms from Old French, including those designating "independent" roles of women, from criminal behavior to military and governmental positions, all appending the suffix *-esse* to mark gender. Among these we find such interesting terms as *arderesse* (female arsonist), *violaresse* (rapist), *championeresse* (champion), *conquesteresse* (conqueror), *guerroiresse* (warrior), and *vindicateresse* (avenger) (164–65). Surridge's objections are not to the feminizing suffixes per se in terms denoting valorous (or even reprehensible) actions, but rather to the "pejorative semantic *connotations now* attached to this method of derivation" (169; emphasis added). In other words, it is not the suffixes *-esse* or *-euse* that are problematic, but the nuances attached to them.[6] The debate is equally familiar to English-speaking feminist linguists, though the list of nouns carrying the troublesome suffix is shorter. In 1911, the suffragist J. Beanland demanded equal semantic representation for women along with the right to vote:

> [A] woman, equally with a man, may be an imbecile, a convict, a liar, a thief, or a fool, without any terminological inexactitude. But when we come to the other side of the shield, she may not be a hero, a benefactor, an administrator, a prophet, or a poet, because these things are masculine prerogatives, and the courage and ability of women must be otherwise expressed. We do not speak of a servantess, a drunkardess, an incendiatrix, or a pauperine; these attributes are not worth claiming a preemption for. But everything denoting prominence or superiority must carefully distinguish between the real thing and its mere imitation. . . . One would think that heroism, like cowardice, would be the same in essence whether displayed by a woman or a man; but while this is tacitly admitted in the case of the vice, with the virtue it is otherwise. Cortez and Pizarro may be heroes; Joan of Arc is but a heroine. . . . And, lastly, you may, if you feel so disposed, speak of a woman as a devil— one of Shakespeare's characters does so—but you cannot under any circumstances speak of her as a god. Only men can be gods. (207)

The Early Moderns likewise wrestled with the terminology of the feminine heroic, and not only in plays but also in poetry and prose, which work together to disclose the competing discourses of the time in regard to the equality—or not—of men and women. In *Haec Homo Wherein the Excellency of the Creation of Woman is described by way of an Essaie* (publ. 1637), William Austin (1587–1634), barrister of Lincoln's Inn, an inaugural nominee for the proposed Royal Academy of Literature (the project was abandoned in 1620), and a prolific author of mostly religious, privately distributed, and posthumously published writings, argued vigorously against his contemporaries' disdain for women: "It shewes, as if a Man should love his head; and hate his braines: Is not She, he? Examine, and you find small Difference" (3–4, B2-B2v); "As, first for name: though . . . they were created male and female, and two Bodies: yet all (in one word) makes but [Homo], one Man which very word Cicero, (the most eloquent of his time,) thought no barbarisme, to bestow upon a woman, and a vertuous Lady; when . . . he calls her Homo singularis pudicitiae ac pietatis. . . . In the sexe, is all the difference; which is but onely in the body. For, she hath the same reasonable soule; and, in that, there is neither hees, nor shees; neither excellencie, nor superiority: She hath the same soule, the same mind, the Same understanding; and tends to the same end of eternal salvation that he doth" (4–5, B2v-B3). The fact that Austin was noted for writings of a religious nature lends an interesting proto-feminist emphasis to his egalitarian polemic,[7] in so far as we have long understood that much English Renaissance misogyny was ecclesiastically driven (Woodbridge, *Women* 129).

An even more remarkable and far more substantial text came from one of Austin's contemporaries, John Paulet (1598–1675), fifth Marquesse of Winchester, grandson of Sir Thomas Cecil, the second Lord Burghley, and Earl of Exeter. Winchester was a Catholic sympathizer and a staunch loyalist during the Revolution, who was ultimately released from prosecution and returned to his estate at the Restoration (*DNB* 15: 535–37). His literary output consisted mainly of translations from the French, three of which survive; the document of interest in the context of this volume is his translation of the Jesuit Pierre Le Moyne's *La Gallerie des Femmes Fortes* (1647) as *The Gallery of Heroick Women* in 1652. Winchester appended a "Translator's Address to the Ladies of this Nation" on the first page, and immediately we see his engagement with the problem of nomenclature: The second paragraph announces that "These Gallant *Heroesses* repaired first from all the Regions of History to the Court of France to lay down their Crowns at the Queen Regents feet: This ceremonie and Duty performed, they had a desire to passe the Sea, and inform themselves of the condition and state of this Island; and finding no Queen here to whom they might render the same obedience, they resolved to address themselves to you, hoping to finde amongst such noble Company, some Ladies, who resemble them at least in part of their Vertues, if not in all." The layered implications of Winchester's ostensibly conventional flattery of his intended readership, including nostalgia for a long-missing queen and an obvious but risky Catholic sympathy, would be very interesting to unpack if time and space permitted. The book would be worth a modern critical edition of its own. It is a carefully structured 308-page folio with tables of organization divided into four sections (or, as Le Moyne, via Winchester, calls them in his preface, "squadrons"). Each presents five "Heroesses" selected from among "The Gallant Jews" (Deborah, Jael, Judith, Salomona, and Mariamne), "The Gallant Barbarian Women" (Panthea, Camma, Artemisia, Monima, and Zenobia), "The Gallant Roman Women" (Lucrecia, Cloelia, Portia, Arria, and Paulina), "The Gallant Christian Women" ("The French Judith," Eleanor of Castile, The Maid of Orleans [*naturellement*], "The Victorious Captive," and, as a unique sixth in this section, Mary Stuart). Prefacing each "Elogy" is an engraving of each figure and the accoutrements of her struggle; within each narrative Le Moyne inserts a "Moral Question" interrogating the particular heroic action for which each woman is noted: for Deborah the question is "Whether Women be capable of Government"; for Lucrecia, "Whether Chastity belongs to the honour of Heroesses and great Ladies"; for Mary Stuart, "Whether great Ladies in Prosperity, be not in a better Condition, then those in Adversity." Finally, in each case, some parallel exempla from contemporary or recent history, intended, as Le Moyne says in his preface, to contextualize these records as perennially relevant and not merely limited to historical, biblical, or imaginative narratives.

Le Moyne sets up a thirteen-page "Panegyrical Address to the Queen Regent" (Anne of Austria) followed by the six-and-a-half-page "Preface" before turning to his narratives proper. It is within these prefatory pages that we find his own painstaking efforts to locate a precise term for his "heroic woman." Winchester, as translator, reverts repeatedly to "Heroesse." But the word used throughout by Le Moyne is *Victorieuse*. This is an important signifier, not least because Le Moyne makes it very clear in his preface that the primary virtue shared by all of his exempla is fortitude or courage. The more usual term, *héroine*, was certainly available to him. His model is a warrior, whether her battle is fought in the field or in the house (witness his division of his subjects into "squadrons"). *Victorieuse* carries a very different weight semantically from the *-esse* feminizer. It would be futile to guess why Winchester opted for "Heroesse"; perhaps with even the best of feminist intentions, he wanted a less relentlessly combative word. Perhaps the awkwardness of a compound such as "victorious one" deterred him, though he does use that phrase once in translating the address to the Queen Regent, and further on tries "Conqueress" and later "Victress." But he gives these up after one instance each in favor of "Heroesse"; it is, after all, less awkward than the term Margaret Cavendish gives the figure of Victoria in *Bel In Campo* (1662): "Heroickesse." Perhaps the only uncompounded signifier in English that can serve as a respectful and respectable improvement over "heroine" is "hero"; the English language does not have a one-word equivalent for *Victorieuse*. Le Moyne's monumental book reminds us, inter alia, that the agon of female heroism often looks like war, and his own language allows him easily to do what English makes difficult—to name the female in terms richly suggestive of a warrior-hero.

"Balls!" said the Queen. "If I had 'em, I'd be King!"

The line comes from Linda Mussmann's 1990 performance piece, *M.A.C.B.E.T.H.*, a highly imaginative de- and reconstruction of Lady Macbeth's voice, silenced as a rational discourse in Shakespeare's play at the end of the banquet scene (3.4) and given back to us only in the echoes of sleepwalking madness in 5.1. When Macbeth says "She should have died hereafter; / There would have been a time for such a word" (5.5.17–18), we are never quite sure what he means by either "should have died" or "such a word."[8] Mussmann gives her the words she "should have" had: "Is a woman who plans a murder less than a man, or more than a woman? Is she a fiend, does she transcend her role? Is she the tragic hero? No, they said, she deserved what she got. *He* is the tragic hero, they said. I am the unacknowledged hero of the story. I am the brains behind the act. I am the one who transcended her role." In terms of Shakespearean tragedy, at least, "the brains behind the act . . . who transcended her role" seems an apt description of the tragic hero. It would apply without modification (except for the pronoun) to Macbeth, Lear, Coriolanus, Othello, Titus Andronicus, and somewhat more problematically to Hamlet (who seems to achieve rather than transcend his role) and Julius Caesar, who, as I have argued (Liebler 85–111), is not really the tragic hero of the play named for him. Mussmann's Lady Macbeth vigorously protests her exclusion from a pantheon in which she has earned a place.

There appear to be three kinds of early modern dramatic exempla for female tragic heroes. One is in plays with eponymous male protagonists (for example, *Hamlet, Othello,* or *Macbeth*), in which female characterizations are presented as an (equal-and-opposite?) "other" to the male protagonist's "self." Another is in plays with eponymous female protagonists: *Medea, The Duchess of Malfi,* or *Mariam,* whose contexts represent a misogyny against which the female stands for a while before it destroys her. The third is in plays whose titles pair and equate male and female: *Romeo and Juliet, Antony and Cleopatra, Troilus and Cressida,* and Marlowe's *Dido and Aeneas,* or *The Changeling,* with its notoriously ambiguous title. Although most of Shakespeare's tragedies focus attention on the singular male protagonists named in their titles, it is worth asking once again what privilege those masculine "selves" enjoy, given their disastrous and also, it should be noted, their demonized or victimized ends. In the three Shakespearean instances of shared titular billing, it is difficult to see how Romeo, Antony, or Troilus are privileged over Juliet, Cleopatra, or Cressida, or to see how they are "more" heroic. In these double-protagonist plays, are the represented challenges or dilemmas, the structures and significations of the agon and the sacrifice, qualitatively different for male and female representations? It is impossible to deny the equation suggested by the conjunctive "and." It does not help to suggest that in such pairs, each member represents half of a single whole, so that each discloses a fractional persona that needs its other half for completion. On the contrary, paired protagonists double rather than halve the tragic action. In the cases of Shakespeare's pairs, the equational point made by the pairing would, I think, have been obvious were it not for the blink-ered critical sexism that Fitz/Woodbridge and others have uncovered.

It is not difficult to see what makes female protagonists tragic, but what makes them heroic? Is their heroism hierarchically different from that of male tragic heroes? Whereas Shakespeare's titular female protagonists only shared top billing, those of many of his contemporaries stood—and acted—alone. Tragedies with foregrounded, singular, unambiguously heroic females were certainly written and performed—some while Elizabeth reigned though more appear after her death—but not by Shakespeare. Webster, Dekker, Marston, Beaumont and Fletcher, among others, recognized the heroic capability of female tragic protagonists. In the light of works by both his immediate and somewhat later contemporaries, Shakespeare's shortfall must be considered an anomaly rather than the norm or the standard.

The putative dominance of an exclusively masculine Elizabethan heroic ethos is problematized at the outset by the fact that a woman ruled the na-tion. Elizabethan England had specifically to negotiate a pervasive doctrinal subjection of women within the context of a female monarchy. Richard, Duke of Gloucester's line in *3 Henry VI,* "A woman's general: What should we fear?" (1.2.68), is one mode of negotiation. It's a good question, despite his obvious sarcasm and the tremendous anxiety it expresses regarding female leadership. Richard refers to Queen Margaret, who, although demonized along with the other females of the First Tetralogy, and although imprisoned by the play's end, survives "to fill the world with words" (5.5.44); as "the mouthpiece of retribution" (Cairncross li), her last spoken line in the play (5.5.82) is a curse. Margaret is one of only two characters in Shakespearean drama to survive through four plays (the other is Mistress Quickly). Such a dramatic endurance suggests a highly successful resistance to the masculine power that fails to silence and suppress her (Liebler and Shea).

During the unstable late Elizabethan period, described as one of "major epistemological transition" (Berry, *Of Chastity* 136), the reality of "A woman [as] general" surely produced complex responses in those led as well as in the leader herself. Elizabeth sometimes represented herself as a tragically heroic woman upon whose shoulders regal troubles weighed heavily. Perhaps it was not only in fear of enemy intrigue that Elizabeth identified herself with

Richard II in the famous conversation with Lambarde (Greenblatt, "Invisible Bullets" 43–44; but cf. Liebler 57–58), but also in their shared sense of the sometimes unbearable burdens of monarchy. Doubtless she too lived with bread, felt want, tasted grief, needed friends, and sometimes cursed the spite of her endangered situation:

> The dowbt off future foes exiles my present joye
> And wytte me warnes to shunne suche snares as threaten mine anoye
> . . . .
> the dawghter off debatte, that discord aye doth sowe
> shall reape no gayne, where former rule styll peace hath tawght to
> know
> . . . .
> my rustye sword throwghe rest shall first his eydge imploye
> to poule there toppes that sekes suche chaunge or gape for future
> joye. (Norbrook and Woudhuysen 95)

and again:

> Revive againe and live without all drede,
> the lesse afraid the better thou shalt spede. (Norbrook and Woudhuysen 101)

Although the "daughter of debate" in the first of these selections was Mary Stuart, for different reasons Elizabeth could have been referring to herself; likewise her encouragement to Raleigh in the second example could well have been soliloquy: "the lesse afraid the better thou shalt spede." Despite the complicated resonance of the queen's heroic persona that at the very least problematized accepted gender-driven differences in social and political roles—the image of Elizabeth in (masculine) military armor has been well noted in both early modern and modern commentary (see Walker; also Frye 3–21)—it was nonetheless an image with which England lived for 45 years.

It is worth noting that during that half-century the dramatic genre that specifically celebrates heroism—that is, tragedy, by Shakespeare and others—rarely imagined a female hero. The data compiled in the Harbage-Schoenbaum *Annals of English Drama* (1964) presents an interesting chronology. From Elizabeth's accession to her death, a period of enormous dramatic production, fewer than 30 tragedies appear whose titles are women's names (this is not to suggest that only eponymous heroes are tragic heroes, only that play titles make good first indices); most of these 30 are listed as "closet" plays, not intended for performance, and about half of them in any case are lost. For about 20 of those first 30 years, nearly all of these female-titled tragedies represent women from Greco-Roman tragedy

(Jocasta, Iphigenia, Antigone, Medea, Octavia) or other Greco-Roman genres, that is, epic or historiography (Dido, Cornelia, Portia, Procne, Cleopatra); most of them appear to be (or in the cases of lost texts are assumed to have been) simply exercises in direct translation or adaptation, including one by Lady Jane Lumley of Euripides' *Iphigenia in Aulis,* done in the year of Elizabeth's accession, possibly the first play in English attributed to a female author or translator.[9]

Then, during the last decade of Elizabeth's reign, we begin to get original drama featuring female protagonists (much of it now lost, some of it anonymously authored), such as Daniel's *Cleopatra* (1593), *The Witch of Islington* (anon., ca. 1580–97; lost), *Black Joan* (anon., 1597, lost), *Branhowlte (Brunhild)* (anon., 1597, lost), Chettle's *The Woman's Tragedy* (1598, lost), Dekker's *The Stepmother's Tragedy* (1599, lost), *A Warning for Fair Women* (? Heywood, ca. 1598–99), Marston's *2 Antonio and Mellida (Antonio's Revenge;* 1599–1601), *Lust's Dominion, or The Lascivious Queen* (? Day, Dekker, Haughton, and/or Marston, 1600), Fulke-Greville's *Antony and Cleopatra* (ca. 1600–1601, lost), Heywood's *A Woman Killed with Kindness* (1603), and two Shakespearean plays in which women share titular billing: *Romeo and Juliet* and *Troilus and Cressida.*

Not until the Jacobeans, with some 18 instances between 1604 and 1625, does the female tragic protagonist command the stage and the page as the titular hero. In this group are a number of lost plays whose intriguing titles alone justify regretting their disappearance: Middleton's *The Viper and her Brood* (ca.1606), *The Proud Maid's Tragedy* (anon., ca. 1612), *A Yorkshire Gentlewoman and Her Son* (? Chapman, ca. 1613), Thomas Carleton's *Emma Anglia Regina* (1620), *The Whore in Grain* (anon., 1624), and Robert Davenport's *The Politic Queen, or Murder Will Out* (ca. 1623–36). This is also the period of Cary's *Mariam* (ca. 1604), Marston's *The Wonder of Women, or Sophonisba* (1605–6), Thomas Heywood's *The Rape of Lucrece* (1606–8), an anonymous *Aeneas and Dido* (1607), Shakespeare's *Antony and Cleopatra* (ca. 1607), Beaumont and Fletcher's *Maid's Tragedy* (ca. 1608–11) and *The Second Maiden's Tragedy* (?Middleton, 1611), Marston and Barkstead's *The Insatiate Countess* (ca. 1610–13), Fletcher's *Bonduca* (ca. 1611–14), Webster's *White Devil* (1612) and *Duchess of Malfi* (1614), Middleton's *Women Beware Women* (ca. 1620–27), Massinger and Dekker's *The Virgin Martyr* (1620), and Middleton and Rowley's *The Changeling* (1622).

With the Caroline dramatists an interesting sort of recycling appears. Caroline tragedians produced a number of classically inspired plays: Thomas May's *Cleopatra Queen of Egypt* (1626), *Antigone the Theban Princess* (1627), and *Julia Agrippina, Empress of Rome* (1628)—all apparently unacted—and Nathaniel Richards' *Messalina the Roman Empress* (1635). Others wrote original tragedies with female titular protagonists: Massinger (*Minerva's Sacrifice*

[1629], *The Forced Lady* [1633]), Ford (*'Tis Pity She's a Whore* [?1629]), Shirley (*The Maid's Revenge* [1626]), Glapthorne (*The Duchess of Fernandina* [ca.1633–42], *The Vestal* [ca.1633–42]), Lower (*The Phoenix in Her Flames* [1639]), Nabbes (*The Unfortunate Mother* [1639]), Jaques (*The Queen of Corsica* [1642]), and the prolific "Anon." (*Andromana or The Merchant's Wife* [ca. 1642]). With the Closing of the Theaters and the Interregnum, few tragedies were written, all apparently unperformed (even privately) or unintended for performance. For most of this period, beginning with Edward Sherburne's translation of Seneca's *Medea* in 1648 and Christopher Wase's of Sophocles' *Electra* in 1649, until about 1656, tragedy seems to have started all over again with translations from Seneca and Sophocles, which suggests that England had to reinvent dramatic tragedy ab initio, and that Greco-Roman stories were considered good (safe?) models to start with.[10] Not only did dramatists turn repeatedly to Greco-Roman models, but specifically to Greco-Roman models of female protagonists. (The pattern stops with the Restoration, when the first tragedy to be licensed for performance was Davenant's 1661 revival of Shakespeare's *Hamlet*.)

Although the aporias in this catalogue may tell us more than the inclusions (they *may*, for instance, suggest suppression from print), we can only work with what we have, and unfortunately the most tantalizing titles in the list belong to lost plays that, had they survived, might have presented an array of tragic female protagonists as heroic as we want them to be. In the plays that *are* extant, how different is the tragic agon of male protagonists in their plays from that of female protagonists in theirs? And why, we must ask with Spenser in my first epigraph, except for Fletcher's *Bonduca*, were there no dramatic representations of heroic females, such as Britomart, from English legend?

It may be useful to begin where the Elizabethan dramatists themselves began: with the Greco-Roman literature whose translations or adaptations were evidently the terminus a quo of Elizabethan tragedy, and with such "modeling" works as Boccaccio's *De casibus illustrium virorum et feminarum* (trans. Lydgate 1494; repr. 1527, 1554, and 1555; of the nearly 50 women mentioned or discussed, more than 40 come from Greco-Roman sources) and his *De mulieribus claris* (ca. 1380), the first such list describing valorous women from antiquity since Plutarch's *Mulierum virtutes*, although as Merry Wiesner has cautioned, the "feminist" import of such paeans is problematized by their masculinist discourse: "the highest praise they can bestow on a woman is that she is like a man" (15). The real historical differences in constructions of gender need to be reexamined; this is no small task. What were those Greco-Roman female subjects understood to represent when these texts were first produced? How do those constructions change by the early modern period? Feminist critics of Greco-Roman culture and its literature have begun to make substantial interventions in this area (see, for example, Rabinowitz and Richlin, eds.). If, for example, the stories of Medea and Antigone are understood to represent the punishments that attend inappropriate behavior (for women, i.e., disobedience, infanticide), willful autonomous actions within cultural contexts that forbid such behavior, their behavior and their punishment reaffirming axiomatic social roles cannot be seen as qualitatively different from what we see in male protagonists like Oedipus, Prometheus, or Agamemnon. They undergo the same kind of agon, commit the same kind of *hamartia* in the face of the same kind of dilemma, suffer the same foregrounded status (Hamlet's "cursed spite"), endure the same responsibility for the disasters that follow their active choices, and have the same kind of impact on their social context. It is certainly possible to see female tragic heroes as neither victims nor bitches, or no more so than male victims and sons-of.

In a passage cited earlier in this introduction, Gerda Lerner called for a "revisionist" view of what she termed the "dialectic" of women's history: "the tension between women's actual *historical* experience and their exclusion from interpreting that experience." Women, she wrote, "are and always have been actors and agents in history. Women have 'made history,' yet they have been kept from knowing their History and interpreting history, either their own or that of men" (5),[11] and offered what for our purposes is a wonderfully fortuitous metaphor for this vision:

> Men and women live on a stage, on which they act out their assigned roles, equal in importance. The play cannot go on without both kinds of performers. Neither of them "contributes" more or less to the whole; neither is marginal or dispensable. But the stage set is conceived, painted, defined by men. Men have written the play, have directed the show, interpreted the meanings of the action. They have assigned themselves the most interesting, most heroic parts, giving women the supporting roles.
>
> As the women become aware of the difference in the way they fit into the play, they ask for more equality in the role assignments. They upstage the men at times, at other times they pinch-hit for a missing male performer. . . .
>
> It takes considerable time for the women to understand that getting "equal" parts will not make them equal, as long as the script, the props, the stage setting, and the direction are firmly held by men. When the women begin to realize that and cluster together between the acts, or even during the performance, to discuss what to do about it, this play comes to an end. (12–13)

Lerner's theatrical "scenario" is, of course, a metaphor for the ways in which historiography gets done and how its lessons are internalized in the modern world. The domain from which her metaphor comes may be—and may always have been—a different matter. In assembling the essays in this volume, all previously unpublished, we hope to take up Lerner's challenge, to extend the implications of this "play of history" to show that while its authors were (mostly) men, some of those men have assigned the "most interesting, most heroic parts" to women. That they were dramatists and not, strictly speaking, historiographers, suggests again, as Gifford once said, that the Jacobean playwrights "were the most clear-sighted politicians of those troublous times" (qtd. in Knights 175). They certainly knew a heroic female when they saw—or imagined—one.

The essays presented here have been organized in the chronological order of the plays they discuss (though with some necessary exceptions), from one of the earliest Elizabethan instances to a late Jacobean one; this seemed the most effective way to suggest a trajectory in constructions of female tragic heroes that bears out the implications of the chronological catalogue indicated above. Taken together, they encompass a wide and varied engagement of dramatists with their subjects. The first four of these essays recognize the crucial inheritance of classical influence, while at the same time underscoring the requisite adaptation of their foundational material to the shifting interests and concerns of a contemporary early modern English culture. We begin almost literally at the beginning of Elizabethan tragedy with Robert S. Miola's study of Gascoigne and Kinwelmersh's *Jocasta* (1566), based on Euripides' *Phoenissae* via Lodovico Dolce's *Giocasta*. Miola situates the Elizabethan play as the complex product of multiple translations and multiple dramatic functions, recuperating an ancient text "in early modern political and moral dress." He reminds us that, from its inception, Elizabethan tragedy based on classical models presented female tragic heroes. Euripides especially, "preeminently the poet of suffering, mythical women," left a notable legacy: 12 out of 19 extant plays with titular female individual or choric protagonists. Through a meticulously close reading of both the Euripidean Greek and its several incarnations culminating in the play performed at Gray's Inn, Miola traces the evolution of *Jocasta*, illuminating the ways in which Gascoigne and Kinwelmersh fashioned not only the titular hero but also her supporting cast—Antigone and the chorus—as the guardians of and spokeswomen for a distinctly Elizabethan cultural morality, one that held human beings accountable for their own responses to the disasters that befall them, that taught by example as well as by exhortation "the serious business of living and dying morally in this world."

Tracing a different path from classical to early modern, Judith Weil follows the figure of Hecuba as avenger, like her "sister" Furies, of familial pollutions and violations of reciprocity, and as guardian—though in very different modes from the figures of Miola's essay—of justice, *comitatus,* and codes of moral and civilizing behavior. Rejecting the view that tragedy is "a prop for patriarchal order," she recuperates the figure of the grieving mother from the conventional trap of victimhood. Drawing significantly upon the important work of Nicole Loraux, Froma Zeitlin, Ruth Padel, and other feminist classicists, Weil investigates the "descendents of Hecuba" in two Elizabethan and two Jacobean plays—Isabella in Marlowe's *Edward II,* Constance in Shakespeare's *King John,* Volumnia in his *Coriolanus,* and Cornelia in Webster's *White Devil*—as agents of tragic action rather than as suffering victims, and considers the "necessity" of their actions as the levering agon of the tragedies in which they appear, despite the fact that none of them is the titular protagonist.

Mimi Still Dixon and Kay Stanton present two distinctly different approaches to the heroic subjectivity of Shakespeare's most complicated and elusive titular female tragic hero, Cleopatra. Dixon locates the Egyptian Queen as subject in a Renaissance dialectic of visual and dramatic arts. Shakespeare's *Antony and Cleopatra,* Mary Sidney's translation of Garnier's *Marc Antoine,* and Daniel's *Tragedie of Cleopatra* are considered separately and in relation to each other, and also in relation to two paintings of the period, beginning with a sixteenth-century painting, attributed to Jean Cousin, of a nude over whom hangs a medallion inscribed "Eva Prima Pandora" that suggests the figure of Cleopatra and merges it with two other of Western culture's most notorious women. Dixon then excavates the tradition of the femme fatale and Cleopatra as one of its archetypes, captivating even while objectified, as a way of explaining the extraordinary fascination that this figure held for the Renaissance. Through carefully nuanced readings of each play, she locates three radically different approaches to the female tragic hero and interrogates the genre of dramatic tragedy as a space for female heroic representation. Unlike his two predecessors, Dixon argues, Shakespeare "does what the theory says he can't": by making us *look* at Cleopatra, he builds her subjectivity, which emerges "because she takes life in a play which questions the very illusions of male autonomy and self-sufficiency . . . upon which . . . tragedy was founded." She concludes by introducing another painting, by Artemisia Gentileschi, in which Cleopatra is surrounded by women; the hand of the (female) artist, "writing men out of the picture," allows us to see her "in relation, like the tragic male hero, to the universe."

Kay Stanton explores her subject through the multiple refractory lenses of Attic and Near Eastern mythology, Tantric and goddess culture, Shakespeare's received Aristotelian precepts, and current feminist theory. She argues that "in his tragedies with couples as protagonists, Shakespeare . . . attempts to restore both the capacity for heroism *and* sexual divinity to the female." Stanton is particularly interested in the complex resonances of the appellation "whore," long part of the received tradition of Cleopatra "studies." Locating this tradition in patriarchal or misogynist Greco-Roman-Judeo-Christian cultures, she explores antecedent (and, as she notes, "for a time simultaneously existing") matriarchal cultures that valorized female sexuality, and identifies in Shakespeare's sexually charged play the vantage of reading Cleopatra as an aspect of Isis, "like the historical Cleopatra," which Shakespeare might have noticed in early modern translations of Plutarch and Apuleius. As Western culture wrought changes upon antecedent religions, a previously understood sanctification of female sexuality transmuted to its denigration, and the "holy" became "whorish." By demonstrating this "devolution," Stanton proposes to recuperate the term "prostitute" to "reclaim both tragic dignity and sexual divinity for Cleopatra as the 'prostitute queen.'"

With Theresia de Vroom's essay on *A Woman Killed with Kindness*, the boundary-breaking capacity of the female tragic hero anticipated in Shakespeare's work finds a multiregistered voice in the presentation of a female tragic hero trapped (and killed) in what appears to be a comedy. With this play, we move into a doubly "domestic" genre: this tragedy about a family of ordinary bourgeoisie is also the first play represented in this volume whose roots are natively English, deriving from medieval cycle and morality plays, Chaucerian narrative, and homily. De Vroom usefully locates this domestic(ated) tragedy within the ambit of "a contemporaneous crisis in gender relations" identified by a number of historians of the period as "the crisis of the family," and suggests that increasingly after 1600 dramatists found such crises an apt matrix for the agon of tragedy. This genre-bending play, she argues, powerfully interrogates a range of patriarchally generated social assumptions about what society (and not only Jacobean society) requires of its citizens in order to thrive. Through a careful explication of the play's active metaphors for domestic life—food, drink, music, and conversation—de Vroom demonstrates how Heywood radicalizes Anne's adultery, usually seen as a deep threat to the very fabric of civilized life, into "a flawed but singularly feminine act of heroism."

Increasingly in Jacobean tragedy, we see evidence of dramatists questioning the culpability, in disturbances of the domestic social order, of "men behaving badly" by instantiating or initiating disruptive, antisocial—i.e., misogynist—behaviors that call for redress by their female counterparts. Arguably this trend in dramatization began with Shakespeare, and certainly we can see it in Heywood's play. As the period progresses, dramatists appear more and more to be locating the impetus for unruly women's behavior in prior unruly and even anarchic behavior by men. Patriarchy may be seen to persist in punishing female unruliness, but in the vision of these later playwrights, the principles of masculine dominance are undermined by the exposure of a set of causal social violations inaugurated by the men in their plays. If men were understood to be the guardians of social order, the playwrights seemed to be asking who is guarding the guards.

John Webster must be considered principal among these Jacobean interrogators, extending still further the critique begun by Shakespeare and Heywood. The next two essays in this volume focus in different ways upon Webster's double apotheosis of the Jacobean female tragic hero. Martin Orkin and Linda Woodbridge both examine closely but through different lenses the richly sexual emphases in *The White Devil* and *The Duchess of Malfi*, respectively. Orkin's essay, "As If a Man Should Spit against the Wind," identifies in its title Webster's presentation of the self-defeating trajectory of hypocritical misogyny; the rest of the line is "The filth returns in's face." Through a close reading of the play's explicit sexual references, puns, and bawdy, he illuminates the ways in which Webster exposes the viciousness of male promiscuity—manifested in this play in the representation of the grotesque *male* body—as itself disruptive of the patriarchal narrative whose project *appears* to be the containment of transgression but in fact is disorder's *fons et origo*. "Against the wind" of conventional presentations of women as the source of misrule, he argues, Webster's women actively if unsuccessfully—that is, heroically—resist such positioning. Webster's critique of unruly masculinity, meticulously analyzed in this essay, "give[s] the lie to patriarchal narrative" in its misrepresentation of both genders.

Woodbridge's essay, "Queen of Apricots: The Duchess of Malfi, Hero of Desire," complements Orkin's explication of demonic masculine sexuality by celebrating the Duchess's exuberant female sexuality. Noting the often contradictory texts regarding sexuality produced during the period by various competing and intersecting interests, she argues that "oversimplification about Renaissance sexual attitudes is endemic in criticism," and proceeds to "complicate existing accounts" of sexuality in this play by adducing one Renaissance discourse that has been neglected in recent criticism: the Neoplatonic humanism of Pico, Ficino, and others, which posited human dignity in an ability to transcend the gravitational pull of physical gratification. But, she notes, because theater requires the bodies of actors, drama never fully denies the body's claims. Instead, "Tragedy stages a collision between the potential of the spirit and the vulnerability of the flesh." Seen against her brother Ferdinand's extreme and paradoxical notions of being human (seen also, Woodbridge shows, in Angelo in *Measure for Measure* and in Marlowe's *Tamburlaine*), the Duchess represents "a healthy and positive alternative to the common Renaissance pattern of aborted ascent followed by a precipitous descent." The play's "Integer Vitae" coda reminds us that the enjoyment of simple—and it should be added, legal—physical pleasures indeed constitutes a heroic act in a world that neurotically insists on choosing between impossible alternatives.

With Laura Denker and Laurie Maguire's essay, "The Morris Witch in *The Witch of Edmonton*," we turn to the latest of the plays under consideration in this volume. Denker and Maguire observe an interesting recombination in this play of the usual binaries, victim/villain and male/female, with a third, witchcraft/Morris dancing. As they point out, in this play the structural positions occupied in the first two of these dyads are "fluid," with gender reversals abounding in regard to who speaks, who is silenced, who is represented as victim, who as villain. The third dyad introduced uniquely in this play positions the magical fertility rite known as the Morris dance, performed (until recently) only by men, alongside witchcraft, attributed conventionally only to women. Both practices were pagan in origin, both were associated with seasonal (i.e., natural) rhythms and fertility. "Witchcraft," the authors note, "is the female side of Morris dancing." One is embraced in early modern culture, the other is shunned; one is considered necessary for communal survival, the other is criminalized. By adding this binary to the more customary ones, Denker and Maguire argue, *The Witch of Edmonton* exposes them all equally as a. bitrary and interchangeable constructs, polarities lamented by the play's authors as "the ideological double bind that traps people's lives, as sons and daughters, as youthful marriage partners, and as single, handicapped seniors." Near the end of the Jacobean period, it would appear, "Dekker, Ford, and Rowley ask us to reassess the taxonomic opposites of gender which structure (and ruin) lives."

The final essay in this collection, Jeanne Addison Roberts's "Sex and the Female Tragic Hero," fittingly caps the volume by, first of all, surveying many of the plays already discussed and their recurrent foci, particularly an increasing emphasis on sexual behavior, and particularly Shakespeare's. Engaging directly with the all-important question of how we can know a female tragic hero when we think we have seen one, Roberts offers a checklist of criteria that might as easily apply to any of her male counterparts: how many lines does she have, how many soliloquies, is her voice distinctive and does she change and develop in the course of her play, is she presented stereotypically, does she suffer dilemma, does she have agency in shaping her own destiny or does she merely suffer as a victim, are there unexplained mysteries in her behavior, and crucially, is the world changed by her death? Roberts then works through each of Shakespeare's tragedies, identifying along the way, as most of the preceding essays have done, the twin poles that support the tightrope female tragic heroes must walk—sex and death—and determining thereby the claim (or its lack) that each of Shakespeare's tragic females has to the status of hero. Not surprisingly, though perhaps for reasons elided in the finely focused analyses of the preceding essays (such is the immense value of Roberts's scientific objectivism), Juliet and Cleopatra both earn the Purple Heart of female tragic heroism; perhaps more surprisingly,

so do Tamora and Volumnia. Roberts concludes with an important reminder that drama, when it matters, is always responsive to the concerns and
anxieties of the culture that produces it. She takes up three plays whose publications (though not in each case their performances) coincided with the
sensational trial of Frances Howard in 1613, reading Marston's *Insatiate
Countess,* Cary's *Mariam,* and Webster's *White Devil* as, if not quite *drâmes
à clef,* nonetheless reflective of the interpenetrations of art and life. Roberts's
study reveals some startling similarities: all three plays deal with many of the
issues that made the Howard case the tabloid-fodder it was—"wives who
have disposed of their husbands and moved on to one, two, or three lovers."
Roberts concludes with what I hope will be the response of this volume's
readers: "a new appreciation of tragic women who do not fit neatly into
stereotypes," unsubmissive boundary-breakers who stand as tall and as
memorably as their brother-heroes.

Notes

1. Readers who share a sentimental interest in this foundational feminist narrative may be interested to know that "Watty Piper" never existed; according to
   Roy E. Plotnick of the University of Illinois at Chicago, the name was a
   "house pseudonym" for Platt & Munk, a company run, when the book was
   published in 1930, entirely by men; "Piper" may have been Munk himself.
   Plotnick supplies a fascinating account of the six-year legal battle over the
   publication rights to this beloved children's book and the contest over its "origins" on his website, http://www.uic.edu/orgs/paleo/littleng.htm. I am grateful to my colleague Corinne Abate for bringing his work to my attention.

2. See, for instance, the essays by Greene, Gohlke, Neely, Klein, Stimpson, and
   Berggren in Lenz, Greene, and Neely's foundational *The Woman's Part*
   (1983); Dympna Callaghan's *Woman and Gender in Renaissance Tragedy*
   (1989); the "Shakespearean Tragedy" section of Valerie Wayne's collection,
   The Matter of Difference (1991); and *Shakespearean Tragedy and Gender,* ed.
   Shirley Nelson Garner and Madelon Sprengnether (1996). Claire McEachern's essay, "Fathering Herself: A Source Study of Shakespeare's Feminism,"
   offers a comprehensive and very useful summary of feminist criticism of
   Shakespeare up to 1988.

3. Jean Howard's equation of misogynist representation and "the representation
   of women who have voice and agency solely as criminals" (109) seems to me
   to raise a further set of crucially important questions about how drama, and
   specifically tragedy, does its work of representation. That is, how do we understand "anti-social" or "criminal" behavior in a representational context of
   a community in crisis where the "law," and consequently its violations, are
   already problematized by the fictional situation portrayed? If the "law"
   and/or its (usually masculine) agents are represented as "wrong"—think of

King Lear or *The Maid's Tragedy* in this context—are the "criminals" then understood to be "right" in opposing them?

4. I follow Kenneth A. Telford's translation. It is worth noting that for Aristotle, tragic heroes are here simply called "agents" of a particular kind of action, and implicitly may be either male or female (although elsewhere in the *Poetics* Aristotle speaks predominantly in terms of the masculine).

5. On the complex resonances of *vir* and its cognate *virtus* as received by English Renaissance dramatists, see Coppélia Kahn, *Roman Shakespeare: Warriors, Wounds, and Women,* especially 14–15 and 33.

6. I am grateful to my colleague Lois Oppenheim of the Department of French, German, and Russian at Montclair State University for bringing this essay to my attention.

7. Kate Aughterson compiles excerpts from Austin's and ten other "Proto-Feminisms" in *Renaissance Women: A Sourcebook.* She does not, however, cite the Winchester–Le Moyne text.

8. Kenneth Muir comments at length on the line's ambiguity in his Arden edition of the play.

9. This play is listed in Harbage-Schoenbaum as extant in manuscript form, probably intended as a closet play, and last edited in 1910 (in German) by G. Becker, "Lady Lumley's Übersetzung von Euripides' *Iphigenie in Aulis,*" *Jahrbuch der deutschen Shakespeare Gesellschaft* 46 (1910): 28–59.

10. Harbage-Schoenbaum indicate very few exceptions during this period: Thomas Killigrew's *The Pilgrim,* and *The Fatal Friendship* by a Mr. Burroughs, both in 1646 (the latter play is in any case lost; the former was apparently performed on the continent but not in England); and a few masculine-heroic instances: Edmund Prestwich's translation of Seneca's *Hippolytus* and an anonymous closet play called *Marcus Tullius Cicero,* both listed for 1651, and Lower's translations of Corneille's *Polyeucte* (1655) and his *Horace* (1656). Where titular female tragic protagonists appear, they are, as in the cases of Sherburne's and Wase's plays, translations from Greco-Roman sources, with one exception: Gilbert Swinhoe's original but apparently unacted play, *The Unhappy Fair Irene,* printed in 1658.

11. Lerner purposely distinguishes *h*istory as "the unrecorded past, with a lowercase h," and *H*istory as "the recorded and interpreted past, with an uppercase H" (4n).

Euripides at Gray's Inn

Gascoigne and Kinwelmersh's *Jocasta*

Robert S. Miola

In 1566 players at Gray's Inn staged the first performance of Greek tragedy in English, Euripides' *Phoenissae* ("The Phoenician Women") retitled *Jocasta*. Advertised on its title page (1573) as "written in Greek by Euripides, translated and digested into act[s] by George Gascoigne and Francis Kinwelmersh," *Jocasta* is actually a translation of Lodovico Dolce's *Giocasta* (1549).[1] Here as elsewhere, Dolce practiced a creative *imitatio,* taking inventions, sayings, and plot structure from the ancients, *togliendo le inventioni, le sentenze, e la testura da gli antichi,* but freely omitting and creating along the way.[2] Dolce based his Senecan adaptation not on the Greek original but on a Latin translation, perhaps that of R. Winter published at Basel in 1541. Gascoigne and Kinwelmersh then presented to their audience a "Euripides" three hands and three tongues removed from the original Greek.[3]

To the modern eye *Phoenissae*—long, diffuse, lacking a central hero—seems an odd choice for the inaugural Greek tragedy on the English stage.[4] Renaissance audiences, however, delighted in the abundance of characters and action. Moreover, they found the play essentially tragic, as Gasparus Stiblinus explained in the annotations to his Latin edition. *Phoenissae* is *admodum tragica, ac plena vehementibus affectibus* [very tragic and filled with violent passions]. It features *atrocitas* [atrocity]: *Quid enim horribilius ac cruentius, quam duorum fratrum mutua caedes? . . . Quid acerbius clade illa & interitu tot heroum & ducum* [What is more horrible and cruel than the mutual slaughter of two brothers? . . . What is more bitter than that destruction and death of so many heroes and leaders?].

What is more pitiable than Antigone seeing her twin brothers and mother *confuso in sanguine se volutantes* [writhing in spilled blood]? Add to such things, Stiblinus says, the sacrifice of Menoeceus, the exile of aged and blind Oedipus, Polynices, *insepultus & infletus, volucribus ac bestiis objectus* [unburied and unwept, cast out to birds and beasts].[5] For early modern audiences tragedy resided properly in horrible events, strong passions, and pitiable sights. It did not have to depict the fall of a great man, as many today expect, misunderstanding Aristotle's comments on the subject. *Jocasta,* as the title suggests, does not feature a man at all, but a woman. In this selection, Gascoigne and Kinwelmersh remain true to the spirit of their author: 12 of Euripides' 19 extant plays have female individuals or choruses in the title roles. Euripides' attention to women and their passions—one thinks of Hecuba, Medea, Electra—did not go unnoticed or unpunished. Such characters prompt the Athenian women of Aristophanes' *Thesmophoriazusae* to prosecute Euripides for his crimes against them.

Choosing to stage a version of *Phoenissae,* Gascoigne and Kinwelmersh well represent Euripides, preeminently the poet of suffering, mythical women. Moreover, their choice fits well into the larger Renaissance recovery of Euripidean tragedy. R. R. Bolgar lists 19 translations from Euripides into European vernaculars before 1600, all of them plays whose titles name women individually or collectively.[6] In addition, Lady Jane Lumley has left a partial manuscript translation of Euripides' *Iphigenia in Aulide* (1555?), the earliest extant English version of a Greek tragedy; George Peele turned one of the *Iphigenia* plays into English verse at Oxford in the late 1570s.[7] The translations of Euripides into Latin tell the same story as those into the vernacular. Erasmus chose to translate *Hecuba* and *Iphigenia in Aulide* in 1506; these plays appeared in 18 editions by 1540. Archibald Hay's Latin *Hecuba* appeared with commentary in 1543. About that time George Buchanan translated *Medea* and *Alcestis* into Latin and borrowed from Euripides for his biblical drama *Jepthes.* By 1556 Martirano, Bishop of Cosenza, rendered into Latin *Medea, Electra, Hippolytus, Bacchae, Phoenissae,* and *Cyclops.*[8]

What shape did Euripides take in Gray's Inn, 1566? What sort of tragic action and heroism did an English translation present? And what did authors and audiences, across many cultural divides, make of Euripides' powerful and passionate women? The opening Argument to the published edition gives a revealing summary of the action:

> To scourge the crime of wicked Laius,
> And wreck the foul incest of Oedipus,
> The angry gods stirred up their sons by strife
> With blades imbrued to reave each other's life.
> The wife, the mother, and the concubine,
> Whose fearful heart foredread their fatal fine,
> Her sons thus dead, disdaineth longer life,

And slays herself with selfsame bloody knife;
The daughter, she, surprised with childish dread,
That durst not die, a loathesome life doth lead,
Yet rather chose to guide her banished sire,
Than cruel Creon should have his desire.
Creon is king, the type of tyranny,
And Oedipus, mirror of misery.

The Argument explains, clarifies, and domesticates the ancient tragedy. The syntax of the opening purpose clause imposes a divine order on the events, situating the various tumults and catastrophes onto a familiar grid of sin and punishment. The gods scourge the crime of wicked Laius and wreck Oedipus for his incest. The Argument thus gives shape and meaning to all the disasters of the play—the war between Polynices and Eteocles, Jocasta's suicide, Creon's banishment of Oedipus, Antigone's self-imposed exile. Not diffuse, the play simply offers more spectacle, passion, suffering, and instruction for the money. Gascoigne and Kinwelmersh preface each of the acts with dumb shows and music to point the moral and adorn the tale. In the printed text quotation marks call attention to *sententiae;* marginal notes explain occasional obscurities and offer sage commentary: "Truth pleadeth simply when falsehood useth eloquence" (*ad* 2.1.301); "No greater honor than to die for thy country" (*ad* 3.2.6). Transformed rhetorically, politically, and morally, *Phoenissae* now *Jocasta* reconstitutes and revalences its women, particularly the chorus, Jocasta herself, and Antigone.

Dolce's titular substitution of Jocasta for Euripides' chorus of Phoenician women indicates a refocussing of tragic interest as well as other substantive changes. The classical chorus has always provided formidable difficulties to translators and directors. Erasmus found the complicated meters and concentrated poetic expression of Euripidean choruses so obscure that he longed for help from Oedipus himself or the Delian oracle.[9] Ignoring Euripidean form and content, Dolce and his English translators wholly refashion the chorus and their songs. Euripides originally changed Aeschylus's terrified Theban women (*Seven Against Thebes*) to a chorus of 12–15 Phoenician women; this group becomes in the Italian version 15 Theban women, and in the English, four Theban dames dressed in black, always on stage. Euripides' Polynices addresses the chorus as "ξέναι γυναῖκες" (278) [foreign women], alluding no doubt to the exotic or un-Greek costume of these Phoenician outsiders from Tyre en route to Delphi, now trapped in the besieged city of Thebes.[10] Euripides' chorus identifies itself as "ἀκροθίνια Λοξίᾳ" (203) [choicest offerings to Apollo], in other words, women chosen to be *hierodouloi* (sacred servants) at Apollo's temple in Delphi. As such, they provide a valuable perspective on the action, one that is cognizant of the mythical past, and attuned to the awesome power of the gods for good and evil. Changing their nationality from Phoenician to Theban, the translators crucially alter the play: the revised choruses speak not as outsiders but as victims. "Seld shall you see the ruin of a prince, / But that the people eke like brunt do bear" (1.Ch.36–37), they comment, this sentence labeled *Argumentum à majore* in the margin of Gascoigne and Kinwelmersh's play.

In their *parodos* (entrance song, 202–60) and four *stasimons* (odes, 638–89, 784–833, 1019–66, 1284–1307), Euripides' chorus evokes Theban myth and history, the long chain of figures and events that underlie the present conflict between Polynices and Eteocles.[11] Repeatedly the dancers entwine past myth and present reality, singing about Io (248, 828), her descendant, Agenor (217), his son, Cadmus (216, 820), the mythical founder of Thebes. To get water, the legend goes, Cadmus slew a dragon, offspring of Ares; at the advice of Athena, he then sowed the ground with the dragon's teeth, whence arose armed men, the Spartoi, who subsequently fought and destroyed each other; five survived to found the city. The story of Cadmus, the dragon, and the warriors echoes throughout the play. To appease Ares for Cadmus's crime long ago, Menoeceus commits suicide; in their mutual slaughter Polynices and Eteocles replay the fratricidal conflict of the Spartoi. Mastronarde (330) points to other significances: Cadmus's arrival in Thebes parallels the divinely inspired and baneful arrivals of the Sphinx, Oedipus, and Polynices.[12] Throughout the play the chorus enforces these parallels by singing of recent Theban history too, recalling the Sphinx, "πολύφθορος πολύτονος / μειξοπάρθενος / δάιον τέρας" (1022–24) [bringer of death, bringer of groans, half-maiden, dreadful monster] and the story of wretched Oedipus (801ff., 1043ff.)—the parricide and unholy marriage that now pollutes Thebes ("μιαίνει δὲ πτόλιν," 1050). The mythological recollections of the choral songs suggest that an intricate skein of past event and character presently entangles the Labdacid house. The chorus bears witness to the working out of vast and mysterious forces, part human and part divine, in the present generation.[13]

The relations between mortals and gods figure centrally in the *parodos* and choral songs. In their first appearance, the Phoenician women declare their devotion to Apollo, for whom they wear the "παρθένιον χλιδὰν" (224) [the maidenly luxuriance] of their hair. Their speech depicts female lives and beauty devoted to the god in joyful harmony. Musically they invoke the magical, animated, and deified world of Delphi (home of Apollo and Dionysus); the myths encoded in language and gesture form a prelude to an escape wish (234–38), which highlights the present danger. The Bacchic dance in green dells at Delphi (cf. 655–56) contrasts with imminent war and bloodshed: "νῦν . . . θούροις μολὼν Ἄρης . . . φέρων / πημονὰν Ἐρινύων" (239, 240, 254–55) [now . . . furious Ares comes, . . . bringing the baneful woe of the Erinyes]. Later, the chorus again contrasts "πολύμοχθος" Αρης" (784) [troublesome Ares], with Bacchus, god of dances, coiffed maidens, and flutes (785ff.). The chorus also fears Strife, a terrible goddess ("ἦ δεινά τις "Ερις θεός," 799) and, in the agitated iambo-dochmiacs of the last *stasimon,* the dread Erinyes again: "ἄποτμος ἄποτμος ὁ φόνος ἔνεκ' Ἐρινύων" (1306) [ill-fated, ill-fated slaughter, the work of the Erinyes]. The chorus invokes Demeter, Persephone (684ff.), and Pallas Athena (1062) for protection. Euripides' chorus depicts Thebes, and by ex-tension, all humankind, as subject to the powerful and capricious gods. They trust and serve Apollo, who, as Jocasta notes at the outset of the play (1ff.), has already brought disaster to the royal house—the murder of Laius, Oedipus's marriage and self-blinding.

Following Dolce's lead, Gascoigne and Kinwelmersh replace the mytho-logical choral songs with proverbial wisdom and conventional moralization. Instead of recalling the legendary history of Thebes, replete with resonant parallels to the present crisis, their Theban women lament human weakness and warn generally against the "greedy lust of man's ambitious eye" (1.Ch.1). Individuals in the unfolding drama illustrate universal truths about vice or, less frequently, virtue. Polynices forgets "quite the duty, love, and zeal / He ought to bear unto this commonweal" (48–49). Eteocles is an "unnoble tyrant" (2.1.244). Oedipus's tragic history becomes a cautionary tale about the archetypal sin: his "swelling pride hath all this jar begun" (2.Ch.35). Creon does not God's will but his own; after he refuses to sacrifice his son Menoeceus, the chorus comments: "But every man is loath for to fulfill, / The heavenly hest that pleaseth not his will" (3.Ch.50–51). Attempting to stop the duel, Jocasta illustrates "the faith and fervent love / A mother bears unto her tender sons" (4.Ch.[1]1–2). The chorus dissects the drama into a se-ries of discrete moral lessons, universally applicable. The specific terrors of the Labdacid house become the timeless struggles of Everyman—passion against reason, virtue against vice, human will against divine command-ment. Characters sometimes generate contradictory lessons. Polynices wins more praise than blame; Oedipus illustrates vicious pride and the fortune that afflicts all men, guilty and innocent; Jocasta is a mirror of maternity and also its most horrible image, wife to her own son.

Revealing the determining power of the past, the Phoenician women di-minish present accountability. Suppressing mention of the past, applying universal moral criteria to characters, the Theban women insist on present accountability. No longer historians, mythographers, and witnesses from the outside, the women in the revised chorus function as victims and homilists. In their view, the comprehensible world runs according to well known and amply demonstrated laws. Ancient tragedy illustrates familiar schemes of causality, especially Fortune's ever-turning wheel:

> When she that rules the rolling wheel of chance
> Doth turn aside her angry, frowning face
> On him, whom erst she deigned to advance,
> She never leaves to gall him with disgrace,
> To toss and turn his state in every place,
> Till at last she hurl him from on high,
> And yield him subject unto misery. (3.Ch.1–7)

The chorus expatiates on the power of fortune in their first appearance (1.Ch.) and in their last, wherein they summarize the moral of the play: "How fickle 'tis to trust in Fortune's wheel" (5.Ch.5). The complex interplay of Theban past and present, of fate and free will, of character and destiny yields to a regular, mechanistic medieval dynamic—up and down, down and up.

Gascoigne and Kinwelmersh's chorus also transforms the pagan gods. They reduce Apollo in dual aspect, beneficent and maleficent, to a mere personification of the sun, "with his glistering rays" (1.Ch.32). Similarly, Ares, originally incensed at Cadmus, bringer of destruction and the terrible Erinyes, becomes a bit of mythological decoration, a colorful metaphor for war: "raging Mars will each of them assist / In other's breast to bathe his bloody fist" (55–56). Alien gods, strange and terrible, simply become the familiar Judeo-Christian god by other names. No longer the god of fertility and dance at Delphi, Bacchus is misidentified in the margin as "the god whom they most honored in Thebes"; this deity defends his "humble thralls" with "tender love" in exchange for praise (59–60). Invoking divine aid (2.1.627–35), the chorus pledges not gold, silver, or sacrifice but consecrated hearts and obedience. Such extraordinary refashioning continues throughout the play; the second act ends with the following choral prayer:

> And thou, great god, that dost all things decree,
> And sits on high above the starry skies,
> Thou, chiefest cause of all that be,
> Regard not his offence, but hear our cries,
> And speedily redress our miseries.
> For what can we poor woeful wretches do,
> But crave thy aid, and only cleave thereto. (2.Ch.36–42)

Dethroning the Olympic deities, this chorus worships the omnipotent Judeo-Christian god in heaven, prime mover and first cause. God, under the name of Jove, "tempers all in heaven on high, / The sun, the moon, the stars celestial, / So that no leaf without his leave can fall" (3.Ch.36–38). He created the world from chaos and now rules by "providence proceeding from above" (4.Ch.30), punishing the wicked and rewarding the virtuous. In such a theologized world, "no man hath wit nor power / To fly from fate"

(3.Ch.30–31). Suffering the storms of life, one can only place all hope in God ("mighty Jove"), "Whereby he wins the wished heaven at last" (3.Ch.32–33). The pun on "haven" and "heaven" reveals the meaning of the metaphor: trust in the one true God leads to salvation in this life and the next.

Gascoigne and Kinwelmersh's Theban women convert the discordant music of Euripidean cause and effect into clean moral melodies. No longer trapped in a mysterious, ultimately unfathomable world, constricted by past events and pollutions, human beings now act as autonomous moral agents in a plain and decipherable universe. Unpredictable, animate, and terrifying gods give place to a divine justice above that rewards and punishes mortals below. This hierarchical division of reality sharply contrasts with the Greek interpenetration of the supernatural and natural, fate and character, gods and human beings. The seer Tiresias calls Oedipus's family "δαιμονῶντες" (888) [driven by a possessing *daimon*]. The present participle (from "δαιμονάω") means literally that they have been "*daimon*-ized" (we borrow the metaphor of possession from a later dispensation). Untranslatable, the Greek *daimon* signifies here both an evil spirit and one's own particular destiny. Tiresias's description thus fuses external and internal causation and suggests just how far later translators and audiences, insisting on two separate planes of reality, had come.

The creation of *Jocasta* from *Phoenissae* entails changes in the lead character as well as in the chorus. Jocasta's initial appearance in Euripides' play must have surprised original audiences familiar with the received tradition, especially Sophocles' plays, wherein Jocasta commits suicide at the discovery of Oedipus's true identity. Her opening speech reviews the woeful history of the Labdacid house, including her own incestuous marriage.

> γαμεῖ δὲ τὴν τεκοῦσαν οὐκ εἰδὼς τάλας,
> οὐδ' ἡ τεκοῦσα παιδὶ συγκοιμωμένη. (53–54)

[He, not knowing—O wretched man—marries the mother who bore him; the mother who bore him, not knowing, lies with her own son.]

Jocasta delivers the prologue of the play in the anguished voice of a victim. Throughout her speech (4, 49, 66, 87), Conacher (234) well observes, she refers to *tyche,* "chance, fate, a god," and its cognates as a motivating force for past events. She begins by begging the sun (Apollo) for help, but ends with a bitter prayer to Zeus:

> χρὴ δ', εἰ σοφὸς πέφυκας, οὐκ ἐᾶν βροτῶν
> τὸν αὐτὸν αἰεὶ δυστυχῆ καθεστάναι. (86–87)

[You must not, if you be wise, allow this one of mortal race to be always cursed.]

Whether referring to herself or Oedipus, Mastronarde observes, Jocasta admonishes Zeus, desperately hoping that the gods will behave according to human notions of wisdom and fairness. "This futile projection of human ideals upon intractable amoral powers is an essential element of Jocasta's tragedy, as it is for many of Euripides' most tragic figures."[14]

Unlike Euripides' queen, the revised Jocasta never dares glance accusingly upward but instead blames the human actors in the Labdacid tragedy. Laius consults the oracle because of his wife's barrenness in Euripides (13ff.); in the revised version Jocasta hints at her husband's culpable habit of curiosity: "Desirous still to search / The hidden secrets of supernal powers / Unto divines [Laius] did make his oft recourse" (1.1.37–39). "Πάντ᾿ἀνατλὰς . . . παθήνατα" (60) [unable to endure all the suffering], Euripides' Oedipus blinds himself; his breast swelling with "the rage of boiling wrath" (1.1.126), the revised Jocasta's husband puts his eyes out. This culpable passion, boiling wrath, incites the later Oedipus to curse his sons for imprisoning him,

> And wishing all th'infernal sprites of hell
> To breathe such poisoned hate into their breasts,
> As each with other fall to bloody wars,
> And so with pricking point of piercing blade,
> To rip their bowels out. (151–55)

Such "Wicked blasphemies / And sinful prayer" (160–61), expressed in a Senecan style wholly alien to the original, thus motivate the current crisis in Thebes. Like the revised chorus, this Jocasta suppresses mention of Theban history and makes moral judgments on those around her.

In Gascoigne and Kinwelmersh's play, Jocasta's opening monologue becomes a dialogue; she tells her story to a servant,

> Because I know that pity will compel
> Thy tender heart more than my natural child
> With ruthful tears to moan my mourning case. (13–15)

Motivating many actions, pity becomes a central theme in her narration and in the larger play: a shepherd "with pity moved" (65) rescues the infant Oedipus. "As a pitiful mother / Whom nature binds to love her loving sons" (190–91), Jocasta intervenes to prevent the bloodshed. Instead of ending her opening speech with a prayer of exasperated admonition, this queen goes inside and asks the gods "With tender pity" to appease her grief (220). Pity, the capacity to suffer with another, thus characterizes the proper relations between humans themselves and between gods and mortals. As Jocasta's opening comments to the listening servant indicate, pity also characterizes the proper audience response to tragedy. In his edition Stiblinus (124) claims that the events of *Phoenissae* can strike and move hearts of iron or adamant (*ferreum aut adamantinum pectus concutere ac mouere*). In the Prologo to his *Giocasta*, Dolce argues that feeling pity for the misery of others (*Hauer pietà de le miserie altrui*) is the duty of every humane person (*Debito ufficio è d'huom, che non sia priuo / D'humanitade*).[15] Stiblinus and Dolce articulate here a cardinal doctrine of Italian poetic theory and practice: the grand spectacles and sufferings of tragic figures ought to stir in an audience *pietà* (pity). The stirring of pity as well as fear, Minturno (*De Poeta*, 1559) explains, expels harmful passions like anger and avarice, checks vain desires for power and pleasure, purges the soul, and brings prudence and equanimity.[16]

The Renaissance conversion of *Phoenissae* into a sentimental tragedy necessitated far-reaching changes in conception, rhetoric, character, and action. Euripides' Jocasta presents a tragedy of intellect, one that starkly reveals the incapacity of human reason to parse the basic facts of human existence. Jocasta uses an all-important participle, "οὐκ εἰδώς" (53) [not knowing], to describe herself and her son contracting the incestuous marriage. Euripides demonstrates more grandly the inadequacy of human reason in Jocasta's great speech of dissuasion later (528–85).[17] Confronting her sons, she employs proverbial wisdom and sophisticated rhetoric to stop the impending war. First she lectures Eteocles on the evils of Ambition ("φιλοτιμία"), an unjust god ("ἄδικος ἡ θεός," 532). She urges him to honor instead Equality ("ἰσότης"), which binds friends to friends, cities to cities, allies to allies (536–37). Equality has given humanity measure, weights, and number; Equality orders the alternation of night and day and the progression of the seasons. This numerical and natural principle of division and order should instruct Eteocles to share sovereignty with his brother as he promised. Sovereignty, like all gifts of the gods, does not belong to him or to any man. In an extraordinary and exciting display of intellect, Jocasta postulates a natural order that humans can imitate by making correct moral choices. She takes a different tack with Polynices, allowing the justice of his complaint but condemning the invasion. Asking if he wishes to be remembered as the man who burnt Thebes, she appeals to his sense of honor and desire for *kleos*, "fame."

In this speech Jocasta superbly demonstrates and champions the power of logos, that is the "word, reason, the essential and articulatable principle of order symbolized by language." But her efforts fail, or rather, prove to be irrelevant. Neither son bothers to answer her. Eteocles tells her there is no time for talk (589ff.), then engages in a blustering dialogue with his brother in about 50 lines of agitated trochaic tetrameter. Deep-searching intellect and rational argument cannot control the passions or prevent calamity. In Aeschylus's *Seven Against Thebes* Eteocles reasonably chooses six champions to defend the city and then finds himself left to face Polynices at the seventh gate. Omitting the strategic selection, Euripides' brothers, eager for the kill, choose to fight each other. After their deaths, Jocasta plunges one of their swords into her body and falls on the corpses. Antigone comments:

> πάντα δ' ἐν ἄματι τῷδε συνάγαγεν,
> ὦ πάτερ, ἀμετέροισιν ἄχη μελάλθροις θεὸς
> ὃς τάδ' ἐκτελευτᾷ (1579–81)

[All the griefs of our house he has gathered, O father, the god who brings this to fulfillment.]

The malevolent force that persecutes the house of Oedipus rides cruelly over human reason and protest. Here figured as a god who intentionally brings the grief to fulfillment (ἐκτελευτᾷ), this force appears elsewhere as a *tyche, daimon, moira* ("fate"), Ares, or the Erinyes. Under these diverse aspects, supernatural power works conjointly with human vice and virtue to create chaos. Jocasta's own life and death prove her faith in the intellect and its capacity to order and comprehend experience to be mere delusion. In the terms of her bitter opening prayer, Zeus is not "σοφός" (wise): there is argument that can avail, no justice for the house of Oedipus, no limit to human evil or suffering, no moral order in the world.

Euripides' translators cast Jocasta in a different role (2.1.396ff.), as we have already noted—that of the grieving, loving mother. They reproduce the basic outline of her great speech, but subtle changes shift emphases and reconstitute the argument. Marginalia reduce the rich, philosophical thought into a series of commonplaces: "Youth seeth not so much as age"; "Ambition doth destroy all"; "Equality doth maintain all things"; "If the head be evil the body cannot be good"; "Content is rich"; "Riches are but borrowed ware." English expressions invoke an alien theology of sin and punishment. Eteocles must rule his "unbridled will" and control "vain desire" (442–43). "Φιλοτιμία" (ambition) is not a deity but a passion, a sin that "most infects the minds of mortal men" (403). Jocasta warns Eteocles sternly:

> Blame not thy brother, blame Ambition,
> From whom, if so thou not redeem thyself,
> I fear to see thee buy repentance dear. (476–78)

Like any good preacher she urges repentance and hopes for the sinner's redemption. Euripides' Jocasta begs her sons to flee the Erinyes of their father (624), significantly recalling the overarching supernatural hostility and the terrible curse on the Labdacid house working through the generations. The revised Jocasta invokes their pity, the compassion natural to all human beings: "O sons, my sons, for pity yet refrain" (544). This Jocasta does not represent human intellect but family values, common sense, and motherhood. Her death, consequently, plays not as intellectual tragedy but as piteous spectacle. The revised Antigone's lyric aria of grief omits the chilling allusion to the corpses as "χάρματ' Ἐρινύος" (1504) [the delights of the Erinyes]; instead Antigone laments her mother, imagined also as mother of the Theban chorus and, by extension, the city:

> Behold, your Queen twixt both his sons lies slain,
> The Queen whom you did love and honor both,
> The Queen that did so tenderly bring up
> And nourish you, each one like to her own,
> Now hath she left you all (O cruel hap!). (5.3.7–11)

Cruel hap victimizes the tender, nourishing, maternal Jocasta. Antigone exonerates her from any imputation of wrongdoing:

> The Hymenei in unhappy bed,
> And wicked wedlock wittingly did join
> The guiltless mother with her guilty son. (41–43)

Because she did not know Oedipus's true identity, Jocasta cannot be considered culpable; she dies guiltless in the "wicked wedlock." The Queen herself articulated precisely this moral principle earlier: "So deeply faulteth none, the which unawares / Doth fall into the crime he cannot shun" (1.1.133–34). One can commit sin, Jocasta argues, only when one acts with full knowledge and full consent of the will. This postclassical and Christian view of sin contrasts with the Greek belief in "μίασμα," a "pollution" spreading down the generations, infecting the house, requiring a cleansing in blood.[18]

Like the chorus and Jocasta, Antigone undergoes radical reformulation at Gray's Inn.[19] In the *teichoskopia* (the sighting from a city wall, 88–201), Euripides introduces Antigone venturing out from her home:

> ὦ κλωινὸν οἴκοις Ἀντιγόνη θάλος πατρί,
> ἐπεί σε μήτηρ παρθενῶνας ἐκλιπεῖν
> μεθῆκε ηελάθρων ἐς διῆρες ἔσχατον
> στράτευς' ἰδεῖν Ἀργεῖον ἱκεσίαισι σαῖς
> ἐπίοχες, ὡς ἂ ν προὐξερευνήσω στίβον
> μή τις πολιτῶν ἐν τρίβῳ φαντάζεται (88–93)

> [Hail, Antigone, a scion who brings glory to the house of your father! Although your mother, at your entreaties, has let you leave your maiden-chambers and go to the outermost two-storied part of the palace to see the Argive

army, yet, stay back, so that I might first check the road lest some citizen appear on the path.]

Delaying her entrance on stage, Paidogogus (tutor) here suggests the cultural codes and constraints that govern the behavior of Greek females, particularly unmarried girls, *parthenoi*. In the opening address he indentifies Antigone in terms of her house and father; clearly she belongs inside, in the "παρθενῶνας" (89) [the maiden chambers]. As the audience well knew, Greek women, especially the *parthenoi*, lived largely within doors, their occasional exits and contacts with men subject to strict regulation and supervision.[20] Having received her mother's permission to go out, Antigone looks to the old man for guidance and protection: "ὄρεγέ νυν ὄρεγε γεραιὰν νέᾳ / χεῖρ'" (103–4) [stretch out, now, stretch out your old hand to this young one]. Here and throughout the dialogue Paidogogus is an old man ("γέρον," 135), Antigone the child ("τέκνον," 139; "παῖ," 154). Wise and experienced, he speaks in the usual iambic trimeter while she, astonished and fearful, speaks (chants?) in an excited mixture of lyric verse forms that convey her shifting thoughts and feelings. She wonders at the brilliant colors of the invading army, the flashing brass (110–11), the white helmcrest of a warrior (119), the gleaming shield of another (129–30). She calls on Artemis for protection (152, 190ff.), nervously hopes that the gates are secure (114–46), recoils in fear at the sight of Hippomedon: "ὡς γαῦρος, ὡς φοβερὸς εἰσιδεῖν / γίγαντι γηγενέτᾳ προσόμοιος" (127–28) [How haughty, how dreadful he is to look upon, like a giant born of the earth!]. At one point she longs to embrace her brother, "ὅπλοισι χρυσέοισιν ἐκπρεπής, γέρον, / ἑῴοις ὅμοια φλεγέθων βολαῖς ἀελίου" (168–69) [outstanding in golden armour, blazing like the morning rays of the sun]. Revising the lengthy catalogue in Aeschylus's *Seven Against Thebes,* Euripides substitutes the emotional and impressionable Antigone for the calm and controlling Eteocles. Recalling as well Homer's *teichoskopia* (Il. 3), he here reverses the roles of knowledgeable female (Helen) and questioning, elderly male (Priam) to emphasize Antigone's naiveté.

Following Dolce, Gascoigne and Kinwelmersh transform the *teichoskopia* into a conversation between Antigone, attended with three gentlewomen, and Bailo, Polynices' governor.[21] Bailo asks why Antigone has left her "secret lodge" (1.3.9) to walk abroad in the armed town instead of going to the temple like the other women. This adaptation shifts the original restrictive cultural context by suggesting that other women are walking in public and that Antigone has simply chosen an inappropriate place and time for her outing.[22] Antigone answers forthrightly: "The love I bear to my sweet Polynices, / My dear brother, is the only cause hereof" (1.3.22–23). The translators greatly expand Antigone's love throughout the scene: She has a "hot desire . . . / To have a sight of my sweet Polynices" (33–34); she wishes to feed her "hungry eyes / But with the sight of my beloved brother" (38–39). Polynices, she recalls, "did ever love me more / Than did Eteocles" (95–96). Not interested at all in the Argive army, Antigone appears as a devoted, loving sister.

This sister, significantly, pleads to no god; nor does she ever tremble in fear. Instead, she wishes that she could shed her "faultless blood" to "stay" her brothers' "dire debate" (28–29): "With glad content I could afford my life / Betwixt them both to plant a perfect peace" (30–31). The mere sight of her beloved brother would be sufficient to allow her to die contented (39–40). This death wish marks her differences from Euripides' cowering *parthenos* and forecasts her future actions. Anticipating the end of the play, the translators have Antigone here express suspicion of Creon, "Him doubt I more than any danger else" (120). Unlike her counterpart, this Antigone from the beginning shows strength, courage, and foresight.

This revised scene replaces the sighting from the wall and the roll call of warriors with sententious conversation and exposition. Only once does the dialogue recall the flashing imagery of the original Greek: Bailo remembers seeing Polynices, "In golden, glistering arms most richly clad" (157; cf. 168–69, quoted above). Instead, Bailo and Antigone discuss the present crisis, identifying the cause as the greedy "desire to rule and reign in a kingly state" (82), condemning Eteocles as a "cruel brother" (70) and "trothless tyrant" (91). Instead of Antigone's desperate pleas to Nemesis and Zeus, the thunderer and wielder of lightning (184ff.), Bailo expresses faith in "heavenly powers": "Sith they be just, their mercy is at hand" (85–86). Euripides' Paidogogus takes a precisely opposite view: Polynices has come "σὺν δίκῃ" [with justice][23]; "ὅ καὶ δέδοικα μὴ σκοπῶσ᾽ ὀρθῶς θεοί" (154–55) [So I fear lest the gods see it rightly]. This servant hopes that God will permit injustice and, consequently, spare the city; Bailo counsels Antigone to "trust in mighty Jove," who, justly, won't allow many to suffer for the offence of one (107–9).

After the death of her brothers and mother, Euripides' Antigone appears as a forceful young woman. She sings a lyric duet of grief with Oedipus (1488–1581). The conversation with her father reverses the situation and roles of the *teichoskopia:* now a matured, independent Antigone informs and comforts an old man. Creon enters, banishes Oedipus, and sets up the wedding of Antigone and Haemon. King and future father-in-law, he commands the *parthenos:*

> κόμιζε σαυτήν, Ἀντιγόνη, δόμων ἔσω
> {καὶ παρθενεύου τὴν ἐπιοῦσαν ἡμέραν
> μένουσ᾽ ἐν ᾗ σε λέκτρον Αἵμονος μένει.}(1636–38)

[Take yourself inside the house, Antigone, and live today as befits a maiden, awaiting that day in which the marriage bed of Haemon awaits you.]

Creon orders Antigone back into the tightly circumscribed world of the Greek *parthenos:* she must go indoors and await the bed of her future husband. Refusing to be so defined, rejecting the limitations of the conventional female role, Antigone disobeys these commands. Rebelling further, she challenges the edict forbidding burial for her brother as "οὐκ ἔννομον" (1651) [not lawful]. Invoking higher laws (1662–63), Antigone defies the authority of the state: "ἐγώ σφε θάψω, κἂν ἀπεννέῃ πόλις" (1657) [I shall bury him, even if the state forbids].

When Creon threatens to punish such treason with death, Antigone responds that loved ones who lie together in death are glorious ("εὐκλεές," 1659). Formerly the shy, childlike maiden, she here claims the due reward of a Greek warrior, fame and glory. Faced with the prospect of an enforced wedding, Antigone threatens to kill her new husband: "νὺξ ἄρ᾽ἐκείνη Δαναΐδων μ᾽ ἕξει μίαν" (1675) [That night will prove me one of the Danaids]. To demonstrate her resolve, she draws Polynices' sword and swears by it. Symbolically assuming male prerogatives, Antigone dedicates herself to honor, violence, and death. Courageous and inflexible, she becomes a tragic hero. Then, revising the tradition, Euripides recasts Antigone as a different kind of hero. Again usurping male prerogatives and violating the codes governing behavior of women, Antigone resolves to accompany her father in banishment.[24] The maiden who first needed her mother's permission to leave the home now decides to protect her blind father in the dangerous and wild world outside the city walls. Astonished at her recklessness, fearing for his son's life, Creon reverses himself and banishes Antigone. Overruling Oedipus's objection that such a task is shameful for a daughter ("αἰσχρὰ . . . θυγατρὶ," 1691), Antigone says that it is proper to the wise ("σωφρονούσῃ," 1692). Laying claim to wisdom, she here practices a virtue of peacetime, one that transcends all gender distinctions.

At the end of the play Antigone's defiance mounts to challenge the notion of moral order and the gods themselves:

> οὐχ ὁρᾷ Δίκα κακούς
> οὐδ᾽ ἀμείβεται βροτῶν ἀσυνεσίας.[25] (1726–27)

[Justice does not regard evil men nor punish their ignorant folly.]

Specifically referring to Creon, Antigone here denies the larger operation of justice in the universe. Oedipus directs her to lead him to Bacchus's haunt; she responds bitterly:

> Καδμείαν ᾧ
> νεβρίδα στολιδωσαμένα ποτ᾽ἐγὼ

Σεμέλας θίασον
ἱερὸν ὄρεσιν ἀνεχόρευσα
χάριν ἀχάριτον εἰς θεοὺς διδοῦσα; (1753–57)

[For whom I once dressed myself in Theban fawnskin and joined the sacred band of revellers honoring Semele in the mountains, giving to gods a thankless offering?]

Devotion to the god and reverential practices have proven a "χάριν ἀχάριτον," a thankless offering, a favor that has won no return. The sufferings of the Labdacid house and Thebes have rendered all such piety and sacrifice meaningless. The family has been destroyed; Menoeceus's death has had uncertain results;[26] the city lies in chaos. Turning a skeptical and accusing glance upward, Antigone's final lines doubt the correlation between human conduct and fate. The gods are amoral and capricious.

Gascoigne and Kinwelmersh recast Euripides' heroic and defiant Antigone into a more conventional mold: she appears as the good sister and dutiful daughter. Heightening the sentiment and diminishing the anger, they emphasize Antigone's tears for her brother (5.5.116, 118). Her kiss of the corpse demonstrates natural sisterly affection, evoking this marginal comment: "She showeth the fruits of true kindly love" (*ad* 5.5.114). Similarly, Antigone's decision to accompany her father here violates no social, familial, or gender codes; instead it demonstrates "the duty of a child truly performed" (*ad* 5.5.141). The defiant Greek hero becomes an exemplary good girl. Throughout the scene, the translators tone down Antigone's ferocity. First, she asserts that she can make Creon repent his rashness by committing suicide (5.5.126); when he scorns her as a fool, she, omitting the allusion to the Danaids, then says that she will kill his son (130). So presented, the threat seems more spiteful petulance and desperate rhetoric than a potential course of action. In direct contrast to her counterpart, this Antigone leaves the scene lamenting her inability to "ingrave the corpse" (222). Creon retains control. Euripides' Antigone finds the world tragically disordered and unfathomable; the revised Antigone sees the operation of familiar principles and well-known laws: "when Dame Fortune frowns, / Be few that find trusty companions" (228–29). She preaches to her father the virtue of patience in adversity (210–14). The last chorus and epilogue likewise dilate upon fickle Fortune and the dangers of the aspiring mind. Accordingly, this play modulates the bitter nihilism of the original close to wistful meditation: there *Dike* does not regard the suffering of mortals or punish the wicked; here Justice simply "lies on sleep" (197), not intrinsically uninterested but momentarily inattentive.

A few years after *Phoenissae* appeared on stage (411–409 B.C.E.), Thrasyllus, an Athenian admiral, dreamed that he and six fellow commanders played the roles of the Seven against Thebes in Euripides' play. A seer informed him that the dream foretold victory in the coming battle but that the seven leaders, like the captains against Thebes, would die. Withholding the prophecy of their own deaths, the commanders reported the omen of victory to their men. They routed the Spartans.[27] From earliest times, apparently, audiences have read their lives and times into Euripides' mythical play. Accordingly, Gascoigne and Kinwelmersh present a Euripides in early modern political and moral dress. The Theban chorus points out various virtues and vices; Jocasta appears as a natural mother and pitiable victim; Antigone turns into a dutiful child who suffers on behalf of her brother and father. Such recuperation of these ancient women illustrates prevailing tendencies of the larger humanist hermeneutic. Editors, translators, commentators, and teachers all sought to subdue the strangeness of antiquity and to produce serviceable texts. To modern eyes the strain of accommodation seems at times ludicrous; but the attempt does reflect a conviction about reading literature largely absent in our critical discourse, despite the posturing. Greek tragedy played as spectacle in Gray's Inn but also as an aid to the serious business of living and dying morally in this world. The stakes of the endeavor were high: the promotion of order and justice in the state, the salvation of individual souls. Transformed from their Greek originals, the women in this play have important, perhaps heroic, cultural work to do.

Notes

1. *Jocasta* first appeared in George Gascoigne's *A Hundreth Sundrie Flowres* (1573); modernizing the spelling, I quote this play and Dolce's *Giocasta* from *Supposes and Jocasta,* ed. John W. Cunliffe (Boston: D.C. Heath, 1906). Citations to Euripides are to *Phoenissae,* ed. Donald J. Mastronarde (Cambridge UP, 1994). Unless otherwise noted, all translations are mine. For the Greek I have consulted The Loeb Classical Library, *Euripides with an English Translation,* ed. and trans. Arthur S. Way, vol. 3 (1912, rpt. 1979).

2. Lodovico Dolce, *Tragedie* (Venice, 1560), sig. Aii^v. On Dolce as translator see Ronnie H. Terpening, *Lodovico Dolce, Renaissance Man of Letters* (U of Toronto P, 1997), 92–94.

3. For the identification of Dolce's Latin text see Cunliffe, xxix. On Gascoigne and Kinwelmersh's *Jocasta,* see C. T. Prouty, *George Gascoigne: Elizabethan Courtier, Soldier, and Poet* (New York: Columbia UP, 1942), 143–59; Bruce R. Smith, *Ancient Scripts & Modern Experience on the English Stage 1500–1700* (Princeton UP, 1988), 81–83, 217–26.

4. A. W. Verrall thought the play notorious for its "remarkable looseness of connexion," *Euripides the Rationalist* (1895; rpt. New York: Russell & Russell, 1967), 233; H. D. F. Kitto called *Phoenissae* "a dramatic pageant" and discussed it as melodrama, *Greek Tragedy: A Literary Study* (Garden City: Doubleday, 1954), 372–83 (373); Helene P. Foley observed that the plot

stood "in need of subtle drugs and a sophisticated hermeneutics," *Ritual Irony: Poetry and Sacrifice in Euripides* (Ithaca: Cornell UP, 1985), 132.

5. *Euripides Poeta* (Basel, 1562), 124.

6. R. R. Bolgar, *The Classical Heritage and Its Beneficiaries* (Cambridge UP, 1954), Appendix II, 512–15: in English, *Phoenissae* by Gascoigne and Kinwelmersh (1566); in French, *Troades* by J. Amyot (1542, not printed), *Hecuba* by Bochatel (1544), *Iphigenia in Aulide* by J. Amyot (1547? not printed) and by T. Sebilet (1549), *Medea* by J. A. de Baif (1570, not printed); in German, *Iphigenia in Aulide* by H. Bebst (1584); in Italian, *Alcestis* by G. Parisotti (1525) and by H. Giustiniano (1599), *Hecuba* by L. Dolce (1543), G. Trissino (1560), G. Gelli (1563), G. Balcianelli (1592), *Iphigenia in Aulide* by L. Dolce (1551), *Phoenissae* by G. Guidi (1532), L. Dolce (1560), *Medea* by L. Dolce (1551); in Spanish, *Hecuba* by P. de Oliva (1533), *Medea* by P. S. Abril (1599). Recent research has modified these counts but confirmed the general trends; we might add, for example, the work of François Tissard, who translated *Medea, Hippolytus,* and *Alcestis* into French (1507); see F. L. Lucas, *Euripides and His Influence* (New York, Longmans, Green, and Co., 1928), 89–117. In addition, Bolgar (524–25) lists 13 translations of individual Sophoclean plays, nine of them featuring women: four versions of *Electra,* four of *Antigone* (not counting Watson's Latin version erroneously categorized as English), one of *Trachiniae.* For Aeschylus (in Latin) see Paul Oskar Kristeller, *Catalogus Translationum et Commentariorum,* 7 vols. (Washington, D.C.: Catholic UP, 1960-), 2: 5–25, 3: 411–12, 7: 293–95.

7. Lumley's translation, without choruses and derived from a Latin intermediary, has been edited by H. H. Child (Malone Society Reprints, 1909) and Gustav Becker, *Shakespeare Jahrbuch* 44 (1910), 28–59. On this play see Lorraine Helms, *Seneca by Candlelight and Other Stories of Renaissance Drama* (Philadelphia: U of Pennsylvania P, 1997), 48–75. We know of Peele's translation from two Latin poems by William Gager; see David H. Horne, *The Life and Minor Works of George Peele* (New Haven: Yale UP, 1952), 42–46. Queen Elizabeth is rumoured to have translated some Euripides (Child, v).

8. Lucas, 97–99; P. Sharratt and P. G. Walsh, *George Buchanan: Tragedies* (Edinburgh: Scottish Academic Press, 1983), 5–7. On the possible influence of Latin Euripides see Emrys Jones, *The Origins of Shakespeare* (Oxford: Clarendon, 1977), 85–118; Louise Schleiner, "Latinized Greek Drama in Shakespeare's Writing of *Hamlet,*" *Shakespeare Quarterly* 41 (1990): 29–48. Schleiner lists Latin editions of Euripides' complete works, 31n.11.

9. Erasmus, *Hecuba & Iphigenia in Aulide* (Venice, 1507), 2ᵛ.

10. On the relation between topography, represented and real, and theatrical space in this play, see David Wiles, *Tragedy in Athens: Performance Space and Theatrical Meaning* (Cambridge UP, 1997), 154–56, 213–14.

11. See Marilyn B. Arthur, "The Curse of Civilization: The Choral Odes of the *Phoenissae,*" *Harvard Studies in Classical Philology* 81 (1977): 163–93.

12. "The slaying of the chthonic serpent at the spring lays claim to the natural riches of the land for civilized human settlement, but the founding acts are also crimes which represent an 'original sin' of civilization from which it cannot be totally freed—a theme which reinforces the play's meditation on the fallibility of *logos* and *sophia* and the power of the irrational/supernatural elements in human life" (Mastronarde, 330).

13. The circumstances of the original production may have amplified this witness if *Phoenissae* played as part of a trilogy that dramatized the curse of fathers through the generations. On this conjecture see D. J. Conacher, *Euripidean Drama: Myth, Theme, and Structure* (U of Toronto P, 1967), 228–29; Mastronarde is skeptical, 13–14, 31–38.

14. Mastronarde, 166; he provides other examples and analogous formulations.

15. Lodovico Dolce, *Giocasta* (Venice, 1549), sig. Aiii.

16. Bernard Weinberg, *A History of Literary Criticism in the Italian Renaissance,* 2 vols. (U of Chicago P, 1961), 739. Derived from Aristotle, Horace, and their commentators, this doctrine circulated widely in the Renaissance; Weinberg cites Robortello (400–401), Trissino (754), and many others.

17. On this speech see Michael Lloyd, *The Agon in Euripides* (Oxford: Clarendon, 1992), 83–93; Mastronarde, 297–98.

18. See Robert B. Parker, *Miasma: Pollution and Purification in Greek Religion* (Oxford: Clarendon, 1983).

19. To place Antigone in literary context see George Steiner, *Antigones* (New York: Oxford UP, 1984).

20. See Sue Blundell, *Women in Ancient Greece* (London: British Museum Press, 1995), 135–44.

21. Dolce plainly identifies Bailo as Polynices' governor (1.3.sd); the English translators identify him as Antigone's governor in the stage directions beginning and ending this scene.

22. Shifting the contexts again, Bailo later refocuses Paidogogus's misogynic comment about female pleasure in gossip (200–201) into a general warning about the power of slander "to blemish the renown of virtue's dames" (1.3.176–77).

23. *Phoenissae* portrays a more sympathetic Polynices than any other surviving treatment (Mastronarde, 27–28); the translators go even further. On *Dike* see Hugh Lloyd-Jones, *The Justice of Zeus* (Berkeley: U of California P, 1971).

24. Ancient scholiasts (Mastronarde, 592n.) and later critics have objected to the apparent contradiction: Antigone decides to bury her brother and incur the death penalty and then to leave the city. Antigone may believe that she can escape death; or the second intention may replace the first.

25. Some editions, including the Loeb, read the sentence as interrogative.

26. On this point see Foley, 106–46.

27. Diodorus Siculus, *Diodorus of Sicily in Twelve Volumes with an English Translation,* ed. and trans. C. H. Oldfather et al., The Loeb Classical Library (1933–67), 13.97.6.

Visible Hecubas

Judith Weil

> It is madness to see them [the Furies]. It may be madder not to.
>
> —Ruth Padel, *In and Out of Mind:*
> *Greek Images of the Tragic Self*

Renaissance tragedies represent fury in diverse shapes: mortal, immortal, monstrous, ordinary, male, female. If these plays are filled with furious significations, how is it possible that anyone could ignore or avoid them? In the study from which the epigraph above derives, Ruth Padel offers one reason when she shows that the ancient Furies, so hideous in aspect and action, appear in Greek tragedies after reciprocity has been violated. To "see" them is to imagine great "damage" in a process of social bonding that often extends across families, cities, and generations.[1] Single them out according to type or focus upon them through a gender-specific lens and Padel's Furies may disappear. In this chapter on the angry descendants of Hecuba I will emphasize incremental and collective elements of their roles and suggest other reasons for their reduced visibility to Renaissance scholars. These include the vitality of Senecan conventions on the Renaissance stage, ethical and psychological views that devalue anger, and a tendency in current critical discourse that Luke Wilson terms "hysteresis," an "elision" of the agencies through which events unfold.[2] I will argue that Renaissance playwrights often distribute the active fury of women among their relatives and henchmen—not to stigmatize these agents as feminine, but, instead, to expand a tragic investigation of how justice and creativity become damaged.

It will be obvious from this preface that I do not "see" tragedy as a prop for patriarchal order, and it will soon be much more obvious that my essay often relies on the perceptions of classicists who, with Nicole Loraux, have been ready to "take a chance on the genre" of Greek tragedy.[3] Their research demonstrates the surprising extent to which tragedies disturb the gender norms maintained by Greek culture. Hecuba will play a major role here, as a figure who can help to identify Greek rages in Renaissance heroines but also as a test case for stretching conceptions of heroism. Hecuba has long stood for the archetypal female sufferer, the helpless widow and mother whose grief for her dead children is overwhelming. Loraux calls her the "paradigm of mourning motherhood" (*Mothers* 40).[4] Part of my project is to suggest that just as no two tragedies are ever quite the same, neither are any two Renaissance Hecubas. In imitating this ancient mother, Renaissance dramatists not only recover the broad scope of her life, from her exposure of Paris on Mount Ida through her loss of husband and children in the Trojan War to her furious revenge on the murderer of her last son. They also displace and rewrite her story, equipping her with agents who enact her rage in ways that are subtle and unpredictable. What these predominantly male agents are to their Hecubas varies with precise social networks that are no longer limited to her biological family.

In the readings that follow I will be more interested in the consequences of women's rage, less interested in how maternal bodies engender suffering and pain. To regard such suffering as necessary is to agree with numerous tragic characters and literary theorists, but it may also be to concede the necessity of the fixations and binary schisms that tragedies can bring into question. As William Arrowsmith points out in his "Introduction to *Hecuba,*" "just because necessity is hard and because the justification it gives—in politics, in love, in war—is unanswerable, it is the justification most frequently debased" (5). Like novelists who turn to tragic themes, playwrights think seriously about the precise interactions through which "necessities" are knotted and untangled. Tragedy, Bernard Williams observes, "is formed around ideas it does not expound" (15), and these ideas encompass social dependencies that vary from culture to culture, play to play. If *Titus Andronicus* were the only kind of Renaissance tragedy and contained the only significant descendant of Hecuba, Tamora Queen of the Goths, it might be fair to decide that wombs are inevitably tombs and that maternal wrath, conforming to a patriarchal gaze, was always barbarous and effeminizing. To unsettle this mode of seeing, I propose to look closely at the rages of Isabella in *Edward II,* Constance in *King John,* Volumnia in *Coriolanus,* and Cornelia in *The White Devil.* But first it will be helpful to summarize several recent discussions of female fury and feminine agency in classical scholarship.

The first dramatic Furies must have put to the test one basic tenet of Aristotelian poetics: that fear (followed by pity) depends upon the spectator's recognizing part of herself in what she sees. For what could be more quintessentially "Other" than the Furies first made visible by Aeschylus in the final play of the *Oresteia?* Like other Furies or Erinyes in Greek literature, their purpose is to punish crimes against "philia," the obligations binding families, kinfolk, friends, hosts, and guests. In the *Eumenides* they embody the implacable wrath of Clytemnestra, killed by her son Orestes in retaliation for her murder of his father Agamemnon, a murder intended to avenge his cooperation in sacrificing their daughter, Iphigenia, before the Trojan War. Probably represented as gorgons with blind, bloody eyes—polluted, doggish, and snake-haired—they must also have been repulsive because of their predatory behavior, their lust for blood.

In an influential essay, "The Dynamics of Misogyny: Myth and Mythmaking in Aeschylus's *Oresteia,*" published in 1978 when she believed that these myths supported gender ideology, Froma Zeitlin treated the Furies as the primal victims of the patriarchal mind, tamed in an Athenian underground after they have hounded Orestes to the shrine of Apollo at Delphi and provoked the intervention of male-born Athena. By 1985 Zeitlin seems to have doubted the aptness of her term "misogyny" and changed her mind about genre. Tragedy, she argued,

> is the epistemological form par excellence. What it does, through the resources of the theater, is to chart a path from ignorance to knowledge, deception to revelation, misunderstanding to recognition. The characters act out and live through the consequences of having clung to a partial single view of the world and themselves. (353)[5]

Other scholars were confronting the Furies, both in the *Oresteia* and in *Hecuba,* where they seem to break loose during Hecuba's horrific revenge on Polymestor, killer of the child she entrusted to his care. These interpretations of enormously complex works deserve much more attention than I can give them here. Elizabeth S. Belfiore's approach to beneficent tragic "fear" through the apotropaic gorgons painted on the bottoms of Greek wine vessels should resonate for Renaissance scholars with Naomi Conn Liebler's account of perverted rituals in "festive tragedy" or with Linda Woodbridge's reflections on the evil eye. Martha C. Nussbaum's treatment of Hecuba as a woman who becomes all the more destructive because of her "fragile" goodness intersects with Adrian Poole's troubling surmise: "One might say of tragedy in general that it is only because we are led to believe that things may go right that when they go wrong we feel such failure to be *tragic,* rather than merely a matter for regret or resignation" (211). Ruth Padel's two studies of tragic madness expose the profound violations of justice that are inseparable from fury, male or female. *Whom Gods Destroy* places Greek tragedy in critical dialogue with later tragedies and with theories of madness that devalue objective causes.

According to Padel, the *Oresteia* "clarifies Erinyes as the concrete, daemonic horror in the human potential for violence. The knowledge that self can damage other, that this force for damage is unlimited, mad, an aberration in the universe that goes on damaging self and others afterwards, is tragedy's heart" (*In and Out of Mind* 175). Because they stand "for other's rights within self, [Furies] are both inside and outside the mind. . . . The center of their persona is self's *awareness* of other's anger" (180). Nussbaum, too, emphasizes the failure of reciprocity that precedes the violence of revenge in *Hecuba*. It is as if such raging women become deranged versions of *kores* or maidens, hideous old children incapable of trust or recognition.

Another exciting investigation is Zeitlin's "The Body's Revenge: Dionysos and Tragic Action in Euripides' *Hekabe*" (*Playing the Other* 172–216). Zeitlin uses a "Dionysiac" approach to "shift the focus away from the judgmental type of criticism that so dominates the interpretation of this the least consoling of Euripides' dramas" (177). Although she emphasizes the somatic power of the maternal body ("No other play forces upon us so insistently the sheer physicality of the self and its component parts," 209), Zeitlin also finds extraordinary interplay among subject positions: "Euripides has constructed a plot that puts maximum pressure on the tension between the stability (and autonomy) of a singular self and the network of reciprocal relations, both manifest and hidden, into which a character is inexorably drawn" (178). "Dionysiac" for Zeitlin becomes a mobile modifier inflecting issues of special concern to feminist critics of early modern tragedy. Like Nussbaum, she stresses the drastic failures of reciprocal vision played out through the two meanings of the word *kore*—the innocent maiden and the pupil of the eye in which others are reflected. ("O woe is me / T'have seen what I have seen, see what I see," says the shattered glass, Ophelia.) She indicates that Hecuba, associated with Dionysius through her Thracian parentage as the daughter of Kisseus, also has a name, "Hekabe," closely linked with "Hekate," so that her fury may invoke the underworld of witchcraft (185). Zeitlin's amoral view of Hecuba's revenge as a Bacchic performance suited to a theatrical festival tends to reduce the ambiguities recognized in other discussions of wrath and justice. But she qualifies her sense of Hecuba's daemonic function—occasioned, in part, by an absence of temples and gods—when she notes that "Stoic sources," Seneca and Lactantius, "understand anger as motivated by the desire to repay wrong unjustly suffered . . . , an appropriate analysis of what happens to Hekabe in our play" (186n35).

As John Kerrigan observes, "revenge and retributive justice are hard to disentangle" (23). This is especially true in a reading of anger like Kerrigan's, haunted by the spectre of Medea and hence of vengeance incommensurate with provocation as well as rebelliously imitative of patriarchal violence. Hecuba's revenge is more collective (which Kerrigan acknowledges, criticizing Nussbaum for treating Hecuba like "a Kantian liberal run wild" 353–54); she acts with a Chorus of enslaved Trojan women. I would add that her revenge complicates gender polarities because Agamemnon, moved by Hecuba through his passion for her only surviving child, Cassandra, grants her control over her enemy, Polymestor. Padel argues that "In Greek tragic plots, madness had two functions—to cause crime and to punish it—which reflect the two weightings of Homeric and tragic Erinyes" (*In and Out of Mind* 177). In *Hecuba,* I think, this difficult balance shifts toward the tragic justice of punishment, offering a model for feminists who might want to take women's wrath more seriously without celebrating patriarchal carnage.

In the *Eumenides,* Athena tells Orestes, "I respect your rights. / Yet these, too, have their work. We cannot brush them aside" (475–76). If her words are more plausible than other claims upon or "appropriations" of justice in the *Oresteia,* it may be because she recognizes a dilemma or "hard course" whether the Furies stay in Athens or get driven off (480–81).[6] Moreover, respecting the Furies in Athenian terms will mean entertaining them as strangers or guests, that is, not as alien others but according to the fundamental values of Greek civility. Insofar as such values survive into Renaissance hospitality, along with a nexus of attitudes about pollution and "oeconomic" space, we might well expect a Renaissance audience to recognize tragic as well as epic elements in female wrath.[7]

There is no denying that angry women are often mocked or trivialized on the Renaissance stage. "As always," writes Michael Hattaway about *The Two Angry Women of Abingdon,* "articulate and angry females are demonized as 'curst'" (109). Ordinary women, Laura Gowing has shown, effectively vented their anger at slanderers by prosecuting them in the church courts.[8] On stage, however, "fury" often becomes a term of male contempt for women's anger. Tragedies in particular seem to concur with advice literature that, as Valerie Wayne notes, associates "women's objections to their circumstances, which could take the form of anger, *with* their weakness, so their resistance was interpreted as a confirmation of their infirmity rather than a justifiable, even necessary response to personal and social constraints on their lives" (173). Again, one may argue that tragic genre should be distinguished from tragic characters, but this argument is unlikely to persuade those who think otherwise if thinking otherwise also includes the belief that anger would have degraded and feminized revengers. According to Alison Findlay, the "view that revenge had an emasculating effect went back to Juvenal's thirteenth *Satire:* 'vengeance is always the delight of a little, weak, and petty mind; . . . no one so rejoices in vengeance as a woman'" (60). Surely such Stoic satire need not be taken as a reliable guide to early modern mentality. Don't bother to punish evil-doers, Juvenal insists—they will either torment themselves with guilt or overreach themselves and get caught. If anger embodies "an inside-and-out-sidedness" (Padel, *In and Out of Mind* 180), it becomes less intelligible when understood too exclusively either as a preoccupation with matters beyond the self (a Stoic view) or as a symptom of inwardness, repression, confinement to the self (a psychologizing, hermeneutic view).[9]

Is it possible to change the ways in which Renaissance scholars "see" anger or the "feminine" agencies of those men who share it with women? Belfiore observes that in the *Eumenides,* "the Erinyes remain the same but our perception of them changes; we are aware first of the negative aspects of the fear inspired by their wrath at pollution, and later of the positive aspects of fear, which can prevent wrongdoing and wrath" (23). The specific plays I am about to consider all invite such altered perceptions; at least one of them illustrates in the "feminine" agency of men that "other" stressed by Zeitlin and Loraux: qualities engaged with, even desired by men who seek a more inclusive humanity.[10] In her introduction to a broad clinical study, *Women and Anger,* Sandra P. Thomas suggests that research on this topic has been preoccupied with the myth that women inhibit or repress their anger and has focussed too narrowly on personal relationships. Pointing out that participants in the study show "concern beyond the self," she argues that a sense of injustice "can produce a very constructive form of anger" (4–6).

Marlowe's *Edward II* has that Euripidean quality that Gordon Braden describes when he distinguishes Greek from Senecan tragic passions: "a diffused communal reality," a "network of social nuance and interconnection" (34, 35). I have chosen to begin with Queen Isabella, who mediates this turbulent "reality," rather than with a more obvious Hecuba figure. Tamora's loyal son compares her with Hecuba in *Titus Andronicus* (1.1.136–41).[11] Loraux begins her pensive monograph on mourning/wrathful mothers with Queen Margaret. But both Tamora and Margaret are also Senecan heroines; they belong to a kind of drama that "reaches its heights not in a vision of ambient, impersonal evil, but in one of furor concentrated, triumphantly embodied in a single character" (Braden 42). Yet even Tamora works through "dispossessed and furious" aliens, her two sons and her lover Aaron (Findlay 64). Margaret's concentrated furor takes effect when Richard exploits the self-destructive weaknesses she identifies in her curses. Loraux invokes Margaret and the angry queens "for those of us who cannot directly feel Greek" (*Mothers* 7). These women who mourn, then rage, illustrate for Loraux a threat that Greek culture could afford neither to permit or ignore—except in the theater. When we turn to *Edward II,* we may get a more Euripidean "feeling" and begin to understand why the Hecuba story maintains its currency in English drama.

Marlowe's play represents the operation of court patronage through a spectrum of male friendships—intimate and erotic, official and domestic, Machiavellian and villainous. Given the fascinations of a patriarchal web, dotted with monstrous men, it may not be surprising that recent readers have diminished Isabella's role. Whether they help or simply use her, none of the contending male characters respects the capacities of the Queen. Gaveston, who occupies her throne and bed, tries to put her in the wrong by insinuating her adultery with Mortimer (1.4.147–48), a ploy that self-justifies Edward in compelling her to plead with the barons for Gaveston's return from exile: "I would wish thee reconcile the lords, / Or thou shalt ne'er be reconciled to me" (1.4.155–56).[12] Edward packs her off to "parley" with her brother, the King of France (3.2.71), who has opportunistically seized Normandy. When her brother treats her with "unkindness"—Spencer bribes his officials to keep him from attacking Edward on her behalf—her unhappiness becomes the occasion for raising an army of English rebels, headed by Mortimer. Successful in upstaging Isabella (4.4.15) and in overpowering Edward, Mortimer assumes that he dominates Isabella and her son: "The prince I rule, the queen do I command" (5.4.47). The Earl of Kent, who has quickly identified Isabella's ambitions with Mortimer's (4.5.21–24), would have agreed. Her angry son, Edward III, is more puzzled by her behavior, but suspecting that she has "conspired" with Mortimer to kill his father, he puts her in the Tower until her responsibility can be determined.

It is tempting to leave Isabella in the dark shadows of the Tower or at least to judge her by the company she has kept. In an astute political reading of *Edward II,* Dympna Callaghan shows that competition between Gaveston and Isabella—between "homoerotic attachment" and "heterosexual alliance" (284)—for "access to the king's body" (287) shores up patriarchal order. "When young Edward comes to power, the juxtaposition of femininity and masculine homoeroticism gives way to a familial and dynastic configuration" (288), purchased, Callaghan argues, through the decapitation/castration of Mortimer, a regicide and "instrument" (289) of a sodomy or chaos in social hierarchy that he both fears and perpetrates. This argument is carefully formulated, but I wonder if Callaghan's term "juxtaposition" and her poetics of materialist feminism don't tend to sort out and clean up the sexual and symbolic chaos actually figured in the relation between Gaveston and Isabella. Castration theory occludes the bond between Isabella and her furious son, even predetermining her guilt. Callaghan replaces the new king's "If you be guilty" and his tearful "I shall pity her if she speak again" (5.6.81, 86) with her own decisive phrase, "having banished his mother and promised her execution" (289).

Keeping Isabella in her "network of social nuance and interconnection" (Braden 35) but dilating the patriarchal gaze, one may suspect that her powers have been underestimated. Immediately after Isabella persuades Mortimer and the barons to repeal Gaveston's sentence of exile, they overhear how Edward "harps upon his minion":

> My heart is as an anvil unto sorrow,
> Which beats upon it like the Cyclops' hammers,
> And with the noise turns up my giddy brain,
> And makes me frantic for my Gaveston;
> Ah, had some bloodless Fury rose from hell,
> And with my kingly sceptre struck me dead,
> When I was forced to leave my Gaveston. (1.4.311–17)

Most readers now credit Isabella with the "reasons of such weight" (1.4.226) that Mortimer urges upon the barons: bring Gaveston home to England because it will be much easier to assassinate him or even find an excuse to rise against the king (1.4.264–66, 279–83). Skilled at bearing a "face of love" while hatching "death and hate" (4.5.23–24), Isabella may have a more immediate connection to the "bloodless Fury" of Lightborn, Edward's murderer, than Mortimer does. Mortimer defers to her judgment when he asks, "Speak, shall he [Edward] presently be dispatched and die?" She seems to anticipate Lightborn's methods with her answer, "I would he were, so it were not by my means" (5.2.44–45). Lightborn, of course, greets Edward in his dungeon-sewer with "The queen sent me to see how you were used, / For she relents at this your misery" (5.5.47–48). Because Isabella is capable of such hypocrisy, how can we be certain that she loves Mortimer? His belief that he controls her may only serve her independent purposes.

One of these purposes, her devotion to her son, persists through her enmity to Edward, making Isabella a far more ambiguous, Euripidean heroine. She treats the prince as if he were the one who had been injured by his father ("O my sweet heart, how do I moan thy wrongs," 4.2.27). In victory, she immediately creates "our well-beloved son, / Of love and care unto his royal person, / Lord Warden of the realm" (4.5.33–35). She repeats that she is willing to destroy Edward and crown the prince if she can thereby secure his "safety" (5.2.17, 43). "Fear not, sweet boy, I'll guard thee from thy foes," she exclaims when Mortimer alarms the new king by executing his uncle Kent (5.4.110). In this revision of the Hecuba story, a mother may suppress her wrath, letting it work out through the brutality of her husband's killers in order to keep herself and her child alive. In some sense, the final explosion of fury from a boy who has always clung to her side is also Isabella's fury. Perhaps that is why Edward III hesitates to treat his mother as a murderess. "I do not think her so unnatural" (5.6.76).

Early in *Edward II* Isabella compares herself to "frantic Juno" and wishes that Circe had changed her shape, presumably to a "Ganymede"

(1.4.172–80). Marlowe's tragedy changes her role and accentuates its classical dimension by developing her antagonism to Gaveston and ultimately to Edward through a complex of pollution metaphors. After Gaveston imagines how he might charm the king by exhibiting "a lovely boy in Dian's shape" bathing in a spring (1.1.60–65), we hear no more about transparent, idyllic waters. Edward and Gaveston outrage the Bishop of Coventry by "christening" him in a "channel" (1.2.187). Mortimer and the barons express their phobia toward Gaveston ("that Proteus, god of shapes," 1.4.410) by comparing him with a "plague" that must be purged (1.4.270), a parasitic fungus ("night-grown mushrump," 1.4. 284), and several transgressive, impure, monstrous creatures: a "vile torpedo" (1.4.223), a "canker" (2.2.18), and a "flying-fish" (2.2.23). Infuriated, Edward cries, "'Tis not the hugest monster of the sea, / Nor foulest harpy that shall swallow him" (2.2.45–46). But when Isabella interacts with the barons and their henchmen, the "foulest harpy" will not be needed. Shortly after Warwick beheads Gaveston "in a trench" (3.2.119) and the barons identify Spencer as a "putrefying branch, / That deads the royal vine" (3.2.162), Isabella joins with Mortimer, who boasts about "This tattered ensign of my ancestors, / Which swept the desert shore of that dead sea, / Whereof we got the name of Mortimer" (2.3.21–23). What "sea" could be more "dead" than the "channel water" with which Matrevis and Gurney barber Edward, obeying the Queen's "charge / To keep your grace in safety" (5.3.14–15, 27–28)? Only the underworld sewers of Berkeley Castle where Edward is compelled to stand for ten days, or the castle moat where Gurney and Matrevis throw Lightborn's body after Edward's murder.

I am suggesting that through metaphor Marlowe organizes a tragic fusion of powers rather than a juxtaposition of distinct political agendas. The impossible contradictions in her "communal reality" transform Isabella into a purifying "Dian" who purges the realm and perhaps herself as well. Less individualized than a *pharmakon* and more aggressive, she attracts and participates in the dangerous agencies of civil war. This queen who unleashes noble watchdogs and disaffected underdogs to hunt down her husband represents Diana in the terrible guise of Hecate, a familiar association, writes Philippa Berry, in "the numerous classical dictionaries and mythographies available at this time" (*Of Chastity and Power* 129).[13] Berry has shown how the dark side of the "Cynthia" cult appears in Chapman's "Hymnus in Cynthiam" where Diana, "an 'All-ill-purging puritie,'" uses her furious dogs to execute "apocalyptic vengeance" and is finally metamorphosed into Hecate, a titanic serpentine figure linked in antiquity with the gorgon Medusa and with potent mother goddesses (141–42). Judith Mossman considers how Hecuba's transformation into a dog associates her with Hecate, by mentioning a surprisingly positive reference in a fragment of Euripides: "You will be a dog, the delight of torch-bearing Hecate" (198; cf. Zeitlin 185, cited above). Tamora, compared to Hecuba, also welcomes identification with "Dian" and her hounds (2.3.61–65). Diana patronized young mothers as well as chaste virgins, but she punished Niobe for boasting that her children were more numerous that those of Latona, Diana's mother. In *Edward II* it is Mortimer who echoes Niobe's overweening pride in Ovid's *Metamorphoses* (VI, 195) shortly before his fall (5.4.68). We should hesitate to see Isabella as a "victim" of patriarchal history (Findlay 167, 169, 172) or as "Mortimer's surrogate wife" (Callaghan 288).

In *King John,* the noble dogs of war briefly play roles that invite us to take a chance on the relevance of Zeitlin's questions about tragic male "femininity": "What do men do that requires, that instigates female intervention?" And, "Why, in the face of a professed inferiority of woman, does the Greek imagination also continually confront the power of the feminine, each time with the need to find some resolution, some accommodation to female demands?" (5). Such questions sound almost too searching for this particular play.[14] The characters of *King John* do refer to Furies, ancestral myths, and Herculean labors, but they do not sustain their passions and commitments, preferring to initiate new and unfinished actions. Legitimacy becomes a vital issue in *King John* because no one can claim it with much persuasiveness. Yet this feudal melée of circumstances also provides subordinate characters— women and followers—with unusual opportunities to alter major events. I would like to look at several passages that are exceptional in *King John* for the odd intensity of the bonds they develop between male and female subjects. These passages suggest that the terror and pity of mothers (Elinor as "Ate," 2.1.63, Constance dead of "frenzy," 4.2.122) revive in the "dogged" rage of warriors and in Hubert's misery at Arthur's death.

Because Elinor and Constance are such dominant presences while alive, it is easy to overlook their spectral agencies after death. When they meet in France they are preoccupied with supporting their sons' claims and with insulting one another in vaunting, epic style. But after Constance loses Arthur to his English captors, her epic anger, bent on shedding blood, begins to shift into a tragic register; eventually, as she anticipates Arthur's death, she becomes the most painful mourning mother in English drama. Shakespeare then seems to break off the deadly process examined by Loraux: the transformation of maternal grief into overwhelming wrath. Instead, he gets rid of the two mothers and Arthur, disappointing his critics. Robert Jones writes that "From this point on in *King John,* virtually everyone loses his way (and not least the critical reader looking for the neatly coherent denouement of a well-made play)" (57). Feminist readers, more likely to prize local female resistance than formal coherence, acutely miss the subversive voices of the mothers. Jean E. Howard and Phyllis Rackin cite Juliet Dusinberre: "the play goes to pieces once the women leave the stage, or once the boys leave it . . . and it never recovers the energy associated with the new world of the Bastard and the new generation: the boys. Or, in our terms, and certainly in Elizabethan terms, the women" (126).

Perhaps because *King John* is generally approached as a history play rather than as a tragedy, its highly charged, Euripedean "network of social nuance" does not stand out, even to a critic like Emrys Jones who is looking for traces of *Hecuba* and of *Iphigenia at Aulis*. Read back to back with *Hecuba,* however, its women, children, and henchmen show up in tragic configuration, temporarily erasing gender lines that have already been blurred, as Howard and Rackin indicate, by the actions of female warriors (122). Maternal mourning does turn into wrath, but those who enact it are men. Shakespeare must foresee how *King John* is about to lose its way when one of these agents-in-waiting, the Earl of Salisbury, brings Constance and Arthur news of the peace plan proposed by Hubert—a marriage between John's niece, Blanche, and the French Dauphin. This follower of John behaves more maternally than Constance herself. Why, she wonders (3.1.20–22), does he look so sadly at Arthur, with his hand on his breast and tears in his eyes? Her ambitions for Arthur frustrated by this sudden friendship between France and England, Constance curses the peaceful "proceedings" (97) and calls on "heavens" to "Set armed discord 'twixt these perjur'd kings!" (111) before the sun goes down. When Pandulph persuades the French king to break his league with John, the newly married Blanche strikes a preliminary tragic note by imagining her *sparagmos:* "each army hath a hand, / And in their rage, I having hold of both, / They whirl asunder and dismember me" (328–30).

With Arthur captured by John, Constance, too, begins to sound more like a Trojan woman, projecting her own sorrow upon Arthur who will "look as hollow as a ghost" (3.4.84) and loving this sorrow in place of her child (93–98). Loraux writes that grief and memory for the "intimacy" of children's bodies can "produce excessive pain for the body-memory of mothers" (*Mothers* 37). In effect, grief over final separation from a child creates an unbearable variant on the pangs of birth. Loraux suggests that when cruel mothers died weeping for their children, ancient audiences would have seen them as justifiably put "out of play" (55–56). Ambitious Constance ought to show some remorse but does not. Hubert and the barons will.

How do the passions of Constance follow Arthur to England and come to life within his male keepers? When Constance goes "out of play," the strong bonds of feudal kinship and service come in. The blinding of Arthur, which would so hideously have violated these reciprocal ties, is averted, thanks to Arthur's skill at manipulating a discourse of obligation and interdependency. However one explains tepid critical responses to Arthur—Pandulph's infectiously cynical attitude toward his prospects, a stage tradition that has sentimentalized him, Hubert's reference to his "innocent prate" or the greater appeal of subverting warriors—it is fair to say that this skill has been overlooked. Wary, prescient, and highly sensitive to strains on reciprocity (i.e., he fears John less than John him, and he loves Hubert more than Hubert him), Arthur can place an enormous "mote" in Hubert's eye (4.1.91) by treating John's agent, assigned to him as his "man" (3.3.73), as if he were instead a master. He reminds Hubert of how he waited upon him during an illness: "you at your sick service had a prince" (4.1.52). Working with a mere hint of compassion in one of Hubert's "executioners" (87), he argues that the very instruments to be used in blinding him are more humane than Hubert: the heated iron has cooled and "like a dog that is compell'd to fight, / [will] Snatch at his master that doth tarre him on. / All things that you should use to do me wrong / Deny their office" (4.1.115–18). By identifying himself with these "officers" and emphasizing his own loyalty ("O, spare mine eyes, / Though to no use but still to look on you!"), Arthur saves his life. Then, instead of sleeping "doubtless and secure" as Hubert instructs him, he assumes a more literal servant role, disguises himself as a ship-boy, and heroically risks death to win freedom by jumping from his prison walls.

In dramatizing reactions to Arthur's death, Shakespeare approximates a Greek sense of tragedy as a group disaster in which mutual blindings, furies, and pollutions multiply. Most significant, I think, is the way that the barons, who have sought to liberate Arthur, "burn in indignation" (4.2.103), their "eyes as red as new-enkindled fire" (163) even before they discover Arthur's body. After they find his corpse, Salisbury says,

> This is the bloodiest shame,
> The wildest savagery, the vildest stroke,
> That ever wall-ey'd wrath, or staring rage
> Presented to the tears of soft remorse. (4.3.47–50)

They "see" Hubert, as John claims to have seen his intended lethal weapon, through "foul imaginary eyes of blood" (4.2.265). Instead of attending "the foot / That leaves the print of blood where e'er it walks" (4.3.25–26), they will hunt John down, as the Furies once tracked "Orestes by blood-drops like a wounded fawn, his 'mother's furious hounds'" (Padel, *In and Out of Mind* 173; cf. her discussion of how Orestes sees Erinys as "the projected image of and from his blood-filled vision of the world," 176). When the Bastard predicts that "Now for the bare-pick'd bone of majesty / Doth dogged war bristle his angry crest, / And snarleth in the gentle eyes of peace" (4.3.148–50), his metaphors connect the barons with Hubert's hot irons, with the executioner who hesitates through "Uncleanly scruples" (4.1.7) and with Hubert's suspicion that the executioners are "dogged spies" (4.1.128). Salisbury claims to be stifled with "uncleanly savors of a slaughter-house, / . . . with this smell of sin" (4.3.112–13). Pollution, disease, childbirth, and rebellion have already begun to fuse through Salisbury's perception that when John's fear of Arthur "breaks" it will "issue" in the "foul corruption of a sweet child's death" (4.2.80–81).

When men weep and rage for a dead child, it is hard to believe that they are merely appropriating women's roles. Purgatorial images of breaking ulcers or bursting bowels in the final acts of *King John* provide savage caricatures of the birth process. Yet if these men cannot share "the body-memory of mothers," they can at least intimate it. The spectacle of Hubert holding Arthur's dead body in his arms is powerfully memorable. Through the anarchic fortunes of war, the barons seem to forget, as Constance never could have, the death of Arthur. Or do they? The final tableau of a tearful young prince surrounded by faithful followers (5.7.103ff.) reconstructs two earlier ones: Blanche and Constance kneeling to beg for peace and war (3.1.308–10), and Arthur surrounded by hostile henchmen with burning rods. The Bastard's final words appear to sanction "needful woe" (5.7.110). Mothers have died but are not altogether absent.

This ritual of kneeling to a young leader will serve to introduce my third example. At the end of *King John,* kneeling helps to compose an image of political solidarity. In the crucial scene of *Coriolanus,* however, the pleading of Volumnia appears to fail so long as she, together with Valeria, Virgilia, and young Martius remain on their knees. Kneeling doesn't seem to work, although Coppélia Kahn, joining Plutarch's narrative to a psychoanalytic one, grants it the power to subdue Coriolanus. Because, she reasons, sons normally kneel to mothers, Volumnia "reverses the usual gesture of indebtedness only to evoke more pointedly the unusual totality of his debt to her so that he will capitulate to her" (*Roman Shakespeare* 157). R. B. Parker has pointed out in his edition how kneeling "runs throughout the action and dialogue of the play" (103). He regards the final gesture as "submissive and aggressive, sincere and challenging" (105). These interpretations are representative in that they explain momentous change of heart through customary practices and attitudes, thereby shutting a window of promise that cracks open for rigid Rome and its overdetermined hero. The tragedy of Coriolanus is not that he listens to Volumnia but that Aufidius and his Volscians can so quickly reverse the transformation Volumnia initiates. To echo her son (5.3.183), what *has* she done, and why is it so surprisingly out of her character and his?

When we think of allusions to Hector and Hecuba in *Coriolanus,* we may realize that even by the epic standards of the *Iliad,* Coriolanus fights with exceptional fury. Volumnia's values, as editor Philip Brockbank suggests (33) and Kahn persuasively illustrates (146–47), seem to derive from Sparta. The first reference to the Trojan hero occurs after Coriolanus, "masked" in the blood of Corioli, also threatens Aufidius with death as a slave in order to "wrench up" his vengeance. Aufidius launches into combat with "Wert thou the Hector / That was the whip of your bragg'd progeny / Thou shouldst not scape me here" (1.8.11–13). He reduces "Hector" to a scourge or whip, often a figure for tragic fury but in this instance little better than an instrument or tool. Volumnia seems happy to imagine her son in such terms when she compares him to "a harvest-man [that's] task'd to mow / Or all or lose his hire" (1.3.36–37), a mechanical grim reaper who gets on with his task more easily after blasting his co-fighters as cowards. Notoriously, she celebrates his "bloody brow" (which the audience will soon see) by asserting, "The breasts of Hecuba, / When she did suckle Hector, look'd not lovelier / Than Hector's forehead when it spit forth blood / At Grecian sword, [contemning]" (1.3.40–43). This mother who wishes she had a dozen sons to risk in war (1.3.22) could hardly be more different from Hecuba who loses 50 and, in the *Iliad,* begs Hector to stay away from battle, reminding him of a lost "blissful proximity" between mother and child by baring her breast (Loraux, *Mothers* 38).[15]

In *Coriolanus* circumstances conspire to fix the hero in an instrumentality, as living sword or whip, which he at times fears and resents. This is not the place to argue that militant Rome, where enslavement is a constant threat and slaves are confounded with a range of dependent positions, would be particularly damaging for a young man who comes of age with almost no experience of mediated, protected vulnerability. At his best, as a "servant" of the state, he can advise his son to "stick i' th' wars / Like a great sea-mark, standing every flaw, / And saving those that eye thee!" (5.3.73–75). At his worst, he becomes a "whip" for Aufidius, convinced as he watches his mother bow that he can "stand / As if a man were author of himself, / And knew no other kin" (5.3.35–37). When he kneels to Volumnia and she promptly kneels back to "Show duty as mistaken all this while / Between the child and parent" (55–56), he rises—and raises her—with a sense that his world has flipped over. But in fact, maternal (Plutarchan) arguments that follow do not move him. "He turns away," Volumnia exclaims, ordering her companions, "let us shame him with our knees. / To his surname Coriolanus / 'longs more pride / Than pity to our prayers" (169–71). Where her first kneeling is an ironic reflex dramatizing her personal humiliation, the second involves a collective suppliancy.

Lest anyone take such a ritual for granted when Hecuba (successfully) performs it upon Agamemnon, William Arrowsmith and Herbert Golder spell out its "sacrosanct" significance for a Greek audience. "Formal supplication requires that one person kneel before another with hands outstretched, one reaching toward the chin, the other touching the knee—an image of vulnerability that says 'I am wholly in your power,' forcing the person in control to recognize in the supplicant the helplessness of the mortal condition that *mutatis mutandis,* they share" (Editors' Foreword to *Hecuba* vi-vii). Because her son, with his severe reciprocity disorder, can't see this implication or anything like it—his son "holds up hands for fellowship" (175)—Volumnia flies into a justifiable rage, a brief fit of fury that succeeds where other words and gestures have failed.

At this point the Roman matron, her confidence badly shaken, her son ethically blinded, suddenly behaves more like an Athenian tragic mother. Getting up, she cries out, "Come, let us go. / This fellow had a Volscian to his mother; / His wife is in Corioles, and his child / Like him by chance" (177–80). This sweep through the relationships Coriolanus could destroy lashes him into compassion. It undoes that bloody self-birth out through the gates of Corioles that so hardened him in his instrumental pride, and it turns him into an emissary of peace, thereby preventing a general massacre. Must we see Coriolanus as a sacrifice to Volumnia and the Roman state (Kahn 158)? Or has his mother brought him to a consciousness of responsibility and given him a choice about what to do next? Is it inevitable or is it rather a tremendous waste and loss when Aufidius breaks down his nascent sense of fellowship, turns him back into a sword, and throws him away?

The White Devil fits one premise about tragedy on which the discussion above has leaned heavily. Webster's play is decentered; it explores the dynamics of relationships within subordination, linking the agencies of women and dependent men through a dense tangle of dog and fury metaphors. These intricate correspondences encourage an awareness like that which Judith Newton and Deborah Rosenfelt endorse when they briefly shift their attention from gender-specific to intersubjected bonds: "Women, like men, appear divided from each other, enmeshed not in a simple polarity with males but in a complex and contradictory web of relationships and loyalties" (*Feminist Criticism and Social Change* xxvi). But *The White Devil* also challenges other premises that I have been exploring. Most tragedies open up space in which to rehearse or contemplate alternative attitudes. Many make it difficult to justify violence before the fact; they defy a willingness to understand them back to front, by refusing to be over until they are over. They test "necessity" to the limits of culture and beyond.[16] Indeed, by featuring excess—what could happen but normally does not—tragedies often falsify the master narratives of theoretical analysis. Or so I would like to think. With corrupt masters apparently controlling its narrative, *The White Devil* eliminates promising transformations or escape routes and normalizes criminal violence. Desperate characters change the compression chambers in which they explode, but their play does seem to be over before it begins.

Given so many post-tragic qualities, the function of the Hecuba legend in *The White Devil* has particularly significant effects. As he wrote his unusual play, working up a contemporary story about Italian court intrigue, Webster rediscovered one of the more terrible elements in the Hecuba legend: not her final revenge or transformation into a dog but her inability to help and protect her children, even when she can anticipate danger. What, he seems to have wondered, would happen to a vulnerable widow and her children in a world of people who had already turned into dogs and furies? Whether he was looking for the Trojan antecedents of contemporary Roman barbarism or thinking his way back to Greece through a practice of imitating other playwrights, Webster managed to give his Italian documentary a Euripidean substructure. This substructure does not have to be clearly visible so long as it actively motivates a "network of social nuance and interconnection."[17]

When Cornelia suddenly interrupts Vittoria's meeting with Bracciano, arranged by her brother Flamineo, she joins her kneeling daughter for "the most woeful end e'er mother kneel'd" (1.2.294)[18]: a maternal curse that echoes Margaret's curse of Queen Elizabeth in *Richard III* (299–300; cf. *Richard III* 1.3.206). Flamineo mocks his mother with "What Fury rais'd thee up?" (1.2.270); Bracciano blames Cornelia with "Be thou the cause of all ensuing harm" (307); Cornelia herself blames "the curse of children" (280) and disappears from the play until act 5. In the meantime, Bracciano's powerful brothers-in-law, Francisco de Medici and Cardinal Monticelso, brilliantly victimize Vittoria and Isabella, Bracciano's wife, in order to destroy Bracciano and secure his patrimony for Isabella's son. Patriarchy as usual, we may decide, until Cornelia once more erupts into action by striking Zanche, the lover of Flamineo, thereby provoking a furious quarrel between Flamineo and his brother, Marcello. Flamineo stabs Marcello in the back, causing him to fall into Cornelia's bosom, just after Marcello has recalled his mother's tale of how, "giving my brother suck, / He took the crucifix between his hands, / And broke a limb off" (5.2.11–13). Webster creates still another potent connection between mother and son when Cornelia's mourning over Marcello's corpse prompts Flamineo to attack Vittoria—whom he would have shot had not Francisco's henchmen executed them both.

This rapid survey is enough, I hope, to suggest that Francisco de Medici, who thinks of himself as a mastermind, does not deserve full credit for purging his *famiglia*. Weaving through *The White Devil* goes the story of how Hecuba exposed her infant son, Paris, on Mount Ida because she had dreamt that he was a burning brand who would ruin Troy. Flamineo knows what his name means: "A flaming fire-brand casts more smoke without a chimney"

(5.4.47–48). He condemns his impoverished mother for sending him to university and blocking his path to "preferment" (1.2.329) through his sister's body. His desperate fury of ambition may not be so far a cry from the wrath that Edward II and Coriolanus inherit from their mothers. Flamineo burns down his family tree and destroys his "house" as thoroughly as any Paris does because he has learned that a prostitute would at least have equipped him with many fathers (1.2.334–38). Instead, he survives under Bracciano's patronage "like a wolf in a woman's breast" (5.3.56) until his patron is poisoned and Cornelia's terrible "howling" drives him to his death, side by side with Vittoria—who courageously bares her breast to her killers, like Polyxena, the sacrificed virgin in *Hecuba*. Webster draws on the agonies of ancient myth to profoundly question the parallel injustices of politic alliance for young women and vicious, enslaving patronage for young men. Again, Hecuba could not have taken revenge on Polymestor without the furious agency of an enslaved Chorus.

The heroism of tragic women like these descendants of Hecuba may vanish if we stare at them too directly. Hamlet, the motive for so many idealized, centered readings of tragedy, wonders what Hecuba, sorrowing wife, has to do with the passions of a weeping player. Perhaps we might wonder whether Hamlet's rage blinds him to the role played by his own mother, Gertrude. Through Rosencrantz and Guildenstern, Polonius and Ophelia, she does attempt to help her son. In tragedy, the heroism of guarding and protecting those assumed to need it can go terribly wrong. Paris is said to have been nursed on Mount Ida by a bear. In *The Winter's Tale,* Antigonus is eaten by one when he exposes Perdita on the seacoast of Bohemia, obedient to his dream-vision of a Hermione who weeps in "fury" (3.3.26) and predicts his punishment for "this ungentle business" (34). If an invisible Hecuba has such power, her visible counterparts must be granted much greater passion and importance.

Notes

1. According to Padel, " Tragedy explores damage within bonded relationships that is worked out by Erinys, daemon of the lasting reality of remembered hurt, of self's self-destructive awareness of other's anger" (*In and Out of Mind* 171). I am especially indebted to the eighth chapter of Padel's study.
2. Wilson uses Anthony Giddens' concept of "practical consciousness" to criticize Foucault and Bourdieu (22). The "hysteresis effect is [. . .] the outcome of a particular rhetorical strategy that seeks to bridge personal experience and the social world through an elision of the person of the agent" (47n19). Frank Whigham brings Giddens and Bourdieu together (*Seizures of the Will* 2–4) in order, I think, to define a sociological "cosmos" in which emergent individuals can seize identities—their own and others'.

3. The context for this phrase from *Tragic Ways of Killing a Woman* (63) is the ending of her "journey" through the "constants" of different tragedies, exploring the "paradox" that women who die nobly must die like men.

4. As a mourner, Loraux points out, Hecuba initiates the lamentation for Hector in the *Iliad* (36) as well as that for Astyanax in *Trojan Women* and for Polyxena in *Hecuba* (40–41). Loraux' brief discussion of Hecuba's revenge and metamorphosis (50) tends to simplify the fury of Hecuba and of the Chorus who assist her: a "female dog is an Erinys only because she is complete motherhood"; when Hecuba becomes a bitch, the "mourning mother has fulfilled her fate."

5. Zeitlin's "Introduction" to *Playing the Other* reflects on her use of terms as part of an overview concerned with how her approach to the study of gender in culture has changed (6–8). Loraux wrote *Tragic Ways* with "only one preconception—that at all costs the sterile opposition between feminism and misogyny should be avoided" (62).

6. *The Eumenides,* trans. Richmond Lattimore, *Greek Tragedies Vol. 3,* ed. David Grene and Richmond Lattimore (Chicago: U of Chicago P, 1960). Goldhill comments on the *Oresteia:* "Each character appropriates *diké* to his or her rhetoric. It is this sort of one-sided laying claim to evaluative and normative words that I term 'the rhetoric of appropriation'" (46).

7. Woodbridge's first chapter, focused on Elizabethan pollution beliefs, draws on the ideas of Mary Douglas's *Purity and Danger* to illuminate political and historical circumstances vital for understanding a wide range of texts. Heal's study of hospitality often describes the ritual and public elements of changing customary practice; the English populace, she observes, lacked a strong ethic of openness to strangers (387). Just how ominous the more mythical significations of house might become has been argued by Orlin with special reference to *Othello* (*Private Matters* 191–245). On the current relevance of Greek pollution beliefs, cf. Padel: "Letting someone in, not to your body but your house, had a body charge with emotional implications that, for the modern Western world, is only comparable in intensity to sex. There were many divinely monitored rules governing relations between host and guest. In our vaccinated age, when researchers through four centuries have worked so long and often dangerously to understand bacilli, and yet we now face another sexually transmitted epidemic we cannot control, we should not underrate the physicality, and pervasiveness, of Greek pollution. Like syphilis or AIDS, it was physical, mysterious, and no respecter of motive" (*Whom Gods Destroy* 153).

8. Lena Orlin stressed the importance of Gowing's research when she criticized an earlier version of this paper written for a seminar, "Critical Genealogies: Feminism and Shakespeare's Canon," led by Margo Hendricks at the International Shakespeare Conference, 1998.

9. In *Poetic Justice* Nussbaum argues that narrowly external or internal understandings of emotion deprive readers and jurors of ethical information needed for "full social rationality" (56, 65–66). For another discussion of ju-

dicial reasoning, deeply informed by classical thinkers, including tragedians, see her essay "Equity and Mercy" in *Sex & Social Justice* 154–83.

10. In "The Feminine Operator," her Introduction to *The Experiences of Tiresias*, Loraux cites Zeitlin on "hypotheses" they share, accepting the idea that "'to play the other' opens the citizen's masculine identity 'to the often banished emotions of terror and pity'" (9).

11. Quotations from Shakespeare throughout this essay refer to *The Riverside Shakespeare*, ed. G. Blakemore Evans, 2nd ed. (Boston: Houghton, 1997). Emrys Jones believes that *Hecuba,* translated into Latin by Erasmus and used as an example in Sidney's *Apology for Poetry,* was probably known to sixteenth-century writers (95–97). After surveying the influence of *Hecuba* through the Renaissance, Judith Mossman finds "strong affinities" rather than "precise links" in English tragedies (236). Mossman also emphasizes Tamora's differences from Hecuba (236n67, 241–43).

12. *Edward the Second,* ed. W. Moelwyn Merchant (London: Benn, 1967).

13. In the *Aeneid,* Juno remembers "Cisseus' daughter" when she plans to wreak havoc in Italy through Aeneas's marriage to Lavinia (VII 319–20).

14. Barbara Hodgdon seems to hint at laissez-faire slackness when she writes, "Much about the play operates like a present-day television commercial, especially those that market a product to a plurality of audiences simultaneously by creating multiple subject positions" (28).

15. Loraux considers Plutarch's Volumnia, not Shakespeare's (18, 30–32), but her discussion of the Spartan Queen Praxithea, from Euripides' fragment *Erechtheus* as quite probably a case of "maximum" unmotherly "excess" in Athenian eyes (13–14) could well apply to Shakespeare's mother on her first appearance.

16. For an arresting view of excess, cf. Loraux on Antigone as a tragic character (*Mothers* 28): "She bears witness to the limits beyond which the thinkable cannot be subverted" (28).

17. In "*The White Devil* and Old Wives' Tales" I argue that Webster gives Cornelia and Isabella power over the design of his tragedy by linking them through allusion to disruptive female figures in tragic and epic tradition and in ancient legend. This becomes more apparent, I suggest, when the contexts of his imitations are taken into consideration.

18. *The White Devil,* ed. John Russell Brown (Manchester: Manchester UP, 1985).

"Not Know Me Yet?" 〰️

Looking at Cleopatra in Three Renaissance Tragedies

Mimi Still Dixon

"Eva Prima Pandora" is inscribed on a medallion that hangs over the reclining nude woman in a sixteenth-century French painting now in the Louvre [plate 4.1]. The picture, attributed to Jean Cousin and possibly the first nude painted in France, attempts to fix with clear verbal symbolism an image whose semiotic meaning is a little more ambiguous. This is Eve, who is also Pandora. Thus the death's head, a reminder that death is the wages of sin, that a woman's body is a "whited sepulcher"; also in the picture are Eve's apples, a serpent, Pandora's jars, one of which she seems to be in the act of closing or opening, as the serpent slides out of it. But recent illuminations of the painting in the laboratory have revealed something more. Another snake has been hidden, almost painted out, emerging from the jar. In the city behind the woman are ancient temples—could it be Alexandria? The pattern of the picture seems to be borrowed from a frontispiece by Holbein where the figure is clearly identified as Cleopatra. She is much like other images of Cleopatra in the period, the serpent wound up her arm in the moment before death. Why has her identity been obscured, merged into the more general moralization offered by Eve and Pandora? Perhaps, as one art historian claims, it is because this painting makes a political as well as a moral statement. Her face and her pose might have called to mind as well the notorious "other woman" who was said to rule the French king, Henry II, as his mistress—Dianne de Poitiers, immortalized in the bronze of Diana by Cellini installed over the entrance to her famous Chateau (Guillaume 191–92).

I don't want to belabor the historical connections, interesting as they are; I wish to look instead at what it means to gaze at such a picture. Our

Plate 4.1   Jean Cousin, *Eva Prima Pandora*. Paris, Louvre. By permission of Réunion des Musées Nationaux.

woman—whoever she is—is typical of the Renaissance nude—her marmoreal whiteness, reflecting the Renaissance identification of the body with ancient statues, airbrushed, as it were, of all particularity and remaining idealized, generalized Woman; she is an erotic space, a blank white canvas waiting for the inscriptions of male desire, her being dominated by the male gaze. Her passive and receptive pose is arranged to be seen, confronting the viewer in what looks to be a rather uncomfortable twist, just tense enough to make it look conscious; her glance is deflected, but indeterminate. Is she thinking of something else, or is she politely looking away so that our view of her is not ruffled by any reflexive gaze? Is she gazing at anything at all? Her body is too conscious of its presence and ours. It is a body to be looked at, offering itself, without any complications, ostensibly inviting our look, serving our visual pleasure. She stares off at a point that is nowhere. She has no thoughts. Or (the viewer thinks) is she hiding them?

And who is looking at Eve-Pandora-Cleopatra-Diane? As John Berger asserts in *Ways of Seeing,* the observer of the classic nude is male. Such paintings are made to serve a male spectator and male patron; they objectify the female body, erase its particularity and subjectivity. "But in all of them"—as I think we can see in our Cleopatra—"there remains the implication that the subject (a woman) is aware of being seen by a spectator" (Berger 49). Sometimes the woman will look back seductively. Sometimes her self-consciousness becomes the theme of the picture, Berger tells us. In Tintoretto's *Susannah and the Elders,* for example, Susannah looks at herself in a mirror, thus becoming a spectator of herself, complicitous with the leering elders and the leering viewer. Berger says that the hypocrisy of such visual fictions reaches a peak with depictions of Vanity as a naked woman admiring herself in a mirror. "You painted a naked woman because you enjoyed looking at her, you put a mirror in her hand and you called the painting Vanity, thus morally condemning the woman whose nakedness you had depicted for your own pleasure. The real function of the mirror was otherwise. It was to make the woman connive in treating herself as, first and foremost, a sight" (51).

What Laura Mulvey and others have said about the male cinematic gaze and its objectification of the female body in service to male visual pleasure can be extended (with important differences) to looking at paintings or looking at the stage. But such specularity is both changing and complex.[1] As culturally inscribed behaviors, both looking and being looked at have a history. In the Renaissance, perspectival painting constructed a unified point of observation, essentially detaching the observer from the object, but in the process both constructing him as the active observer of the scene in a mathematically rationalized space and at the same time obscuring this act of construction. The development of perspective in Renaissance painting has been seen as a metaphor for the early modern construction of the autonomous male subject; as I want to suggest, looking at the Renaissance nude serves as a useful trope for the problematics of knowledge and power relations in the early modern era. If what is at stake in exploring female tragic heroism on the Renaissance stage is precisely the possibility of staging female subjectivity, such looking relations are critically important. Does *looking* at Cleopatra on the stage inevitably prohibit our *seeing* her?

When the unitary viewer is confronted with an erotic object, the dynamics of looking and the potential of constructing a self—a male subjectivity—in relation to a female other become particularly charged and consequential. Her subjectivity must be effectively erased to enable him to experience his own; the seer effectively dominates the object of vision. What is at stake is the self-image of the viewer; enhanced by the passivity of the female, he is active, autonomous, rational, independent, self-controlled. But this subjective stance is in fact threatened by the very act of erasing the subjectivity of the "not-me," the objectified other. Her repressed subjectivity becomes unknowable, her mind and her intentions inscrutable, and her body takes on a dangerous power uncontrolled by a conscious mind. Thus the contradictions between the symbolic and the semiotic in the *Eva Prima Pandora*. The moral condemnation of her cannot frame the temptations she offers, the magical power she holds—her body enchants, casts spells, seduces. It implicates the viewer in a charged way in the radical ambiguities of looking, the contradictions and ambivalences of perspective. This notion of ambivalent perspectives is particularly resonant in the Renaissance, an era of suddenly multiplied points of view and a potentially relativized and expanding globe.

The femme fatale, I would argue, has a privileged place in the cultural history of images, a position that helps to account for the renaissance of Cleopatras in the early modern period. According to Mary Ann Doane in *Femmes Fatales,* the seductive woman "is the figure of a certain discursive unease, a potential epistemological trauma. For her most striking characteristic, perhaps, is the fact that she never really is what she seems to be. She harbors a threat which is not entirely legible, predictable, or manageable" (1). Representations of the femme fatale thus transform "the threat of the woman into a secret, something which must be aggressively revealed, unmasked, discovered" (1). Her presence raises questions about "vision and its stability or instability." She is an "ambivalent figure because she is not the subject of power but its *carrier*. . . . Indeed, if the Femme Fatale overrepresents the body it is because she is attributed with a body which is itself given agency independently of consciousness. In a sense, she has power *despite herself*. . . . The Femme Fatale is an articulation of fears surrounding the loss of stability and the centrality of the self, the 'I,' the ego" (2). Doane is discussing the popularity of the dark, oriental seductress in the nineteenth century and in contemporary film, and she connects this with modernist cultural anxiety about the male body, male agency, and the newly articulated concept of the unconscious. "Her power is of a peculiar sort insofar as it is usually not subject to her conscious will, hence appearing to blur the opposition between passivity and activity" (2). But we can see similar anxieties expressed not just in representations of Cleopatra, but popular Renaissance images of Delilah, Salome, Omphale, Venus, or even of the ravished or raped nymphs, or the innocent Dianas, Susannahs, and Lucreces, whose narratives are explicit about the misfortune of being seen, but who nevertheless, while protesting their innocence, reveal their dangerous and seductive bodies.

This use of the other's body to work out conflicts or anxieties of the self is a dangerous game. Images cannot be held at a distance. Even if she doesn't look back, even when she's artfully framed, the woman possesses visual and erotic power in relation to the viewer. In *The Power of Images,* David Freedberg argues persuasively that whatever we tell ourselves about our detachment from the visual object, we can't repress our responses, even our empathy with it. In earlier visual regimes, the medieval for example, it was understood that the icon could send out its visual rays to the worshiper and transform him. But given the fiction of objectivity in the modern era, the viewer is rendered particularly vulnerable to the threat of the image, or the subjectivity of the other. Cleopatra, of course, is doubly "othered" as a dark, exotic figure, oriental or African, the subject being just as vulnerable, dependent, and thus threatened in relation to racial and cultural others upon whom he has projected rejected and repressed aspects of the self. Thus Cleopatra becomes an overdetermined figure, the feminine and the exotic fusing in her as they would later in Freud's image of the unknowable female psyche as a "dark continent" (Freud 212).[2]

Shakespeare's *Antony and Cleopatra* is a complex play in part because it foregrounds these issues of sexual power and visual perspective, of subjects and objects and knowledge relations. By doing so, it avoids the simple resolutions of the moralizing or romanticizing representation. To return to our picture of the naked Cleopatra: Shakespeare brings the invisible male viewer into the picture, and turns the gaze on him as well. Thus male anxieties about the loss of power or selfhood are seen in the context of male objectifications of others. And that loss is frequently imaged in the play in terms of seeing: Antony can't see his own shape, is feminized by being looked at, becomes a spectacle of shame when his sight of Cleopatra causes him to lose control. "His goodly eyes that . . . glowed like plated Mars, now bend, now turn / The office and devotion of their view / Upon a tawny front" (1.1.4–6).[3]

From the very opening of the play with its commands to "behold and see," we are enjoined to look. But, as Janet Adelman tells us, the play never gives us a stable point from which to judge appearances; it never rests in a single perspective, but is propelled by its own uncertainty principle. This radical ambivalence threatens the culturally privileged Roman (male, European, imperial) point of view, which is continually dislocated by Cleopatra and the feminized, othered, oriental. Cleopatra, of course, is the supremely self-conscious object. She exploits her power as visual object with her unrelenting theatrics. Her personal and political strategies depend on the power of theatrical spectacle. She takes the cliche of the femme fatale to such an extreme that it doubles back on itself—returns to her a kind of agency and conscious will that the passive and inscrutable seductress of convention does not have. Whether at Cydnus or in her tomb, she plays to the viewer.

One of the central mysteries of Shakespeare's tragedy, its suspense, lies in discovering Cleopatra as a subject—a subjectivity that is a minimal condition, I would argue, for tragic heroism as it is usually defined. Cleopatra remains so perfectly in control of the lines of sight in the play that we can't really see her for seeing her. As Mary Ann Bushman says, Cleopatra herself becomes visible—beyond the roles and spectacle—only in a few moments of failed performance, "failed speech" or "incompleteness" (40). We glimpse her interiority only in the gaps between performances. And this is indeed ironic for a heroine who fulfills most of our requirements for the construction of subjectivity—she speaks amply and royally, and she dominates. As Helen Mirren put it so colorfully, Cleopatra "is the best-written female role ever. She's full of fire and spark and has balls" (qtd. in Garber 37). Yet her power is clearly threatening—though she speaks, we don't know her. And Cleopatra's excluded subjectivity in a sense structures the play. We wait for a soliloquy that doesn't come. The play "creates in the audience a desire for soliloquy, for a moment of stasis that interrupts the continual role-playing and reflects on it. Yet this desire for soliloquy never gets fulfilled; instead her speeches invite the audience to complete her" (Bushman 40). We have to imagine a Cleopatra. And in doing so, we construct a female tragic hero, despite strong cultural inhibitions against doing so.

It may help to see how Shakespeare's exclusion of Cleopatra's soliloquy and subjectivity works if we compare this play with two very different dramatic treatments of Cleopatra from the same period. In 1592, the Countess of Pembroke published her own translation of Robert Garnier's *Marc Antoine,* a translation that Shakespeare probably knew. Mary Sidney's play is a Senecan tragedy that opens with Antony's defeat at Actium and ends with Cleopatra lamenting Antony's death and resolving "To die with thee and dieing thee embrace: My bodie joynde with thine, my mowth with thine" (ll. 1964–65).[4] However we might interpret Mary Sidney's decision to translate this tragedy, and even acknowledging, as several critics have said, that Sidney is a woman "written by men," her choice of this particular play to fulfill a masculine agenda presents us with multiple ironies. It is a strange choice, perhaps even a defiant one, much as that defiance may be hedged by gestures of femininity.

Most European women seem to have had little sympathy for Cleopatra, to have seen her competitively as the "other woman." As Kim Hall argues, English women had an interest in "othering" the African queen and identifying with the wronged wife Octavia; they racialize Cleopatra as a way of consolidating their own precarious status (177–86). Thus Aemilia Lanyer uses Cleopatra as a recurring foil to her virtuous patronesses; in the "Salve Deus Rex Judaiorum" Cleopatra reveals her lustful duplicity as a "black Egyptian" (l. 1431). Elizabeth Cary too in *The Tragedy of Mariam* makes Cleopatra foil to the virtuous Mariam, underlining their differences not just in terms of character but color. If in these women's writings the othered woman is blackened, in Mary Sidney's sympathetic treatment of Cleopatra, the heroine's beauty is described as flawless "faire alablaster [*sic*]" (l. 421).

In further contrast not just to these versions of Cleopatra but to Shakespeare's as well, Sidney/Garnier's Cleopatra speaks her heart out. If only because of the conventions of Senecan drama, Cleopatra speaks in lengthy, self-revealing monologues, thus amply satisfying the "anticipation of soliloquy" so effectively frustrated in Shakespeare. Indeed, this interiorizing of Cleopatra in this play comes close to being the whole point, the central dramatic irony. In this portrait, Cleopatra turns from her recumbent pose and spills her heart out—not to the audience exactly, but the to absent Antony. However, the cost of this shift from object to subject, from other to self, is her complete domestication. Cleopatra can't become a subject until she becomes a loyal English wife. Moreover, Octavia, whose presence might contest that position, almost completely drops out of the picture. Along with the deracializing of Cleopatra comes her revision from femme fatale to patient Griselda or falsely accused Constance.

Cleopatra's final gesture in Sidney's play is to sacrifice everything for Antony—her children, state, people—to follow him to the banks of the Styx where he waits for her. The good wife is unequivocally devoted to her "holy mariage."

> Antonie by our true loves I thee beseeche,
> And by our hearts sweete sparks have set on fire,
> Our holy mariage, and the tender ruthe
> Of our deare babes, knot of our amitie:
> My dolefull voice thy eare let entertaine,
> And take me with thee to the hellish plaine.
> Thy wife, thy frend. (ll. 1945–51)

In her long laments in act 2, it is not duplicity that characterizes this Cleopatra but complete sincerity, not theatrics but intimacy. As she laments Antony's lack of faith in her constancy, his belief that she betrayed him with

Caesar, his blaming her as the cause of his downfall, her focus is on the distance between how she is seen and her interior emotional reality.

> That I have thee betraide, deare *Antonie,*
> My life, my soule, my sunne? I had such thought?
> That I have thee betraide my Lord, my King?
> That I would breake my vowed faith to thee?
> Leave thee? Deceive thee? . . .
> . . . I ever had that hart?
> . . . .
> Rather, o rather let our Nilus send,
> To swallow me quicke some weeping Crocodile. (ll. 388–98)

These are no crocodile tears. Cleopatra's love is selfless, her protestations without irony. She is devoted only to Antony's love, "thy love alas! thy love, / More deare then Scepter, children, freedome, light" (ll. 409–10).

Her debate with her women as they try to dissuade her from suicide underscores the excessive and heroic (or sentimental?) nature of her self-abandon. Charmian asks, "what helps his wrack this ever-lasting love? . . . Ill done to loose your selfe, and to no end" (ll. 547–49). Cleopatra answers, "Without this love I should be inhumaine" (l. 557).

> CH. Live for your sonnes.
>   CL. Nay for their father die.
> CH. Hardharted mother!
>   CL. Wife, kindhearted, I. (ll. 555–57)
> . . . .
> CH. Our first affection to ourselfe is due.
> CL. He is my selfe.
>   CH. Next it extends unto
> Our children, frends, and to our country soile.
> And you for some respect of wively love,
> (Albee scarce wively) loose your native land,
> Your children, frends, and (which is more) your life.
> With so strong charmes doth love bewitch our witts. (ll. 587–93)

Cleopatra figures here in something like a general defense of woman, contradicting Antony's bitter blame in the opening scene of the play. Though we see Cleopatra actively willing the actions that she will finally take, this picture of the heroine essentially erases the threat of female power because of Cleopatra's strong insistence on sacrificing that power for Antony. "He is my selfe" (588), she proclaims, after all, so that despite her strong assertion of selfhood, despite this moment of conscious control and decision-making, her "selfe" essentially dissolves into Antony.

Where Cleopatra's monologues all address the absent Antony, Antony's address himself—the disillusioned Antony in dialogue with his former self, who has been the naive dupe of the scheming seductress. She is a "traitres," a perjurer, the whole cause of his downfall in betraying him to Caesar. She is his scapegoat: the Delilah who sheared off his hair, the Omphale who unmanned her Hercules, the Eve who flaunted her apples, the Pandora who let pleasure and despair out of the box. The story of othering—the efficient deflection of anger, in this case, from a male "competitor" to the female other—is told in stark images.[5] Imagining himself paraded through Rome by Caesar, Antony refuses to give Caesar his triumph:

> Thou only *Cleopatra* triumph hast,
> Thou only hast my fredome servile made,
> Thou only hast me vanquisht: not by force
> (for forste I cannot be) but by sweet baites
> Of thy eyes graces, which did gaine so fast
> Upon my libertie, that nought remain'd
> None els henceforth, but thou my dearest Queene,
> Shall glorie in commaunding *Antonie.* (ll. 31–38)

One couldn't find a more vivid revelation of cultural anxiety about male autonomy and selfhood than in the imagery of this scene. Antony is stripped naked—

> . . . nought remaines . . .
> But these same armes which on my back I weare.
> Thou should'st have had them too, and me unarm'de
> Yeelded to Caesar naked of defence. (ll. 23–26)

The imagery of seduction is inextricably woven into his loss of power: Cleopatra has invited him into her bed merely to get his clothes off so she can serve him up naked to his enemies. Cleopatra's face and eyes haunt this scene with the active/passive power Doane attributes to the femme fatale. Her body and face can enervate, enchant, and poison him. He once broke from her spell "as one encharmed / Breakes from the enchaunter" (ll. 79–80) by the sheer force of reason and will, but even in the battlefield her image comes over him "stealingly" and "entred againe thy soule, and day and night, / In watch, in sleepe, her Image follow'd thee" (ll. 103–4). What is expressed elsewhere in the play as a philosophical debate on man's freedom and bondage is adumbrated here in images of entrapment and helplessness: Caesar, Antony tells himself, "enwalles thee round / Cag'd in thy hold, scarse maister of thy selfe, / Late maister of so many Nations" (ll. 128–30). Cleopatra's duplicitous, inscrutable selfhood plays the foil to his (threatened) unified identity: She, "nor constant is, even as I constant am" (l. 142). Again, her female duplicity—her individuality is even effaced here—is a property of that body, the image that haunts his mind:

> But ah! by nature women wav'ring are,
> Each moment changing and rechanging mindes.
> Unwise, who blinde in them, thinkes loyaltie
> Ever to finde in beauties companie. (ll. 145–48)

Thus the issue for Antony remains one of masculine selfhood and honor, rather than love.

> Whereby my faire entising foe entrap'd
> My hedelesse *Reason*. . . .
> *Pleasure,* nought else, the plague of this our life,
> . . . .
> Alone hath me this strange disastre spunne,
> Falne from a souldior to a chamberer,
> Careles of vertue, careles of all praise.
> Nay, as the fatted swine in filthy mire
> With glutted heart I wallowed in delights,
> All thoughts of honor troden under foote.
> So I me lost. (ll. 1140–58)

Antony dies, finally, to redeem his honor: "Die, die I must: I must a noble death, / . . . / I must adorne the wanton loves I us'de, / With some couragious act: that my last day / By mine owne hand my spots may wash away" (ll. 1238–43).

The play's final speech is Cleopatra's, however. Even the chorus disappears at the end of the play, so that her pathos, her constancy, her heroic sacrifice, color our final impression. All of the moments that are heavily ironized in other versions of the story are devoid of irony in Sidney's tragedy. The raising of the dying Antony into Cleopatra's tomb, for example, is a moment of deep pathos—the messenger who describes it testifies to the weeping of the gathered citizens who watch the drama, and the heroic strength of the women who struggle to raise him. There are moments in the play of parenthetical qualification—"wively (though scarce wively)" (ll. 590–91)—though they have the effect of apology rather than disparagement. Cleopatra is at once a passionate, sexual woman, a queen, and a sympathetic private subject, one who opens herself up to the spectator, and does indeed, as she vows in her final line, pour forth her "soule":

> Then let me kisse you, you faire eies, my light,
> Front seat of honor, face most fierce, most faire!

O neck, o armes, o hands, o breast . . .
A thousand kisses, thousand thousand more
Let you my mouth for honors farewell give:
That in this office weake my limmes may growe,
Fainting on you, and forth my soule may flow. (ll. 1993–2000)

Despite his dedicatory testimony that his *Tragedie of Cleopatra* has been written as a companion piece to Sidney's *Antonie,* Samuel Daniel's play gives us an entirely different Cleopatra—a stereotypical femme fatale, who serves as a warning for men who love too much. It is tempting to see a bit of subversion going on here—Daniel quietly revising or erasing his powerful patron's inscription of female subjectivity in the guise of complementing it. Yet at the same time, Daniel's *Cleopatra* continues in its own way this expression of concern about male selfhood and autonomy.

If Cleopatra speaks in Daniel's play, it is only to admit her complicity in the fall of Antony, of Egypt, and perhaps eventually of Rome. She and Antony are moral exempla, tragic overreachers who show us how "greatnesse" can go awry in its pride and self-indulgence. Daniel's play is a tragedy in the precise sense that it fells the proud and shows us the way the wheel of fortune turns, "for never any age hath better taught, / What feeble footing pride and greatnesse hath" (ll. 513–14).

For sencelesse sensualitie doth ever
Accompany felicitie and greatnesse.
A fatall witch, whose charmes do leave us never
Till we leave all in sorrow for our sweetnesse. (ll. 553–56)

Antony is dead, and Cleopatra remains to personify that "fatall witch," a feminized image into which we are invited to pack all the dangers that are vaguely gestured at in the ambiguous syntactical reference of the line—sensuality, greatness, pride, "Lust and ease," "unwary Peace with fat-fed pleasure," "dissolute impietie," "New fresh invented ryots," and on and on. "My lascivious Court . . . / Affoorded me so bountifull disport, / That I to stay on Love had never leisure: / My vagabond desires no limites found, / For lust is endlesse, pleasure hath no bound" (ll. 159–64), she confesses, admitting in soliloquy that she never loved Antony until his death:

We suncke each others greatnesse both together;
And therefore I am bound to sacrifice
To death and thee, the life that doth reprove me:
Our like distresse I feele doth simpathize,
And even affliction makes me truley love thee.

> Which *Antony,* I must confesse my fault
> I never did sincerely untill now:
> Now I protest I do, now am I taught—
> In death to love, in life that knew not how. (ll. 144–54)

The confessional Cleopatra articulates precisely the tacit message that John Berger reads in Renaissance portraits of Vanity: "I saw my state, and knew my beautie; / Saw how the world admir'd me, how they woo'd, / I then thought all men must love me of duetie; / And I love none" (ll. 156–59). Caesar later reinforces the moral—Cleopatra is driven not by love, but by hatred and ambition: "That made thee seeke all meanes to have us scattred, / To disunite our strength, and made us feeble. / And therefore did that breast nurse our dissention, / With hope t'exalte thy selfe, t'augment thy state" (ll. 631–34). Though Cleopatra's suicide in Daniel's play is finally complex and overdetermined, none of her reasons for dying are particularly sympathetic. She does the right thing, but only because she has few other alternatives: "hereby yet the world shall see that I, / Although unwise to live, had wit to die" (ll. 195–96). Yet she remains proud, more concerned about her freedom than her loss of Antony: "So shall I shun disgrace, leave to be sorrie, / Flie to my love, scape my foe, free my soule; / So shall I act the last of life with glorie, / Die like a Queene, and rest without controule" (ll. 1184–87). Pride remains her dominant emotion: "No, I disdaine that head which wore a crowne, / Should stoope to take up that which others give; / I must not be, unlesse I be mine owne" (ll. 71–73).

One might argue that this Cleopatra is more like the morally complex male tragic hero, but there is, I think, a significant difference. While at times in the play her gender seems irrelevant, as she is strongly identified with her historical role and with an argument about "the great," she fails to achieve the minimum of internal coherence that might lead us to see her as a sympathetic individual. Though she speaks, she never receives a sympathetic hearing, and seems indeed strangely alienated from herself, often serving as a self-condemning mouthpiece for the play's moral interpretation of history. The shifts between Cleopatra and the choruses of the play are instructive—it is the suffering of the "people," the Egyptian masses, who have both the last word and our sympathy, although at the same time, they serve as a direct warning to the English auditor about how civilizations destroy themselves by gazing at "the hideous face of sin." Cleopatra remains too dangerously "other" in the play—too dark, seductive, exotic—for empathy. Even her moments of triumph are distanced from us, narrated through or to Dollabella, who has fallen under her spell. If the connection between seduction by the woman and the threats of cultural others is hinted at in *The Tragedie of Antonie,* it is almost an obsession in Daniel's play. He pairs two kinds of seduction—temptation by woman's beauty and temptation by the exotic Egypt's decadent and seductive luxury. The explicitness with which he articulates the latent psychological threat of contamination by the other is rather extraordinary. "Mysterious Egypt, wonder-breeder" has been rendered "servile" by its treasure and pleasure. This sounds like a justification for empire, an excuse for the strong to conquer the self-weakened, the sinful. It is Cleopatra's sin that has destroyed her "Race"—that is, her seed, her bloodline and succession to the throne—"To cut off all succession from our land / For her offence . . ." (l. 571). But Egypt threatens the victors with contamination by proximity—as the chorus warns the conquerors who reap Egypt's treasure, this "poison"

> may so farre infect their sences,
> That Egypts pleasures so delightfull,
> may breed them the like offences.
> And Romans learne our way of weaknes,
> be instructed in our vices:
> That our spoiles may spoile your greatnes,
> overcome with our devises.
> Fill full your hands, and carry home
> enough from us to ruin Rome. (ll. 1249–57)

The parallel between the femme fatale and the seductive orient is clear. Both are desired, both threaten to contaminate and destroy the self.

What can these two earlier versions of Cleopatra tell us about Shakespeare's tragic queen and about the possibilities for female tragic heroism on the early English stage? Sidney's Cleopatra speaks her mind; she is, indeed, a fully textualized subject. To become a sympathetic one however, she must be whitewashed of her threatening alterity, warped into a more familiar model, the self-sacrificing, misprized wife, a version of what Lisa Jardine calls the "saving stereotype of female heroism" (*Still Harping on Daughters* 169). What Jardine dislikes about this role is that the heroine's agency merely reiterates traditions of female passivity, her subjectivity inauthentic because it serves male needs: "Lucrece 'frantic with grief' is, in patriarchal terms," she says, "most reassuringly the female hero" (193). Jardine also suspects the way such heroines are able to jerk our tears: "I suggest that even today we are tempted into responding to Hermione and to Hero as most grand when most wronged" (193). Ironically, it is this easy access to sentiment that leads traditionalists to dismiss such figures of pathos as "melodramatic" rather than tragic. Evoking a too facile sympathy, pity without fear, as Aristotelians might say, such heroines fail to achieve in themselves or demand of the spectator a complex recognition, and allow us to indulge uncritically in what Robert Heilman calls the simpler "monopathic" response of "self-pity."[6] In a variety of dismissive characterizations of melodrama as improbable, excessively emotional, weak, sentimental, self-indulgent, or trivial we can hear an implicit association of the genre with women's speech. Thus melodrama, along with other "lesser" forms, plays the female to tragedy's male. No matter how ready the heroine is with words, she seems to wither under this critical gaze.

This may be a literary-critical version of blaming the victim. In fact, female heroes are unlikely ever to fit criteria for the honorific title of tragedy, because "tragedy" defines a very specific kind of literary experience. The tragic hero must not only be complex in a particular way, but must stand in complex relation to the viewer—distant enough for critical reflection, but close enough that his errors, limits, his outright contradictions are owned by the spectator and from this privileged internal perspective, forgiven. Tragic heroism thus represents both a particular kind of subject and a particular perspective on that subjectivity. But both of these—the roles we can play and the emotional responses we can have—are obviously conditioned, their possibilities limited, by gender and culture. Thus female heroism falls into a familiar double bind, where, as Lisa Jardine points out, the qualities that make the weeping woman a hero in our culture and in our criticism are "precisely those qualities that negate the possibility for heroism in the male" (193). My point is that even women writers, like Sidney, were likely to create female heroes who fail to achieve a complex subjectivity because, given women's cultural position, any representation of a woman is bound to be refracted through a male gaze. Built into the construction of female heroism at this historical moment is an implied debate with the inevitable misprisions of the male spectator, a debate that splits the picture, forces the viewer into one of two camps, two radically contradictory perspectives. Sidney's play is paradigmatic of this cultural divide: the male perspective is fully articulated by Antony's accusations, which Cleopatra defends. For Sidney, Cleopatra models heroic resolve, albeit in the service of the other (who is "herselfe"), but it is a defensive posture.

Is what we call tragedy, then, and what we valorize as the most profound literary experience, simply a form developed specifically to explore the problems that inhere in the male cultural position—the problems (and illusions) of the free human being, seeing himself in relation to fate, destiny, metaphysical reality, temporality? If so, then the feminist critic may, indeed, not want to find a tragic woman just like a man, but explore instead the limitations that inhere in the way the tragic problem is posed in the traditions that grow out of our particular culture. In *The Subject's Tragedy*, Linda Kintz argues that Greek tragedy grows out of a specifically male cultural problematic. "Something *befalls* [the hero]—that is, he is the object of another subject, be it fate, the gods, logic, language—and the pathos of the tragedy lies in the crucial moment of the hero's passivity. . . . It is the recognition of this moment of passivity, of the logically feminine moment, which seems to constitute tragic recognition" (61). This feminization of the hero, however, is compensated in tragedy "by ritualizing and controlling his experience of passivity" and by reassurance that "no matter what other disruptions or reversals he may face, Oedipus is always guaranteed the possibility of being the active character on stage" (62).

The problem for the woman on the early English stage is not one of self-recognition—she already knows what the hero has to learn. Though this "saving stereotype of female heroism" is easily dismissed, its project is a different one; it works out the woman's need to become visible as a subject, to *be* recognized, to have her sacrifices recognized *as heroic actions,* as choices, not reflexes, and brings her subjective experience and her culturally submerged knowledge to center stage.

If the cultural situation of women and the explosively gendered position of Cleopatra as archetypal femme fatale make inevitable a bifurcation of the heroine into the suffering victim or the monstrous victimizer (that is, make inevitable the oversimplifications that preclude tragic effects), how does a playwright work against cultural bias to create a heroine who is, in the complex sense we have come to appreciate, a "subject"?

"Not know me yet?" asks Shakespeare's heroine in the very center of the tragedy. It is a question that should by now resonate for us, thus shifting the burden of questioning from the woman to the critical gaze of those who look at her. I want to suggest that Shakespeare achieves Cleopatra's tragic subjectivity in a paradoxical way, through her silences. If we go back to our trope of the seductively painted nude, he does what the theory says he can't—he builds Cleopatra's subjectivity by making us look, by making her silent bodily presence on stage the object of our attention and speculation.

Beginning with the aftermath of the battle of Actium in act 3—precisely where the Sidney/Garnier tragedy opens—Cleopatra falls significantly silent, shifting from actor to observer. Yet here, I think, even more than in her performances center stage, we can't help but look at her. For the central dramatic question from here to the end of the play is one only she can answer—has she betrayed Antony? Will she? *Can* she love? But all she gives us are a few brief half-lines, mostly questions that (ironically) mirror back Antony's accusations. Though onstage from 3.11 to the end of the act, through almost 300 lines, Cleopatra says very little. Beginning in 3.11 with Cleopatra's tentativeness in approaching Antony, with its implied sense of fault ("Ah stand by!" [l. 41] and "Oh my lord, my lord, / Forgive my fearful sails! I little thought / You would have followed" [ll. 54–56] to "Oh my pardon!" [l. 62] and "Pardon! Pardon!" [l. 68]), Cleopatra continues to play a supportive role to Antony as he disintegrates before our eyes. In 3.13, alone with Enobarbus and her attendants, she probes their responses: "What shall we do, Enobarbus?" (l. 1); "Is we or Antony at fault in this?" (l. 2); "Prithee peace" (l. 12), she replies to Enobarbus's long indictment of Antony. When Antony enters, already convinced she will be sending his head to Caesar, she says merely, "That head, my lord?" (l. 19). In the dialogue that follows with Thidias, Caesar's ambassador, Cleopatra's responses remain terse and ambiguous. Her brief "Oh!" (l. 60), an apparently spontaneous exhalation, deepens the mystery and complexity of the interior it implies. Even more striking are her responses to Antony's subsequent accusations of her betrayal later in 3.13—"Good my lord—" (l. 114); "Oh, is't come to this?" (l. 120); "Wherefore is this?" (l. 126); "Have you done yet?" (l. 157); "I must stay his time" (l. 160); "Not know me yet?" (l. 162). Though Antony is immediately satisfied when she at last responds at length to his doubts that she is "coldhearted toward me" (ll. 163 ff.), knowledge of Cleopatra may be a more complex issue for the play's spectators.

Though throughout the play as a whole Cleopatra speaks enough to satisfy any historian of female subjectivity, her words always bear an oblique relation to herself. Ironically that habit of indirection, so long seen as female duplicity with Cleopatra its very exemplum, works to create her interiority. This is most obviously seen in the silences of these scenes, where *knowing* Cleopatra becomes essential to the meaning of the whole action, especially to our interpretation of Antony. When we are forced to read the subtext and imagine a Cleopatra in the gaps and between the words, we ourselves construct that interior, a truer and more authentic self,[7] precisely because it is not offered up for display. The work we and the actor do together in this process creates the kind of intimacy with a female character that seems impossible given the cultural dynamic. Such characters, after all, *are* ourselves to the extent that we must actively infer, empathize, and project our own emotion in constructing them. Unlike the earlier closet dramas, Shakespeare's is a work of the theater, which moves beyond words and remembers the body. As Cynthia Marshall argues, "interiority has a necessarily physical dimension in the theater" (99). It is precisely in that space between "the semiotic and the symbolic, between the body and language" that a "subjective identity, and its fullest dramatic achievement, character depth" (95) are created. By provoking an interior "knowledge" of her, Cleopatra's silences prepare us to read her final performances with renewed insight and from a much more sympathetic perspective.

And what do we imagine between words and body—who is the Cleopatra that we recognize in the final scenes of the play? A history of debate about that very issue should make it clear that, within a range of possibilities, we read differently—even Antony's reading, his "satisfaction" with Cleopatra is not the last word. One of these possibilities is illluminated, I hope, by reading the passionate soliloquies of Mary Sidney's queen against the silences of Shakespeare's. For Shakespeare's queen falls silent just where Sidney's play opens. In Cleopatra's "Not know me yet?" I hear a distinct echo of the Sidney/Garnier Cleopatra's much fuller text: "That I have thee betraide, deare Antonie, / My life, my soule, my sunne? I had such thought? . . . / That I would breake my vowed faith to thee? / Leave thee? Deceive thee? . . . I ever had that hart?" (ll. 388–93). Is Sidney's Cleopatra, with her single-minded devotion, the unspoken subtext of Shakespeare's play? Except that in the difference of dramatic technique, there comes a significant difference in our perception of her depth and complexity.

Cleopatra, unlike so many violated virgins and victims on stage, can't claim personal integrity through purity or impermeability of body, but she has, paradoxically, a wholeness that the tragic hero Antony lacks—precisely, I think, because he has given it over to her (as he had earlier to others, his male spectators and competitors). Playing the very role that Virginia Woolf attributed to all women, that of the mirror who reflects men back at twice their natural size (35), Cleopatra nevertheless has a self—perhaps because she takes life in a play that questions the very illusions of male autonomy and self-sufficiency, questions upon which, I have ventured, tragedy was founded. What may be unique about Shakespeare's play is the way these questions are formed in terms of gender. It has become a psychological commonplace that the need for mirroring is a human condition, that is it only through refraction that we know ourselves. The self we know best in this play seems, paradoxically, to be the woman.

～～　～～　～～

I want to end with a picture, one that provides an alternative to the traditional nude with which we began [plate 4.2]. It also provides an interesting counterpoint to Mary Sidney's Cleopatra, and, I suggest, may illustrate a woman artist's ability to move beyond the male gaze in representing the female subject. Artemesia Gentileschi painted two Cleopatras, an early and more traditional portrait, and the one figured here, probably from the early 1630s, later in her illustrious career. Gentileschi is one of those fascinating female artists who have been completely written out of history even though she was admired and celebrated in her own day. In *Artemesia Gentileschi: The Image of the Female Hero in Italian Baroque Art,* art historian Mary Garrard argues that the painter's refiguring of such biblical or mythic subjects as Susannah, Lucretia, Judith, and Cleopatra transformed them into powerful heroic agents very different from the ambiguously eroticized figures painted

Plate 4.2 Aremisia Gentileschi, *Cleopatra*. By permission, formerly Matthiesen Gallery, London.

by her male counterparts. Gentileschi claims particular authority to speak as a female subject because of what we know about her personal history. Garrard prints transcripts of the rape trial that her father won against her rapist, a fellow painter, a victory due in part to her own heroics under torture in the trial (as the *sibilli* tightened around her fingers, the 17 year old refused to give in, yelling across the court to her counteraccuser, "This is the ring that you give me, and these are your promises!" [462]). All of Gentileschi's paintings are remarkable for the way they unapologetically express the reality of the woman's point of view, a reality that becomes particularly vivid in her Susannah, recoiling from the leers of the elders, or her Judith, angrily decapitating Holofernes, pictures that seem intimately related to her personal experience. Her Cleopatra, however, does not struggle. In fact, this painting, unlike most, including her earlier one, captures Cleopatra after her death, beyond action, will, desire, and words. In spite of that, she comes across as a subject, not an object; hers is not a body to be looked at, not one that traces the desires and fears of the onlooker, but one that expresses the life, the inner world, of the woman. Why? Perhaps because of the unglamorized realism of the body, relaxed into deep sleep, her pallid face drained of blood, her breasts flattened by gravity, her legs slim and boyish, her arm gracefully curved as if to enclose herself within herself. Mortal as she is, Cleopatra yet seems powerfully self-possessed, a subject to be reckoned with, admired, lamented. As Garrard points out, there are intimations of immortality in this picture, a habit of Gentileschi to see the divine in the ordinary, the immanence of the infinite (274–77). The snake, the basket of flowers, the crown, are emblems of the great goddess; the iconography borrows from Diana, Natura, and a Sleeping Nymph. The two women form her sympathetic audience, just discovering her, suggesting a female circle of empathy, writing men out of the picture. To me this suggests an inwardness and a powerful selfhood that is specifically female. Discovered by her women, Cleopatra seems to be dreaming herself. Is this the shift of perspective that Virginia Woolf asked of Shakespeare's sister, to see women not always in relation to men (118), but in relation, like the tragic male hero, to the universe?

Notes

1. I am glancing casually at what has become a long and complex discussion in feminist film studies, literary studies, psychology, and art history, about the gaze and the ways in which it is both gendered and historically inflected. Laura Mulvey's "Visual Pleasure and Narrative Cinema" initiated the discussion among feminist film theorists, but it was soon followed by others, including E. Ann Kaplan, *Women and Film: Both Sides of the Camera,* Theresa de Lauretis, *Alice Doesn't: Feminism, Semiotics, Cinema,* Mary Ann Doane,

The Desire to Desire: The Woman's Film of the 1940s, Judith Mayne, *Cinema and Spectatorship* and the collections, *Camera Obscura: The Spectatrix* (1989), and Linda Williams, ed., *Viewing Positions: Ways of Seeing Film.* For a perspective on the history of "visualities" see Martin Jay, *Downcast Eyes: The Denigration of Vision in Twentieth-Century French Thought.*

2. See Doane's discussion of this much quoted Freudian image in *Femmes Fatales,* 209ff.

3. All quotations are from the New Arden edition of *Antony and Cleopatra.*

4. All quotations from Sidney's translation are from Bullough's edition.

5. The following lines in the play testify to the overwhelming anxiety of male competition; women are essentially subsumed in male relations:

> Bloud and alliance nothing do prevaile
> to coole the thirst of hote ambitious brests:
> the sonne his Father hardly can endure,
> Brother his brother, in one common Realme.
> So fervent this desire to commaund:
> Such jealousie is kindleth in our hearts,
> *Sooner will men permit another should*
> *Love her they love, then weare the crowne they weare.*
> All lawes it breakes, turnes all things upside down:
> Amitie, kindred, nought so holy is
> But it defiles. (ll. 1010–20)

6. I am using Heilman to represent a traditional and highly prescriptive and evaluative critical position on tragedy that is in some ways still with us. Heilman, to be fair, tried to avoid such invidious comparisons, but they still seem implicit in his work (at one point he even describes the pleasures of melodrama as "neurotic"). Though discussions of tragedy have moved on to less universalizing positions, even more recent works have reacted against the underlying critical assumption about tragedy's superiority. Thus Dympna Callaghan argues that "There is no need for a female hero nor should feminists try to create a new critical paradigm in order to accommodate one. Heroes are merely the chief characters of plays, not the timeless representatives of the bravest and the best; and tragic action is not the zenith of aesthetic experience, but, in Madelon Gohlke's phrase, 'a particular kind of heterosexual dilemma', leading to mortal ends unmitigated by transcendence or apotheosis" (*Women and Gender* 68). For more recent work on melodrama, see Peter Brooks, *The Melodramatic Imagination,* as well as a still growing body of feminist film theory on melodrama and the woman's film. Feminist approaches to tragedy include, besides Callaghan, Catherine Belsey, *The Subject of Tragedy: Identity and Difference in Renaissance Drama;* Nicole Loraux, *Tragic Ways of Killing a Woman;* Shirley Nelson Garner and Madelon Sprengnether, eds., *Shakespearean Tragedy and Gender;* and Linda Kintz, *The Subject's Tragedy.*

7. Both Maus and Marshall explore the ways this "inner and truer selfhood" (Marshall 94) is suggested, paradoxically, on the stage where "it is always perforce inwardness displayed: an inwardness, in other words, that has already ceased to exist" (Maus 32), since for the Renaissance, "Inwardness, inaccessibility, invisibility, all seem to lose their authenticity as soon as they are advertised or noted by another" (33). According to Maus, "the English Renaissance stage seems deliberately to foster theatergoers' capacity to use partial and limited presentations as a basis for conjecture about what is undisplayed or unplayable. Its spectacles are understood to depend upon and indicate the shapes of things unseen" (Maus 32). The point of the distinction between inner and outer is to privilege the inward, "something imagined to be more real, more true, more primary" and by definition, "unspeakable" (Maus 1), which "implicitly devalues any attempts to express or communicate it" (1), the "exemplary instance of this devaluation [being] the theater" (1). Marshall points to the ways that "seams" or "gaps" between actor and character, visible and invisible, require a more active collaboration or "collusion of several sorts" (101) from the Renaissance audience. Inwardness, for Marshall, is a "theatrical effect."

The Heroic Tragedy of Cleopatra, the "Prostitute Queen"

Kay Stanton

For centuries, Roman writings routinely and disparagingly called the historical Cleopatra *regina meretrix,* Latin for the "prostitute queen" (Anderson and Zinsser I: 56), so the Roman male characters in Shakespeare's *Antony and Cleopatra* accurately anticipate their emerging cultural tradition in likewise regarding her. As inheritors of that tradition, male *and* female literary critics have resisted granting Shakespeare's Cleopatra full status as tragic hero.[1] That reluctance is epitomized in this seeming oxymoron of "prostitute queen," by which "prostitute" easily trumps "queen"; the pun on "queen" as "quean" ("whore") in early modern English concisely enables the same function.[2] As Linda Fitz [Woodbridge] observes, it is Cleopatra's "frank sexuality" that "damns her" in critics' estimations, disallowing her serious consideration even as queen of Egypt, let alone as tragic hero ("Egyptian Queens" 303–9).

The same Greco-Roman tradition that would propagandize against the historical Cleopatra as "prostitute queen" also defined and refined the genre of tragedy, not only in terms of the necessary social preeminence and general high moral character (but for a flaw, usually pride) of the almost exclusively *male* hero, but also on a phallocentric model whose stages— exposition, rising action, climax, falling action, denouement—parallel those of male sexual arousal and release.[3] Aristotle's discussion of catharsis, in this context, suggests that the (predominantly male) audience members voyeuristically (though probably subconsciously) participate in a grand-scale sex act through vicarious identification with the male hero as he swells up to superhuman height and attempts to fuck the mysterious abyss that gave him birth and that will reclaim him in death (with "fuck" chosen deliberately here for its aggressive, female-contemptuous, vulgar connotations for the male coital role).

Shakespeare's tragedies both follow and explode this model. In the two with couples as eponymous protagonists,[4] the female characters not only share heroic tragic stature with their male counterparts, but also surpass them—because both Juliet and Cleopatra achieve mental and spiritual androgyny.[5] In that they deliberately choose to synthesize masculinity (evidenced by Juliet's use of Romeo's dagger and Cleopatra's appropriation of Antony's sword), they enter the Aristotelian-determined tragic scheme. In that they do not therefore reject, but instead revel in, expression of their female sexuality, they heroically transcend the male tragic model. Furthermore, Cleopatra recoups a pre-Aristotelian tragic ritual tradition, precisely through being the "prostitute queen."

Although Aristotle's writings have enduring interest and value, we now recognize as misogynistic his assertions of women's inferiority and the necessity to rein in female sexuality, opinions that perhaps bolstered his authority in later patriarchal cultures. We may, however, assume Shakespearean sanction for sidestepping, modifying, or overriding Aristotle not only by the bard's typical practice of ignoring the Aristotelian unities but also by the implications of his canon's two direct references to him, both positioning Aristotle as antagonistic to sexual pleasure and fertility.[6] As Philip Traci rightly remarks, Shakespeare seems intent "to foil" those approaching *Antony and Cleopatra* from a "strictly Aristotelian point of view" (38). The play, I believe, urges us to seek beneath and beyond the phallocentric model of Aristotle for a gynogenic schema with a female tragic hero climaxing on top.

Cleopatra's deserved status as tragic hero can be recovered through less focus on demonstrably repressive and misogynistic Aristotelian tradition and more on tragedy's roots and psychic functions. Naomi Liebler identifies tragedy as "part of a genealogy of related encodings that begins in ritual, myth, and folklore, whose interests are the same and whose vestiges remain visible even in the most complex and sophisticated plays," wherein protagonists' and several of their community members' destructions result because "sociopolitically important rituals" have been "perverted or ignored" (*Shakespeare's Festive Tragedy* 51). Similar neglect has long been typical of scholars, who have generally valorized "male" ceremonial rites of political power and initiation and neglected, attacked, and demeaned "female" rites involving fertility. Such exclusion, however, is *not* endorsed by Shakespeare. As Liebler affirms, "Shakespeare's festive tragedies" exhibit "explicit concerns with rites of fertility, seen as rites of survival and perpetuation, as well as communal rites of passage," though such rites are sometimes "appropriated by 'male-dominated' interests" (225). We need not search long or far to find these male-centered appropriations and effacings in action, though recent feminist work in ritual/mythic areas assists in excavating women's impact in literature and history.

Most expanded definitions of *tragedy,* such as those in literary handbooks, explain its genesis (just before lauding Aristotle) as in this typical example: "Probably tragedy originated in Greek religious rituals to celebrate Diony-sus, in whose honor the chorus, dressed as goats (the animal sacred to the god), or satyrs (his mythical half-goat, half-human companions), danced and chanted verses. (The word *tragedy* means 'goat song.')" (Hornstein, et al. 452). Conspicuously absent is the information that Dionysus was a "phallic god, worshipped for his sexuality," who "presided over ecstatic experience and the casting off of inhibition," and that "his was originally a mystery cult for women" (Dening 74). These otherwise "repressed Greek matrons," his priestess-followers (maenads) carried representations of the god's phallus in religious ceremonial processions and ritually performed "sexually explicit and even vulgar actions aimed at stimulating the fertilizing power of the god" (76). Even from this information (and more will follow below), we might reasonably extrapolate that the tragic genre's roots are in *female* sexual passion, or at least that tragedy is a *hermaphroditic* genre, as carvings de-picted Dionysus with masculine *and* feminine elements (74). The historical Antony deliberately associated himself with Dionysus (Hughes-Hallett 89–90), and *Antony and Cleopatra's* Romans regard Antony as effeminized.

Shakespeare specifically references Dionysus solely in Roman manifesta-tion as Bacchus, four times only in his canon, twice in *Antony and Cleopa-tra,* during the scene on Pompey's galley. After Pompey laments his party's being "not yet an Alexandrian feast," Enobarbus asks, "Shall we dance now the *Egyptian Bacchanals* / And celebrate our drink?," whereupon Antony proposes that "all take hands / Till that the *conquering* wine hath steeped our sense / In soft and delicate Lethe" (2.7.97, 105–6, 108–10). Their grievances and jealousies set aside, the assembled power figures, hand in hand, listen to a boy's song beginning, "Come, thou *monarch* of the vine, / Plumpy *Bacchus* with pink eyne!," with all joining in the refrain "*Cup* us till the world go *round*" (2.7.115–16, 119). The conquerors identify wine as "conquering" *them,* the Greco-Roman Bacchus and his rites are called "Egyptian," and their only moment of harmonic accord comes in their sung entreaty in unison that Bacchus "cup" them into cyclical motion. The cup and cyclicality are feminine archetypes, so the incident resonates of Cleopatra, whom the play links with Venus (2.2.210), as it does Antony with Mars (1.1.4; 2.2.6; 2.5.119); Harmony (Harmonia) was born of the Venus/Mars coupling, and Aphrodite-Venus was grandmother of Diony-sus-Bacchus. With Lepidus drunkenly incapacitated and Caesar complain-ing that "Strong Enobarb / Is weaker than the wine, and mine own tongue / Splits what it speaks" (2.7.124–26), Antony seems champion of the world-class drinkers on Pompey's galley, but Cleopatra had earlier claimed ability to outdrink Antony: "I drunk him to his bed, / Then put my tires and mantles on him, whilst / I wore his sword Philippan" (2.5.21–23). Thus—fittingly, as the historical Cleopatra was held to be a Dionysus-descendant (Hughes-Hallett 89)—Cleopatra is the play's most Dionysian character, not only by her superior drinking ability, but also by her theatricality and agency in enacting and bestowing androgyny, especially through her appropriation of the sword-phallus for her own pleasure, which contextualizes other sexualized images of her.

Caesar is the play's least Dionysian character, as seen not only in his complaint quoted above but also in its continuation that "The wild disguise [of drunken revelry, suggestive also of the masks and costumes for Dionysian rites] hath almost / Anticked us all" (2.7.126–27). Critics have sometimes identified Antony with the Dionysian and Caesar with the Apollonian modes,[7] but the play may further represent by its conflict between the "competitors" the shift between the two modes for dominance both of culture and the rituals of tragedy. Dening reports that Dionysus worship evolved into retreats to the wilderness, where participants feasted, drank, and danced themselves into an ecstatic state. In the festival's climax, as an act of communion with the god, they bare-handedly tore a sacrificial animal apart and ate its raw flesh, representing the body of Dionysus. Earlier, a young boy had been used as the sacrificial victim. The rite was one among many pagan customs that the Christian church later borrowed and adapted. Eventually the festival came under state control, with the rites, still orgiastic, held twice a year at Delphi, Apollo's home, but with participation limited to official female representatives from Greek cities (76). The movement first of the Dionysian festival to the wildest possible place is paralleled in Enobarbus's attribution of Bacchanals to Egypt; the human sacrifice victim is suggested in the boy singer on Pompey's galley; the subsequent state-initiated moving of the festival to Apollo's Delphi and restricting to official female participation is analogous to Caesar's ultimate triumph over Antony and Cleopatra and the restrictions and redefinitions of female sexual power that followed. The sacrifice's appropriation in Christian communion's ingestion of the symbolic body and blood of Christ is also anticipated by Shakespeare's having Caesar himself state the necessary condition for Christ's impending birth during his reign: "The time of universal peace is near" (4.6.5).

If we can watch the triumph over the Dionysian by the Apollonian ritually reenacted before us in *Antony and Cleopatra,* we thereby also witness the spectacle of female sexual power being its most dramatic sacrifice, seen by tracing Cleopatra's Dionysianism back through Dionysus's grandmother Venus and further to the ancestors of Venus-Aphrodite herself, which include Isis, another of Cleopatra's associations. Ancient authors often distinguished *two* Venuses: Venus Coelestis, source of universal harmony, and Venus Vulgaris, goddess of sensuality (Wells 158). In the second form, Roman Venus echoes Greek Aphrodite Pandemus as patroness of prostitutes; sacred ritual prostitution was practiced at Aphrodite's temples (Grigson 111–24). Although to the Roman populace Venus remained the goddess of love and sexuality, sacred prostitution was abandoned in Rome, as inappropriate to the state's propagandistic celebration of the "more respectable Venus Genetrix, Venus the Mother, Mother of Rome, divine ancestor of the imperial line," as treated in Virgil's *Aeneid,* showing how Caesar Augustus, "descendant of Anchises and Venus," would "renew Latium's golden age" (221). This information elucidates why, though he complains and moralizes over them, Caesar participates in the Dionysian rites on Pompey's galley, since they relate to Venus Coelestis, the source of universal harmony, and why Caesar, at the play's end, bequeaths some limited measure of dignity on "prostitute queen" Cleopatra, who "O'erpictur[es] that Venus" (2.2.210), as the historical Caesar would appropriate for political purposes a sanitized Venus as his divine ancestor. Furthermore, as many note, beneath representations of Virgin Mary as Mother are images of Venus Genetrix, superimpositions tracing the near-total early Christian effacement of female sexuality as well as the divinity-shift from female to male, the mortality from male to female.

The implications of Venus (and through her, Aphrodite and Cleopatra[8]) for the Roman Empire and its cultural inheritors, then, have tremendous significance. Grigson documents that the Romans traded statues of naked Venuses in Britain (224), and Wells states that in the Renaissance the Mars/Venus myth became "an allegory of the Creation itself" (158). Thus Shakespeare's associations of Cleopatra with Venus would have resonated powerfully for his audience, whom he educates further on goddess worship by Cleopatra's self-presentation as Isis (3.6.17–18). Dening notes that Isis represented the Egyptian throne, "the hieroglyph for which is her name and the image of which rests upon her head." The Christian image of the Madonna as throne from which child-emperor Jesus blesses the world derives from Egyptian imagery depicting the Pharaohs seated on the lap of Isis, from whose suckling they receive "divine nourishment." If painted red, the hieroglyph for Isis "signified both the female genitals and the Gate of Heaven" (60). As Gajowski observes, Cleopatra dies seated on the Egyptian throne, and, "like the Isis of Egyptian iconography, she represents that throne," taking her "'place i' th' story'" (3.13.46) beside "the legendary figures who live in ancient myth," which include Thetis, Isis, Venus, and Dido (118). To Cleopatra's accretion of female-divine images, we might add another goddess as relevant: Nut, Egyptian mythology's earliest ruler over the heavens, typically pictured (see Plate 5.1) arching over her husband, earth-god Geb, who, lying on his back, tries to reach her with his erect penis (Dening 59). Shakespeare may have deliberately invoked this image (which anticipates representations of Isis over Osiris) in presenting the dying

Plate 5.1 Nut as the sky, arching over Geb, the earth, as depicted in the Papyrus of Tanienu (Egypt, ca. 1000 B.C.E.). Copyright British Museum. Photo by permission of the British Museum, London.

Antony, lifted up to Cleopatra (skylike as fire and air elements only, 5.2.289, and the "Eastern star," 5.2.308), with the queen lamenting that "The crown o' th' earth doth melt" since Antony's "pole is fall'n" (4.15.65, 67).

The later Egyptian myth of Isis and Osiris, discussed by Plutarch in his account published in English translation in 1603, is undoubtedly referenced in *Antony and Cleopatra,* as some commentators have recognized (Steppat in Spevack, et al., *New Variorum* 657).[9] Briefly summarized, the story is as follows. Twin offspring of Nut and Geb (whom Plutarch calls Rhea and Cronus, passim), Isis and Osiris first had intercourse in their mother's womb (the original divine incest) and loved each other from then on. Their jealous brother, Set (called Typhon by Plutarch), tricked Osiris into lying in a coffin, which was then closed and thrown into the Nile. Isis searched throughout the country for her beloved husband's body. Although she finally found it, Set intervened again and tore it into 14 pieces. Isis then recovered and reassembled all the pieces—except the phallus, which a fish had eaten. With her magical powers, Isis fashioned an image of it, which she used to conceive her divine child, Horus. Then, performing the very first rites of embalmment, she restored Osiris to eternal life. We may easily see the parallels in *Antony and Cleopatra,* with Set/Caesar as Osiris/Antony's brother (-in-law), whose attempts to destroy him result in Cleopatra as Isis using a created image of her consort to restore him to life in her dream account to Dolabella and to conceive through her imaginary version of Antony such that she suckles at her breast their child, the asp uniting her and her "husband" Antony through the death satisfying her "Immortal longings" (5.2.281) by granting imagined eternal life.

Rites of the Isis/Osiris myth paralleled those of Dionysus, as annually Osiris's death was reenacted in a public ceremony, with a phallus-representation carried in solemn procession (Dening 60). These similarities were definitely evident to Plutarch, who habitually equates Osiris and Dionysus (passim); thus through ancient cross-influencing, the "Bacchanals" *were* in a sense "Egyptian." Besides its parallel in the processional, the phallus in this Egyptian story that is severed by a male family member, drowned, and resurrected through the female to become divine also suggests the myth of Aphrodite being born from the spume produced when Cronus threw the severed genitals of his father, Uranus, into the sea. These myths can be seen as subtextually woven into, and ultimately unraveling, Roman male anxieties over Cleopatra's supposed castrating influence on Antony as depicted in *Antony and Cleopatra,* true to historical record of Octavius's propaganda campaign against the pair (Hughes-Hallet 56–57).

The key to understanding how Shakespeare "screws" the phallocentrist Aristotelian model of tragedy is found by following the procession of *Antony and Cleopatra's* phallic symbology, epitomized by Antony's "sword Philippan" (2.5.23). Michael Neill, noting that Venus's triumph over Mars was "essentially an allegory of emasculation" (116), discusses how the sword, as "received symbol of masculinity" (111), expresses an Aristotelian male-heroic self-conception that "realizes itself in 'doing'—as though it were capable of recognizing itself only as an entity projected into the outside world" (112). Yet, although there is much nervous anxiety by the Romans, Antony included, over Cleopatra-as-Venus's castrating effect on him, Cleopatra only *borrows* his phallus/sword for her (and/or their mutual) pleasure. The actual castration is initiated by Antony's self-mutilation and completed by Dercetus's theft of his sword, showing that it is obsessive fixation on an exclusively male heroic ideal that actually annihilates a man, by "spending" his essence in ways disallowing his projection of his fleshly existence into the future, fears of the self-destructive effects of mingling with the female to the contrary.

Yet a male's union with a female, the *only* means of immortality through fleshly rebirth, entails entering her "throne," recognizing it as a seat of power, and trusting that he will reemerge intact after losing his phallus in its liquid depths and commingling with her essence—a difficult threat for an exclusively male-heroically determined sense of identity to face. As Neill notes, a threat to gender boundaries threatens such male identity itself, as "an annihilation of the self which is ultimately no different from death," linked to the pun on death as orgasm. Thus Enobarbus's satiric lines on the queen's "celerity in dying" (1.2.151) suggest that the "threat" of Cleopatra ultimately lies in "the mysterious female affinity with Death" that allows her "to die and die again" (Neill 109). Enobarbus, of course, thereby also mocks Cleopatra's tendency to respond hyperbolically and sometimes recklessly to whatever crosses her will, which may indeed represent her "tragic flaw" in the Aristotelian model. Yet, although she has "died" metaphorically and "femininely" many times, for her literal death she determines to "*do* 't after the high Roman fashion" (4.15.92), which she later elaborates as "To *do* that thing that ends all other deeds, / Which shackles accidents and bolts up change, / Which sleeps and never palates more the dung" (5.2.5–7), a "doing"-emphatic description consonant with the male-heroic idea of death as existential annihilation of the self. Just before greeting her means of suicide, she reasserts, "My resolution's placed, and I have nothing / Of woman in me"; calling herself "marble-constant," she adds that "now the fleeting moon / No planet is of mine" (5.2.238–41), discarding even the lunar feminine associations of cyclicality. What more could she (and Shakespeare) *do* to prove her heroic princely quality in manifesting a seminal truth implicit in Caesar's earlier sneer that the renownedly heroic Antony "is not more manlike / Than Cleopatra, nor the queen of Ptolemy / More womanly than he" (1.4.5–7)?

In choosing the male-heroic pattern for death, Cleopatra demonstrates that she has completely assumed, and is justified in being granted, full heroic status on the male model. Our lingering sense, however, that something is wrong about this attribution shows not that the female's heroism is incomplete, but that the heroic model itself is incomplete by definition as only male. Dissolution of gender boundaries does not unnerve Cleopatra as it had Antony: "O thy vile lady! / She has robbed me of my sword" (4.14.22–23). The female willingness to transcend gender points up the contrasting cowardice of the male "heroism" so fixated on potential loss of the phallic sword to the "O," the supposed "no-*thing*-ness" of the female. Yet, as Antony eventually puts it, "I, that *with* my sword / Quartered the world" can "condemn myself to *lack* / The courage of a woman," having "less noble mind / Than she which by her death our Caesar tells 'I am conqueror of myself'" (4.14.57–62). In Antony's realization, "lack" pertains to the phallic-equipped male, not to the supposedly "lacking" female, in contrast to what Enobarbus ("between [women] and a great cause they should be accounted nothing," 1.2.140), Aristotle, Freud, Lacan, and other proponents of male supremacy would have us believe. To his credit, Antony's ultimate sense of phallocentrism's incompleteness impels his preference to die in his female mate's space rather than in the male realm that has attempted to claim him exclusively.

The tragedy of Antony goes beyond Aristotelian tradition in his glimmer of understanding that his death's real waste is in nonsimultaneous orgasm. Unlike most male tragic protagonists, he finally recognizes mutual orgasm with the female as a consummation devoutly to be wished, not only for the shared moment of ecstasy, but also because the odds of conception—thus fleshly rebirth of the phallus—thereby increase.[10] Antony, however, is in effect a premature ejaculator, for Cleopatra is multiple-orgasmic: she rouses from her "death" frustrated that her male partner has gone limp before granting her full satisfaction, rendered in her lament that "The soldier's pole is fall'n" (4.15.67). The female protagonist has to bring about her climactic death herself, through the phallus-appropriation that her androgyny instructs her toward, as relates to the Dionysian and Isis/Osiris rites (and Aphrodite-Venus birth story) involving material and spiritual resurrection for both sexes through female sexual power.

Although Cleopatra and Juliet deliberately cross gender boundaries and resolve to die in the male-heroic mode, their physical female sexuality, rather than canceling or castrating the male mode in their actual final deaths, instead *envelopes* it, as the vagina does the phallus in sexual congress and the abyss does the traditional Aristotelian male tragic hero in death. Thus in his tragedies with couples as protagonists, Shakespeare attempts to restore both the capacity for heroism *and* sexual divinity to the female, which seen, puts the male mode into a perspective that is subsumed by her, as evidenced in the fact that although each male character holds primary position in the title, the last words of *Romeo and Juliet* are "Juliet and *her* Romeo" (5.3.310), and in the last speech of *Antony and Cleopatra,* Caesar speaks of Cleopatra and "*her*" Antony" (5.2.358, my emphasis). In the end, then, like Nut over Geb, the female is "on top."

In *Antony and Cleopatra,* as in *Romeo and Juliet,* the male protagonist as phallus, represented as "I," is invoked to rise within the yonic circle, represented as "O."[11] Burgundy's advice in *Henry V* to King Henry on wooing Princess Katherine explains these images: "If you would conjure in her, you must make a circle; if conjure up love in her in his true likeness, he must appear naked and blind" (5.2.294–96). The "true likeness" of "love"—that is, Cupid/Eros as the projectile erotic impulse—is the naked erect male member, which is "blind" when standing within the circle. Virginal Katherine, Burgundy adds, cannot be blamed for resisting "the appearance of a naked blind boy in her naked seeing self" (5.2.298–99). The male protagonists of *Romeo and Juliet* and *Antony and Cleopatra* are naked blind boys attempting to penetrate the "O," the circle, the sphere, the void, the abyss, the "nothing"; the plays' female protagonists, as shown below regarding Cleopatra, are naked seeing selves who learn to perceive and bestow illumination by the erotically stimulated third eye.

In *Antony and Cleopatra,* two servants discuss the male power figures' comparative potency, with the Second Servant preferring "a reed that will do me no service" over "a partisan I could not heave," and the First Servant observing that "To be called into a huge *sphere,* and not to be *seen* to *move* in 't, are the *holes* where *eyes* should be, which pitifully disaster the cheeks" (2.7.12–16). Such is the fear of cosmic insignificance, of not being "seen" to "move" in the grand "sphere," even for the most prodigiously ithyphallic of men. Cosmic potency *does* eventually accrue to Antony—not by his own actions, but through Cleopatra's desiring dream vision after his death: "His face was as the heavens, and therein stuck / A sun and moon, which kept their course and lighted / The little O, the earth" (5.2.78–80). The female protagonist is the projective-reflective means, through her magic visionary yonic circle, of illuminating the sphere for her consort, and that circle spirals into further ascendance and widening circumference with added revolutions of female divinity.

The heavenly yonic "sphere" in the estimation of Shakespeare's male tragic figures, however, can also be interpreted by them as a pit of hellish disaster, with that depiction emerging when the male senses that his consort's sexuality is not solely owned and controlled by himself. Furious that Cleopatra has allowed Caesar's messenger Thidius to kiss her hand, Antony calls her a "kite" (3.13.90), castigates her over her former lovers, and tells the subsequently beaten Thidius that Caesar can easily anger him now, "When my good stars that were my former guides / Have left their orbs and shot their fires / Into th' abysm of hell" (3.13.148–50) because of Cleopatra's behavior.

As "kite," Cleopatra is both a whore (in slang usage) and a predatory bird signaling his "fall" (3.13.157) into a hell made for him by her wantonness. He does not yet "see" that the nonexclusively owned sexuality of his mate will not only be integral to his resurrection but will also confer upon him the title of "emperor."

As feminist research in various areas now confirms, the misogynistic stance of Greco-Roman-influenced Judeo-Christian cultures that women are degraded by being, or potentially being, whores—in descending from Eve/evil as attending on the serpent/Satan—was a weapon used to justify male dominance and authority by effacing, revising, and/or gender-reversing earlier evidence of female leadership and association with deity. Primary divinity supposedly resided exclusively in the male god, as father-creator, who made only men, not women, in his image, thereby necessitating that priests be male. By deeming female liberty "whoredom" and vilifying it so entirely, patriarchs convinced women to accede to male control of their sexuality and power, enforcing that control in no small part by brandishing the deadly sword of the "whore" label (as do *Antony and Cleopatra*'s Roman men) at any signs of female longing for freedom or authority.

Preexisting and for a time simultaneously existing matriarchal cultures held almost entirely opposite views on female sexuality, as shown by Merlin Stone in *When God Was a Woman*. Recurring accounts, from Sumer and Egypt's earliest historic periods and surviving into Christianity's first centuries, depict the goddess's earthly incarnation, the high priestess, as a woman who chose annual lovers or consorts and retained the more permanent position of highest rank for herself (131). These accounts habitually treat the subject, derived from the early female religion's original rituals and customs and retained in Christianity's annual mourning for Jesus, of "one of the most ancient practices recorded—the ritual sacrifice of an annual 'king,' consort of the high priestess" (132). We may extrapolate from recently understood evidence that it is *this* sacrifice, to the *goddess,* that directly underlies the rites of Dionysus (and Osiris) leading to the development of the dramatic genre of tragedy.

In these matriarchal cultures a man was king *only* by means of sexual congress with the goddess's high priestess and only for a limited period of time, usually a year (or so long as he retained his sexual potency *and* her favor). Their sexual union, the *hieros gamos* (sacred marriage) is discussed in Sumerian, Egyptian, Babylonian, and classical Greek history. Following the sexual ceremony, the man, as consort of the priestess, became the "king" (Stone 133). A dream may have inspired selection of the high priestess's "king," because Isis, who absorbed and epitomized the traits and rites of many earlier erotic goddesses, called her initiates through dreams (Green 67). The vision of Antony as an "emperor" is the product of an erotically charged dream, thus a mystic revelation of such a sacred sexual union beneath and/or beyond patriarchal surface reality. Cleopatra tells Dolabella, "I dreamt there was an emperor Antony. / O such another sleep, that I might see / But such another man!" (5.2.75–77). It is the female's mystic sexual power that confers the title of "emperor"—with the implication that Cleopatra *could* conceivably, like the goddess-incarnate priestess-queen, later bestow the title upon "another man," just as she had in a sense earlier conferred it upon Julius Caesar.

Male castration anxieties in *Antony and Cleopatra* may be further illuminated by Stone's conjecture about the castration-death link in stories of Osiris, Attis, and others. An Anatolian myth states that after a man had coitus with the goddess (represented by her high priestess), he could then never have sex with another woman, because he would thereby transfer the goddess's sacred powers to her. Attis's voluntary castration of himself, from fear of infidelity to the goddess, suggests that in certain areas castration was a substitute ritual allowing the temporary consort-king to live (148). Such may be the reason why Shakespeare has his Antony claim to Cleopatra that he has "Forborne the getting of a lawful race" (3.13.108) for her sake, even though the historical Antony did sire children with Octavia (Hughes-Hallett 24). Shakespeare, however, allows his Cleopatra to be like the historical Cleopatra in representing herself as the incarnation of the goddess Isis, who had the magical ability to restore the severed phallus of Osiris and to conceive by it. In some accounts, Isis did so while in the form of a kite mourning over Osiris's body (Ions 59). Antony, who testifies to Cleopatra's magical powers by referring to her positively as "great fairy" (4.8.12) and negatively as "grave charm," "spell," and "witch" (4.12.25, 30, 47), also, as mentioned above, derogatorily calls Cleopatra a "kite" when raging over her seductive behavior, surely being utilized to secure leniency and some property rights from Octavius for Antony, herself, her son by Julius Caesar, and her children with Antony. Isis also manifested herself in kite-form after employing seductive wiles on Set, enemy of herself and Osiris, to secure the inheritance of Horus (Manniche 56). In kite-form perched atop the dead Osiris, however, Isis, "with the beating of her wings, created the wind—the breath of life—conceiving a child from him as he lay resting there, breathing her breath and so suspended from death," and thus "for all those whose soul has left their bodies through the mouth, breathed out as the last breath, Isis hovers with her life-giving wings offering the first breath of eternal life" (Baring and Lashford 245).[12] Similarly Cleopatra, wishing her "lips" had "that power," entreats the dying Antony to "Die when thou hast lived, / Quicken with kissing" (4.15.39–40). Kissing, symbolic of coitus, is discussed as facilitating the merging of souls in Castiglione's *The Courtier* and elsewhere.

Manifested as a kite over Osiris, Isis represents the Ba ("soul" or "life force") bird. In the mystery of Osiris, the Ba, phallus, and seed all join in a creative act allowing the deceased to come forth through copulation (Reeder 78). In Apuleius's *The Golden Ass* (translated into English by Adlington in 1566), Isis tells Osiris that, unlike any other god or goddess, "*I played the part of a man, although I am a woman,* to let your name live on earth, for your divine seed was in my body" (ctd. in Manniche, her emphases, 54). Thus, to confer immortality, Isis, like Cleopatra, becomes androgynous, and each does so sexually, "on top" of her dead male consort, with the hint that she could do so for others also.

The magical resurrection of Osiris that Isis accomplishes expresses itself in various ways, some involving grain. Baring and Lashford state that reapers wept and invoked Isis to mourn with them when the first ears of corn were cut, signifying the dismembering of the god's body in the corn (238), but the grain's new life was understood as Horus, Osiris renewed through Isis (236). As a god who was dismembered but resurrected through spring's reviving vegetation, Dionysus, god of wine and fertile crops, mostly fits the qualifications of "king" in the ancient goddess rites of the sacred coupling, but with some alterations. His story, briefly summarized from classical accounts, is as follows. Dionysus was saved as a fetus from his dead mother, Semele (Harmonia's daughter) by his father, Zeus, who sewed him into his thigh. After his birth from it, Dionysus was torn to pieces by the Titans, at the instigation of Hera, who was jealous of Semele. Dionysus, however, was revived by earth-mother Rhea, then transformed into a kid goat and brought up by nymphs. In adulthood, he traveled extensively, accompanied by maenads, teaching cultivation of the vine for wine production. Later, having become an Olympian, he raised his mother from Hades. Those who refused to recognize his divinity or opposed his orgiastic rites were made insane and/or otherwise destroyed, often by a dismemberment recapitulating his own.

In his work on the Isis/Osiris myth, as noted above, Plutarch identified Osiris with Dionysus, who was related to Demeter, the grain goddess, in the Eleusinian mysteries. Baring and Lashford explain that the Greeks found parallels between Isis searching for and finding Osiris and Demeter searching for and finding Persephone (268). Many scholars believe that what was "found" in both instances was an ear of corn, symbolic of earthly fertility's rebirth. A recent amazing "finding," discussed by Green, contributes to the resurrection of the female in drama's history. It is *The Songs of Isis and Nephthys,* an Egyptian "script" for the performance by temple priestesses of an Osirian drama. Apparently composed in the fourth century B.C.E., it was thus performed during Aristotle's lifetime, circa 384–322 B.C.E. Green notes that Greek historian Herodotus, living circa 480–425 B.C.E., wrote of seeing an Isis festival, with enactments of Osiris's dramatic mysteries being "like those of Dionysus" (65). Scholars regard Euripides' *The Bacchants,* dealing with the tragic punishment of Pentheus, who imprisons Dionysus and is torn to pieces during a bacchanalian orgy by his own mother, Agave, as the play most closely resembling in form the Dionysian mysteries from which Greek tragedy sprang; it is usually dated 408–6 B.C.E. Thus when tragedy as we recognize it, in its Greek androcentric glory, was born, there had been and continued to be an Egyptian gynogenic dramatic tradition, known to the Greeks, in which survived earlier goddess rituals similarly performed in many places.

In *Sacred Pleasure,* Riane Eisler collects and extrapolates upon other related pieces of the story, determining that the subject of the earliest recorded drama (63) and of the Eleusinian, Dionysian, and Orphic mysteries was the sacred marriage (137). Celebrated by thousands of worshippers from about 800 B.C.E. to as late as the year 150, the Eleusinian mysteries, like prehistoric myths, dealt with birth, sex, death, and regeneration as interrelated (137). But, Eisler notes, the Eleusinian myth changed, reflecting cultural conflicts between goddess-worshipping agrarian peoples and their warlike invaders (137) as the phallic sword's violent mode began to triumph over that of the mutually generative grain.

In these declensions, the mysteries' central myth, originally involving the marriage between a female and male deity and the journey to and return from the underworld realm of the dead, changed first into the Demeter-Persephone story, wherein sexual union, having become a violent rape, is a subplot to death and resurrection (Eisler 138). Dionysus was added rather late to Demeter's rites, probably not before the fourth century B.C.E. (138)—thus very close to the point when Greek dramatic tragedy emerges. Eisler laments not only that "neither the Dionysian nor Orphic Mysteries any longer celebrate the Goddess's creative female sexual power," but also that the "key female role in these Mysteries is now that of a destroyer rather than creator," as "it is the maenads (which in Greek literally means 'raving women') who dismember the dying and resurrecting god," thereby "reinforcing the Greek view of women as naturally destructive and dangerous creatures who must be strictly controlled or 'tamed' by men, lest they do to them what in these myths they do to the god" (139–40). As the Dionysus story manifests itself over time in dramatic tragedy, this female sexual force even as destructively associated is so further effaced to disallow women *any* power over men that literary critics rarely if ever even recognize its presence.

Without detecting this female subtext, William Storm does, however, comment that tragic drama fails to portray the full Dionysian life-cycle of annihilation followed by resurrection. The Dionysian rhythm, "as dictated by the seasonal cycle and by the god's own experience in legend," is broken by tragic drama at dismemberment, as demonstrated in that defining tragedy *The Bacchants,* at whose end Agave hopes that her son's remains can be reassembled, but "there is nothing to be done; the work of the god is accomplished" (22). Thus, Storm determines, tragedy is distinguished not by its heroes' deaths but by their dismemberment, by "the fragmentation and the dispersal, not just of the body but of the essential self" (21). Shakespeare depicts dismemberment, fragmentation, and dispersal literally in his first tragedy, *Titus Andronicus,* and the same elements symbolically in arguably his last tragedy, *Antony and Cleopatra.*

In *Titus Andronicus,* in which a militaristic Roman male-heroic code clashes against the strong will and sexual assertiveness of an "outsider" queen, bodies are violated, slaughtered, dismembered, and eaten, with blame on both sides. In the mayhem's wake, Marcus entreats the survivors, "O let me teach you how to knit again / This scattered corn into one mutual sheaf, / These broken limbs again into one body" (5.3.70–72). This passage not only points toward the kind of resurrective reassembling that Storm finds implicit in Dionysianism yet lacking in tragedy, but it also concisely describes exactly what Isis does for Osiris and what the gynogenic ritual dramas probably included but the phallocentric tragedies evolving from the same rituals omit. Although *Titus Andronicus* articulates the process for moving beyond tragedy, it is not fulfilled until *Antony and Cleopatra,* which positions another sexually assertive, strong-willed, "outsider" queen against adherents to a militaristic Roman male-heroic code.

In his version of dismemberment and dispersal, Antony insists, against ocular evidence of his appearance in united human form, that he "cannot hold this visible shape" (4.14.14) because of his humiliation over defeat by Caesar and belief that Cleopatra has betrayed him, and after being told that she was loyal but is dead, he cries for his "sides" to "cleave" and his "Heart" to "Crack" its "frail case," then tells his "Bruisèd pieces" to "go" (4.14.39–42) as he determines to die. Antony does, though, assume that he and Cleopatra will together rule the underworld, imagined now not as a grotesque "hell" but as a place of springlike splendor: "Where souls do couch on flowers, we'll hand in hand," making the "ghosts gaze" with their "sprightly port," such that "Dido and her Aeneas shall want troops, / And all the haunt be ours" (4.14.51–54). Yet Cleopatra does not leave him as ruler merely of the underworld, but, like Isis, collects her consort's dismembered pieces and sexually resurrects him to be a godlike "emperor," with her dream reproducing the Osirian/Dionysian agricultural renewal that triumphs over winter/death: "For his bounty, / There was no winter in 't: an autumn 'twas / That grew the more by reaping" (5.2.85–87). To restore his lifeless phallus, like that of Osiris the irretrievable piece, Cleopatra's sexualized magic imagination creates a new one that is "nature's piece 'gainst fancy" (5.2.98).

Antony, then, had wrongly assured Cleopatra that "I and my sword will earn our chronicle" (3.13.178); their fame, indeed their immortality (lasting at least to our time), is earned instead by her transformative powers, presaged with Julius Caesar. In Egyptian myth, Osiris manifests in the grain, Isis in the crops, and Isis as consort is called "Green Goddess" (Baring and Lashford 236–37). Cleopatra describes her time with Caesar as "My salad days, / When I was green" (1.5.76–77). If the sword is the phallus of choice that male tragic heroes employ to fuck the abyss, goddess-representative Cleopatra's power transubstantiates sword-fucking into plowing: "She made great Caesar lay his sword to bed; / He plowed her, and she cropped" (2.2.237–38). This passage echoes lines from the Sumerian Inanna hymns, among civilization's earliest literary works, dated at 2000 B.C.E. and reflecting traditions from 7500–3500 B.C.E. (Eisler 67). After choosing shepherd Dumuzi as her king-consort, Inanna invites him to "plow my vulva, man of my heart!" and, with the act accomplished, vegetation "flourished" (qtd. in Eisler 69). Thusly continuing earlier traditions associating the sacred marriage with the rising of plants from the goddess's womb every spring (Eisler 69), the Inanna cycle furthermore deals with nature's periodic death, symbolized by the descent of Inanna, Dumuzi, and her sister Gestinanna into the underworld, from there every year to be reborn (70). This story evolved not only into the Isis/Osiris myth, but also, as the dominator model of the blade gained in cultural power, into the Demeter/Persephone/Dis myth.

Cleopatra, however, in her ultimate death proves herself the consummate magician by transubstantiating the phallic blade once again, this time into a snake, the asp employed for her suicide. Although she had resolved to "do 't after the high Roman fashion" (4.15.92) and does indeed attempt to stab herself with a dagger, in 5.2.38, Cleopatra eventually realizes that she should not merely imitate but must triumph over Roman militaristic heroism—and over the potential future "absurd attempts" of puppeteers, "scald rhymers," "quick comedians" (5.2.226, 215–16), and female-impersonating boy actors to trivialize her and Antony's story in the comedy of ridicule. She must triumph, then, not only over the Roman mode now mastered and epitomized by Octavius Caesar, but also over time and the kind of art that could make her, as Anne Barton notes, "a mere parody queen in the epic pageant of his own imperial greatness" (51), for "all of time that matters" (52). Therefore Cleopatra must die "ostentatiously as a tragedy queen" (51), but with her last obstacle on her death-path being "Comedy," personified by the clown who brings the asps (52). Thus, in Barton's appropriate phrasing, "Comedy simply flowers into tragedy" (52). That flowering not only evidences metamorphosing genres, but also eventually yields fruit from the tree of knowledge of good and evil in enhanced understanding of the snake's "place i' the story" (3.13.46) as transubstantiated phallus.

The snake as Cleopatra's chosen death-instrument is a complex symbol with multiple associations, superficially contradictory. She initially calls it "the pretty worm of Nilus" (5.2.243), which recalls Antony's epithet for her as "'serpent of old Nile'" (1.5.26). Thus it seems both indigenous to Egypt and representative of herself, particularly as Egypt's queen. Indeed, the crown that she had just sent Iras to fetch undoubtedly includes a representation of the royal uraeus, two raised serpents, long a symbol both of Egyptian rulers and of Isis, in whose "habiliments" (3.6.17) she will surely again dress for her death tableau. The clown, though, usually employs the male pronoun "he" for the snake and twice "wish[es]" Cleopatra "joy" of "the worm" (5.2.260, 279), suggesting it as symbol of the phallus employable for her sexual pleasure. But his statement that "there is no goodness in the worm" and linkage of it to the "devil" and his dealings with "woman" (5.2.266–67, 273) evoke the serpent's temptation of Eve. For those many commentators over time wanting to damn Cleopatra, her turning to the serpent and figs "proved" that she was a no-good temptress causing Antony's fall, just as Eve had caused Adam's as well as that of all (hu)*man*kind.

What has been pieced together and interpreted from goddess culture, however, allows a very different interpretation. Noting that myths of many lands specify that existence began with a serpent and that several Sumerian tablets call the goddess "Great Mother Serpent of Heaven" (199), Merlin Stone details various goddesses' serpent associations, showing that with the imposition of dominance by Indo-European invaders, myths began to depict a male deity killing or otherwise triumphing over a serpent, as comprehensive symbol of goddess religion. She determines that the Old Testament's authors followed that pattern in their propaganda that woman was disposed to serpent-associated evil and whorishness, particularly when independent of male ownership and control.

Several elements in Stone's analysis invite correspondences to *Antony and Cleopatra*. Partly but not only because Adam and Eve were said to clothe their nakedness with fig leaves soon after the fall, Stone submits that in earliest times, the tree of knowledge of good and evil was not an apple but a fig, specifically the *ficus sicomorus,* sycamore fig, also called the black mulberry, whose reddish-colored fruit grows in grapelike clusters (215). This prospect illuminates Cleopatra's mention of the "juice of Egypt's grape" (5.2.282) shortly before reaching for her death instrument from the basket of figs—which were associated with Dionysus (216). Osiris was first buried in a mulberry coffin, which was later placed inside a living sycamore tree, symbolic of Isis-Hathor as his mother/wife, who could thereby provide him with the food of eternity (215). This tree was known as the "Living Body of Hathor on Earth," the "flesh and fluid of the Goddess" (215). Thus the fig was probably eaten as a type of "communion" with the goddess, perhaps inspiring Jesus's "flesh and blood" communion (216). Furthermore, Egyptian murals depicted the goddess within this tree, dispensing to the dead its sacred fruit as the food of eternity (215). *Antony and Cleopatra*'s many metaphors comparing Cleopatra to food, as well as her asking the clown whether the snake will "eat" her (5.2.271), could relate to this information.

Hathor-Isis, "Lady of the Sycamore," was also revered as "the Eye of Wisdom and the Serpent Lady" (Stone 214–15), which contextualizes the clown's remark to Cleopatra that the snake emerging among the figs can be "trusted" only "in the keeping of wise people" (5.2.265–66). Goddess culture habitually associated the serpent with wisdom, prophetic counsel, oracles, and dreams of the future (199), accessible by the priestesses (210). Furthermore, the oracular shrines' sacred serpents may have been the actual instruments of divine revelation, as recent scientific evidence documents that the bite of certain snakes triggers in an immunized person an hallucinogenic state involving super-acute hearing, "seeing" of visions, and poetic ability. Thus the venom may have caused a priestess, especially if in an "expectant state of mind," to sense communication with the "very forces of existence" and to comprehend past, present, and future events with superior clarity (213). Cleopatra seems in such an "expectant" state not only in her "dream" of "emperor" Antony, but also shortly before her death when she says, "Methinks I hear / Antony call; I see him rouse himself / To praise my noble act" and "hear him mock / The luck of Caesar" (5.2.283–86). Perhaps she had experimented with snake venom in small doses previously, as directly after quoting the "serpent" epithet for herself, she says, possibly not only as metaphor, "Now I feed myself / With most delicious poison" (1.5.27–28), and her physician apparently told Caesar that she studied "easy ways to die" (5.2.356). That could explain why, in contrast to Charmian, Cleopatra does not die until bitten by *two* asps, and why she asks, "Have I the aspic in my lips?" (5.2.293) when Iras falls dead immediately after Cleopatra's kiss but before the queen has employed an asp.

Besides the serpent, sex had to be vilified in the Eden story, since the goddess, as many sources note, also supervised all sexual acts (homosexual as well as heterosexual). Stone interprets that because the serpent-associated goddess was honored as "the tutelary deity of sexuality and new life," Genesis's writers depicted "the advisory serpent and the woman who accepted its counsel, eating of the tree that gave her the understanding of what 'only the gods knew'—the secret of sex—*how* to create life" (217). The goddess disapproved of monogamy (Dening 57), and, according to Stone, Judeo-Christian patriarchs' zeal to institute a male-kinship system through certain paternity led to their characterizing sex as immoral, the "original sin" (218). Goddess culture instead regarded sex, the goddess's "gift to humanity," as "sacred and holy" (155).

Sexual customs of goddess culture included what many call "ritual prostitution." Although Stone complains that the term "prostitute" encourages misinterpretation of a word that from the original languages literally translates as "holy" or "sanctified" woman (157), Dening states that "prostitute" originally meant "to stand on behalf of," or represent, the goddess's power (54). Together, these inceptive meanings not only clarify the practice's religious significance, but can also assist in reclaiming both tragic dignity and sexual divinity for Cleopatra as the "prostitute queen." Ritual "prostitution" was similarly practiced in the worship of goddesses Inanna, Ishtar, and Isis, each said to have spent some time on earth as a prostitute, and, as briefly noted above, of Aphrodite-Venus, patron deity of prostitutes.

A woman wishing to become a conduit for the divine energy was initiated into ritual prostitution's mysteries by sacrificing her virginity in sacred marriage with a male priest, or, if the priest had castrated himself as voluntary sacrifice to the goddess, with a representation of the divine phallus (Dening 56–58), which parallels Isis's and Cleopatra's completion of their respective mysteries' path with a phallic substitute. Although Enobarbus marvels that "the holy priests / Bless [Cleopatra] when she is riggish [in a sexual desire/arousal state]" (2.2.249–50), if they are holy priests of the *goddess,* it makes perfect sense, as does Cleopatra's being attended by eunuchs, like Mardian, who nonetheless has "fierce affections" and meditates on "What Venus did with Mars" (1.5.18–19).

Prohibited from ordinary marriage, the goddess's priestesses used their sexuality only in practice of the sacred marriage, sometimes enacted with male priests, impersonally, not as women and men, but as incarnations of female and male deities (Dening 54–56). At many temples priestesses also performed the sacred marriage with any male worshippers desiring direct contact with the goddess's power as mediated through them (56). Such practice of the sacred marriage was for male worshippers an ecstatically rejuvenating experience, for the priestesses a ritual offering to the goddess, and for the temple a source of considerable income (56).

Income from these worshippers may have had a spiritual transformative significance, as gold, honey, speech, and sexual fluids are semantically interlinked (Friedrich 79). Perhaps relatedly, some accounts state that Isis replaced Osiris's phallus with one of gold, made into living flesh by her magical powers (Ashcroft-Nowicki 157).[13] Enobarbus describes Cleopatra, "when she first met Marc Antony" and "pursed up his heart," as dressed in "cloth-of-gold of tissue / O'erpicturing" "Venus," and her barge's "poop," "like a burnished throne," was "beaten gold" (2.2.196–97, 209–10, 201–2). Later, irritated Caesar reports that in Alexandria, Cleopatra, the "whore," appearing in "th' habiliments of the goddess Isis," and Antony "in chairs of gold / Were publicly enthroned" (3.6.69, 17, 4–5): Antony had been upraised to share the prostitute queen's golden goddess throne. For Osiris and Antony, as for ritual prostitution's male worshippers, sexual contact with the goddess-representative led to elevation and acknowledged value through an alchemical-like golden transformation.

Although Greco-Roman and Judeo-Christian patriarchs first suppressed and eventually almost obliterated goddess religion in Western culture, it did survive in the east, not only in Egypt through Cleopatra's time, but also even to the present in India, in the philosophy and practices of Tantra, discussed by Philip Rawson. Its most significant rituals involve conversion of the participants through coitus into images of the male deity and the goddess (79). Tantric art often represents the goddess astride a male corpselike figure, whose penis is embedded in her vagina (130); this image parallels those discussed above of Nut over Geb, Isis over Osiris, and Cleopatra "on top" of Antony. In the Tantric image, the goddess represents "active creation," and the remote male "continually fertilizes her into being" (130), though his lingam (phallus) is actually self-originated in the goddess's yoni (vagina) (140). The goddess's "self-originated lingam," paralleling the phallus-substitutes of Isis and Cleopatra discussed above, functions as the "Pure Mirror" of the male's image (183). Indian icons habitually delineate the divine couple "either as a male and a female, He with erect organ, She holding a mirror, or as a single double-sexed being," center-divided, "the right half male, again with an erect organ, the left half female" (183). The first form parallels the "mirroring" of "'serpent of old Nile'" (1.5.26) Cleopatra holding a phallic-associated "worm of Nilus" (5.2.243), and the second corresponds not only to Isis's and Cleopatra's androgyny, but also to the male-female Dionysus carvings.

Tantric and Egyptian mythologies, compared by Edward Bynum, share emphasis on bird and serpent mystical symbols (29), represented too in Isis's and Cleopatra's parallel kite and snake associations. In both mythologies, bird and snake evolve into "the inner fiery serpent who rises, takes flight, and transforms the world," called the uraeus in Egypt, the Kundalini in India (129). According to Bynum, the Greeks took from Egyptian culture many mystery-school teachings, but not the Kundalini phenomenon, perhaps because their "predilection for rationality and the mood of bodily doubt" disallowed ego transcendence "except in brief periods of Dionysian and Eleusian cult ecstasy," when they did "openly attempt to 'embody the gods'" (137). The historical Cleopatra's biographers agree that she immersed herself much more into Egyptian cultural teachings than had any other Ptolemaic rulers, and, as mentioned above, the crown that Shakespeare's Cleopatra wears in her death tableau surely displays a uraeus representation. Bynum documents that the headdress signified Pharaohs' knowledge of this serpentine power, also involved in alchemy and the Osirian resurrection (129). The historical Cleopatra, then, almost certainly understood Kundalini, and both she and Shakespeare's Cleopatra can be seen as manifesting it in death.

Kundalini involves spiritual transcendence not so much *from* the physical body as *through* the fully sexually awakened body. According to Earlyne Chaney, Kundalini is the "soul nerve," the "highest energy of the infinite, coiled up and dynamic, at the base of the human spine, where contact is made between the infinite divine creative energy and the finite physical sex energy" (20). While coiled, Kundalini stimulates the reproductive organs, but, for the physically incarnated soul to attain its highest spiritual potential, Kundalini must uncoil, upraise, and travel upward, becoming "the Serpent of Wisdom, the Plumed Serpent, bringing power, enlightenment and cosmic energy up the spine to burst into enlightenment in the Third Eye" (20). This language closely parallels that applied to the ancient serpent-goddesses. Chaney identifies Tantra's main theme as "the sublime marriage between Shakti, the [internal] feminine goddess, and Shiva, the [internal] male god" (23). With Kundalini's upraising, one attains "union of the male-female principles in the highest state of Buddhahood" (24). Thus a Kundalini-awakened person becomes double-sexed, androgynous, as does Cleopatra.

Androgyny through Kundalini can be produced by sustained coitus culminating in a third-ventricle brain orgasm, opening the third eye (Chaney 43–44) for "'the birth of the Christ within'—the true Immaculate Conception," as the "divine Christ-seed" germinates through union of "the spiritual sperm of the pineal—the Sun Seed—and the spiritual ovum or divine egg emitted by the pituitary—the Moon Seed" (31). Indian Shakti/Shiva equates to Egyptian Isis/Osiris (Bynum 133), so this process parallels the mating of Osiris as Sun with Isis as Moon to produce the divine child, Horus. The historical Cleopatra had coins struck representing herself as Isis and Caesarion, her son by Julius Caesar, as Horus, and later she and Antony posed for portraits as Isis and Osiris (Hughes-Hallett 84); she thus seemed intent on manifesting herself as Isis with an appropriate great man as Osiris. Neither Julius Caesar nor "premature ejaculator" Marc Antony could satisfy such desire for Shakespeare's Cleopatra, though her reconstructed "emperor" Antony, whose luminous face shone of both "sun and moon" (5.2.79), will. Indeed, it is a rare couple that attains mutual simultaneous brain orgasm (Chaney 44). Once Kundalini has been awakened, however, meditation on the beloved deity can continue the process (45). Cleopatra's dying visions of her reconstructed Antony may so function; her line "Husband, I come!" (5.2.287) suggests that she has finally merged in spiritualized orgasm with her deified consort, and her asp can symbolize their divine child, conceived and delivered at accelerated rate.

Kundalini stimulation can provoke a possession state, so in her death scene Cleopatra may finally *be* "possessed" by Isis. In possession state, an initiate experiences "body and consciousness being entered into by a god or being or force that exists on a higher plane or deeper, more subtle order,"

Plate 5.2 Goddess with serpentine energy emerging from her vulva (South India, ca. 1800). Ajit Mookerjee Collection. Photo courtesy Thames and Hudson Ltd., London, from *Tantra: The Indian Cult of Ecstasy,* by Philip Rawson, published by Thames and Hudson, London and New York.

enabling sight of either "beings" or "forces" (Bynum 145). Shakespeare's Cleopatra sees both: her deified Antony on the "other side" and herself as forces of "fire and air" (5.2.289) only, when, like the fire and air Kundalini snake itself, she sheds the outer skin of her "other elements," bequeathing them to "baser life" (5.2.289–90). Charmian seconds her "fire and air" self-identification by calling her the "eastern star" (5.2.308). Both descriptions confirm risen Kundalini, which "radiates light to all the radiant one contacts" (Chaney 22), proving state of grace, detectable by and sometimes benefiting onlookers (58). Even Octavius Caesar describes the dead Cleopatra appearing "As she would catch another Antony / In her strong toil of *grace*" (5.2.347–48).

The goddess-figure from Tantric art shown in Plate 5.2 parallels Cleopatra in her death scene. Some critics have suggested that lines like "Look, where they come" (1.1.10) tease audiences/readers with the prospect of witnessing Antony and Cleopatra in sexual congress. With Plate 5.2 as a gloss, we may realize that Shakespeare does indeed deliver an onstage sexual act, but audiences, readers, and critics have been blind to it—because it is gynogenic rather than phallocentric. Through it, we can see that "Have I the aspic in my lips?" (5.2.293) puns on her vaginal lips and that the snake is Cleopatra's "Husband" for whom she will "come" (5.2.287) in taking "joy of the worm" (5.2.260, 279).[14] By additionally calling the asp her "baby" (5.2.309), Cleopatra manifests an interpretation of the pictured goddess-figure as birthing the snake, relating to the ancient serpent-associated goddess tradition of the "king"-consort as both lover and (literal or symbolic) son, a tradition retained in the Isis/Osiris story, with Horus as both child of Osiris and resurrected Osiris. In parallel fashion the asp is both the reconstructed Antony and Cleopatra's divine child by him. The pictured goddess, however, may most easily be interpreted as double-sexed, with the snake as erect phallus, which relates to Cleopatra's androgyny and her assuming male-heroic tragic stature even by the Aristotelian phallocentric standard—which revelations of the gynogenic bases underlying and encompassing it problematize. Furthermore, as noted above, this double-sexing represents Supreme Being, both the originating Deity and the corresponding human deity within, achieved by the ultimate orgasmic *hieros gamos* of Kundalini. If in Christian tradition Jesus represents all that is God embodied in man, then for goddess tradition Cleopatra can represent all that is Goddess embodied in woman—not in spite of but *through* her sexuality, *through* her being the "prostitute queen." So can we now at least see her as a "hero"? Or must she ask us, as well as Antony, "Not know me yet?" (3.13.160)?

We can begin to honor Cleopatra's heroism by celebrating her metamorphosing sexual power, particularly regarding drama's genesis in ritual. More than any of Shakespeare's (or anyone else's) male tragic heroes, she restores tragedy to its Dionysian and pre-Dionysian roots, making *Antony and*

Cleopatra epitomize what Liebler calls "festive tragedy." By his staging of Cleopatra's enactment of a profound ritual comparable to and recapitulative of the Dionysian, Eleusinian, and Isis/Osiris mysteries, Shakespeare shows that rebirth can be the gynogenic festive epilogue of phallocentric Aristotelian-tragic death.

As Isis had done for Osiris, Cleopatra had gathered up the bruised and scattered pieces of Antony and, through the magic circle of her sexuality, heroically proved herself his savior by resurrecting and deifying him. In her own death, she heroically accomplishes the same for herself: the collection, recreation, and deification of the multiple components of herself that had been dismembered and scattered—not only by the Romans in their deliberate withholding of respect for her royalty, but also by critics attempting either to epitomize her in her sexuality to damn her, or to efface it by domesticating her as "mere" Roman wife. Uniting all elements of her "infinite variety" (2.2.246) in her climactic act, she metamorphoses her political defeat into a majestic triumph over Caesar, Rome, death, time, and the arts not only of ridiculing comedy, but also of the great genre of tragedy itself, furthermore encompassing Greco-Egyptian history, Dionysianism, goddess culture, Greco-Roman heroism, Greco-Roman and Judeo-Christian myth, creation, damnation, salvation, mysticism, divine incarnation, ritual prostitution, and immaculate motherhood to "Become themselves in her" (2.2.29). To adapt 5.5.68 of *Julius Caesar*, THIS was the noblest orgasm of them all!

Cleopatra achieves this sublime climax herself through Kundalini sexual union with the serpent and her own androgyny that includes Tantra's images of the goddess's self-originating lingam and of the male deity's unseen phallus that stimulates the triumphant orgasm enabling her to conceive, as their "divine child," what Antony had called "new heaven, new earth" (1.1.17). That phallus belongs to the only one of her consorts truly deserving to be her correspondingly androgynous son-lover-king: William Shakespeare. The "screwing" of phallocentric Aristotelian tragedy is accomplished by the play's ultimate manifestation of phallic symbology, mightier than the sword: the pen of the bard, through supreme uprising of his "I" in the "O" of the Globe, in the spirit of gynophilic love-making rather than phallocentric fucking.

Neither Cleopatra's tragedy nor her triumph is hers alone. So long as we women ourselves continue to efface the stature of Cleopatra, we blindly contribute to the tragedy of our own effacings, degradings, and dismemberments. Our efforts in such form may be "heroic" on the male model, but not contributive to the festive divinity that we could embody and draw our male counterparts up to share. Shortly before her death, Cleopatra had asserted that "'Tis paltry to be Caesar; / Not being Fortune, he's but Fortune's knave, / A minister of her will" (5.2.2–4). The goddess most in contemporary women's power to embody is Fortune, one of Isis's forms (Pomeroy, *God-*

desses 218). If we adhere to the Romans' view of Cleopatra, we maintain Caesar in his position at the top of Fortune's wheel. But if we recognize Cleopatra's heroism, and, like Charmian, articulate her point of view when her lips are mute, we spin the magic circle of the goddess's wheel and thereby elevate ourselves, making Cleopatra's triumph our own.

In a visionary sense, *Romeo and Juliet*'s and *Antony and Cleopatra*'s endings show that the female can go on after the self-castrating death of phallocentrism, aided by, though not dependent on, the phallus that we may symbolically fashion in a festive Dionysian/Isis-like mode for ourselves, whether or not by that we choose to identify ourselves as devotees of the goddess and whether or not we take Shakespeare as the matter with which to fashion that new, divine, resurrected-resurrective phallus of creative revisioning, as, in my eyes, he offers himself to become, for our increased agency in the world and joy in our sexuality's divinity. His Cleopatra is the hero who can inspire us to (re)create new heaven, new earth—for ourselves, our consorts, and the literal and/or symbolic children that can be born from such a partnership model of mutuality in power and love. In return, we can at least mend her crown as the "prostitute queen."

Notes

1. Fitz [Woodbridge] made the first prominent case for Cleopatra as tragic hero. Feminist critics often cite her exposure of sexism, yet many remain unconvinced that Cleopatra possesses tragic stature. See, e.g., Adelman's *Suffocating Mothers* (190–91; 341n56) and Kahn's *Roman Shakespeare* (138).
2. See Rubinstein on "queen"/"quean" in Shakespeare's and his contemporaries' works (209–10). On Shakespeare's uses of the word "whore," see my "'Made to write "whore" upon?'"
3. Though I have seen no other commentator make this point regarding drama, Scholes asserts that music and fiction imitate sex through the "fundamental orgastic rhythm of tumescence and detumescence, of tension and resolution, of intensification to the point of climax and consummation" (26). Winnett rightly responds that "female pleasure might have a different plot" (507).
4. Space limitations prohibit fuller discussion here, but Cleopatra's androgyny, heroism, and goddesslike sexual divinity are demonstrably anticipated in Juliet.
5. See Kimbrough, who argues that Shakespeare's works depict androgyny's "full range," from "the personal/societal to the psychic/mythic" (5).
6. See *Shrew*, 1.1.32–39; and *Troilus*, 2.2.166–73. All quotations of Shakespeare come from Bevington's edition; all emphases within them are mine.
7. See the *New Variorum*, ed. Spevack et al., Steppat's Appendix, especially 655–60, dealing too with Isis, Osiris, and so on. On the Apollonian and Dionysian modes generally in tragedy, see Storm.

8. The historical Cleopatra, like many of her female Ptolemaic ancestors, associated herself with Aphrodite-Venus, whose birthplace, Cypress, was under Ptolemaic control (Pomeroy, *Women* 30–31).

9. For Plutarch's treatment of this myth, see Griffiths's translation and commentary. For more recent and thorough analyses of the Isis-Osiris myth's relation to *Antony and Cleopatra* than found in Steppat, see Adelman's *Suffocating Mothers* and Bono's *Literary Transvaluation*. My analysis, though informed by these commentators' work, involves very different implications.

10. The idea that female orgasm was necessary for conception was prevalent during the Renaissance and had appeared sporadically in medical writings for centuries beforehand. Medical science now shows that, though not integral to conception, it *does* increase the likelihood.

11. Willbern observes that female-associated "sexual, bodily senses of Shakespeare's Nothing and O" interlink with "various myths of symbolic origins" (250). The circle emblematized mother, woman, and Mother Earth (Cutner 156). The straight line, represented by the letter I, or number 1, symbolized the male; in Egypt, the line attached to the circle depicted the sacred "Bar of Isis," or the union of the sexes (158).

12. Nut was often depicted with wings, spread over the dead, who lay in her "starry bosom"; coffins' inner lids pictured her body's firmament, signifying that the "soul of the deceased might join the blessed dead who became the stars on her belly" (Ions 50). Commentators on Egyptian mythology agree that Isis absorbs all of both Nut's and Hathor's qualities. I am grateful to my friend Prof. Tim Alderman, of West Virginia State College, for directing me to material on Egyptian mythology cited in this essay.

13. Ashcroft-Nowicki's *The Tree of Ecstasy* provides specific directions for a couple's performance of "The Raising of Osiris" sexual ritual (155–67); its elements may well parallel those of the ancient gynogenic dramas.

14. Interpreted thusly, the staged sexual act may also have political import. Alexander the Great (whose conquest of Egypt enabled rule by the Ptolemies, the last being Cleopatra), to establish his divine lineage, asserted that his mother, a maenad, conceived him by coitus with Zeus in snake-form (Pomeroy, *Women* 29). Besides Caesar's claiming Venus as divine ancestor, his mother declared that she was impregnated with him by Apollo in snake-form (Hughes-Hallett 93). Cleopatra's snake-coupling, then, might pay tribute to Alexander's mythic Dionysian-related conception and mock the supposed Apollonian conception of Octavius Caesar.

Female Heroism in Heywood's Tragic Farce of Adultery

A Woman Killed with Kindness

Theresia de Vroom

I will begin this paper with two reasonably reliable critics of Thomas Heywood's play, *A Woman Killed with Kindness* (1603). The first is the anonymous author of the "blurb" on the back of the New Mermaid's edition of the play who describes *A Woman Killed with Kindness* as follows: "The play is notable for the restraint with which Heywood deals with his theme, and for the spirit of reconciliation, rather than violence, in which tragedy ends."[1] The second is my eight-year-old son, who, on seeing a copy of the play on my desk, read its title aloud and said quite matter-of-factly, "That's impossible!" The argument I will advance is that while the former view is the one most commonly held by critics, that the play's end is a model of forgiveness, restraint, and reconciliation, it is the latter view that should concern feminist readings of the play. If it is essentially impossible to "kill with kindness," if the play's title can be read ironically or even parodically, then the play's subject might also be read in a different light.[2] The figure of the adulterous wife may be tragic, immoral, even sinful, given the cultural, social, and religious context in which the play was written, but the act of adultery by this married woman, punished by her husband's "kindness," is at the same time more complex. In *A Woman Killed with Kindness,* Anne's adultery is crucial to defining and defending her fledgling heroism and it is key to understanding the tragedy of the heroine of the subplot, the hapless Susan.[3] Against a comic backdrop that mocks the masculine and patriarchal world on which this marriage is necessarily based, a brief vision of female heroism emerges, a heroism that quite radically suggests that "kindness" is really cruelty and that adultery is a flawed but singularly feminine act of heroism.

A Woman Killed with Kindness is variously appreciated as an exposition of the virtue of constancy in marriage, of nobility and restraint in punishment, of obedience and of the Christian prescription for mercy and forgiveness; at the same time, the play fits uneasily into these perspectives. The vision of kindness at the end of the play, for example, is of a heroine publicly disgraced and living in exile, banished by her husband from her children, her home, and the society in which she lives. She has lost everything that constitutes her identity save, for the time being, her physical self, while her adulterous accomplice is free to plan a trip abroad and with it, his advancement at court.[4] And yet the heroine's husband does not treat her with physical violence, but with the "kindness" of the play's title, a reprieve that is nonetheless directly linked to her death. Taking her cue from her husband, Anne kills herself "kindly" by refusing to eat or drink. But this "kindness" is also clearly problematic. While Frankford's punishment of Anne may be a civilized improvement on physical violence, it also may be more cruel because of its psychological nature. It is a punishment that makes the criminal her own victim and in the process, leaves behind no evidence of how the penalty has been exacted. Frankford punishes Anne politely, passively, and silently. Without his raising a finger, his wife acts out her own punishment for him.[5] He comes off as a good spouse, patient and restrained, while she is doubly guilty. She is not only an adulterer but a suicide. Frankford's punishment in this light seems to be greater than his wife's crime for not only does Anne lose her life but she also jeopardizes her salvation. To "kill with kindness" may be both the most innocuous and precise form of revenge and Frankford says as much. When he decides not to use physical violence against Anne, he tells her rather that he will "with usage / Of more humility torment thy soul, / And kill thee with kindness" (13.155–57). His is a revenge of great cruelty masked as restraint.[6]

The genre of *A Woman Killed,* the domestic tragedy also called "the murder play," is first found on the popular stage toward the end of the sixteenth century. Its subject, nonetheless, is already visible, as H. Adams and others have shown, in the medieval morality play, whose pattern of temptation, sin, repentance, punishment, and mercy is closely followed in the domestic tragedy (Adams viii; Comensoli 27–35; Smith 138–47).[7] Like the medieval morality play, the primary purpose of the domestic tragedy was to provide a moral example, in this case drawn from people as ordinary as the citizens of its audience.[8] The homiletic superstructure of the domestic tragedy was often the same: disaster comes to the family because of the actions of an adulterous woman, a structure that would be reversed in the citizen comedies where redemption depends on a woman's constancy (Harbage 235).[9] The genre also has roots in the medieval morality plays, especially in the model of the exemplary obedient wife as portrayed by the popular story of

Griseldis, in Chaucer, Petrarch, and Boccacio, but also in the later dramatic depiction by Chettle, Phillips, and Haughton (Comensoli 19–64).[10] The homiletic potential of the tale of Griseldis was easily adjusted to include the Anglican prescriptions for the constancy of women, their submission in marriage, the rewards of long-suffering patience, and so forth.

Nonetheless, the genre of the domestic tragedy is a hybrid. It is at once morality play, tragedy, domestic vignette, melodrama, and homiletic set-piece.[11] And therefore, because it is many things at once, a pastiche or collage of many generic interests, it vacillates between loyalties. And while these plays seem to have clear didactic purposes, to preach the importance of feminine fidelity in marriage, some ambivalence toward the moral superstructure remains. These traces of ambivalence may also have been inherited from a medieval model. Beside the morality plays and the tales of calumnized, long-suffering women such as Griseldis, the medieval cycle plays contained material that would influence the portrayal of domestic life in the citizen tragedies of the sixteenth and early seventeenth centuries. The depiction of marriage in the cycle plays, particularly the marriage of Joseph and Mary (as well as Noah and his wife), provide well-known and often humorous critiques of the instability of one of the most important models of domestic life, the marriage between the parents of the Savior. The tropes are familiar enough: Mary is young, pregnant, and virtuous, the mother of God, while Joseph is a cuckold, an impotent and hen-pecked husband, an old and tired man who is asked to believe that his young wife has conceived a son by the power of divine intercession alone (de Vroom, "Unequal Couples," passim). Like the domestic tragedies to come, the medieval cycle plays were serious depictions of the underpinnings of morality and mystery, or of fidelity and love in marriage, but at the same time, they could not always resist the comic temptations implicit in any marriage, particularly that of the unequal and unstable couple, Joseph and Mary.[12]

Another important social aspect that may effect the composition and meaning of the genre of the domestic tragedy is what seems to be a contemporaneous crisis in gender relations. Many observers in the early seventeenth century thought that marriage and the family were in crisis. Scholars as well have documented and discussed the various and growing forms of social disorder, particularly as it concerns women between 1560 and 1660, a period that saw rapid population growth, inflation, and the extensive transfer of land (Burke, Donaldson, Macfarlane). Witches and scolds are primarily a phenomenon that occurred in this hundred year period as was the singling out of women who had been abused or beaten by their husbands in a version of the charivari called the "riding" of a whore. Steven Ozmet, speaking more generally about the crisis concerning marriage in Reformation Europe, writes:

Humanists, reform-minded Catholics, and especially Protestants decried the amount of domestic litigation, particularly that of contested first marriages, and a casual demeaning of marriage and family life they perceived all around. It was surely not accidental that these "defenders of the estate of marriage," if such they may be called, appeared at a time when perhaps 40 percent of all women were single (an estimated 20 percent spinsters, 10–20 percent widows), and infant and child mortality high (perhaps two-thirds to one-half of all children died by age five). Nor was it accidental that women found new advocates in an age when their physical vulnerability had made them the target of politically self-aggrandizing secular and ecclesiastical witch-hunters. . . . (Ozmet 1)[13]

In more general terms, D. E. Underdown has observed that "The flood of Jacobean anti-feminist literature and the concurrent public obsession with the scolding women, domineering and unfaithful wives, clearly suggests that the patriarchy could no longer be taken for granted . . ." (116–17); and further he suggests "the possibility of a crisis in gender relations around 1600" (122). In the same vein, S. D. Amussen writes that despite the tensions that threatened the social order, particularly in the family unit,

the gender order was never challenged explicitly, and the inferiority of women never denied. . . . The governors of England, from parish officers to those in parliament, sought to impose order on a society which was changing, and apparently disintegrating before their very eyes. . . . The analogy between family and state, gender order and class order, offered an effective response to disorder. . . . [Their] effort was successful, and even if the threat was less than they had feared, the dimensions of the fear itself should not be underestimated. (Amussen 216)

Whatever the precise nature of the "crisis" of the family, how real the crisis in gender relations was, or how much of it was merely perceived as real, the effect would be the same in the sense that the relation between men and women seemed no longer to be stable; the world was falling apart at its core. If the titles of plays after 1600 can be taken as evidence, then women as the subject of drama as indicated by the inclusion of their name or gendered referent (whore, witch, virgin, duchess, and so on) in the title of a play underscores the increasing anxiety about their conduct. Along with *A Woman Killed,* their titles are such as: *The Honest Whore I and II; The Virgin Martyr; Women Beware Women; The Witch of Edmonton; The Duchess of Malfi; The Roaring Girl; The Dutch Courtesan; 'Tis Pity She's A Whore; Epicene? or the Silent Woman;* to name a few. These titles are plentiful and telling in that they include women's names or the subject of women in a way almost nonexistent before 1600.[14]

The rise of the ritual of the charivari in this same period, the humiliation, punishment, and ultimate absorption of deviant couples was on the rise and concurrent with popularity of the iconographic description of the subject across Europe and England (Thomas; Thompson; de Vroom, "Unequal Couples"). The "charivari," usually taken as a French form, had its versions across Europe. In England these rituals were variously known as "a riding," a "skimmington ride," "rough music," or the "riding of the stang." The rituals, frequently occurring at night, were largely punishments for crimes associated with deviance in marriage, the most usual subjects being: age difference in couples who were about to marry; the censure of premarital sex; the exposure of adultery and cuckoldry; the punishment for wife beating; and the humiliation of the scold and/or the hen-pecked husband. While there are many elements that can make up a charivari, two are prominent and relative to our discussion of Heywood's play. One is the riding of the subject. In a charivari, humiliation was always displayed by riding the person: in a procession, on a horse, an ass, or a substitute horse, a pole or cowl-staff, or even in a cart as in the "carting of the whore." And second, a charivari was noisy. As the "rough music" of its English name suggests, the ritual was loud and cacophonous; it was music made with bawdy songs, banging pots, drums, pieces shot off, the clanging of bones and tongs and pots, shouting and hooting. The opposite of learned music, a reflection of harmony and order in the universe, the noise of the charivari was the announcement of disorder based on the conjugal crimes of its victim(s).

Comic elements derived from the medieval dramatic tradition, the ritual undercurrents of the charivari, and so on, provide a counterpoint to the didactic and moral message of Heywood's play. In *A Woman Killed with Kindness,* marriage is tragedy masked by comedy—but comedy of a particular kind. The tragic action of plot and subplot of the play is predicated on an undercurrent of farce, contained first of all in the bawdy folk humor of the servants but more extensively in the bourgeois rituals of Frankford's house: the hounds, the horses, the falcons, card games, dances, and dinner parties accompanied by the learned and rough music of the play. It is in the manners of the bourgeois culture that the values of marriage repeat themselves as farce.[15] Humor in this play stands to expose the marriage between Anne and Frankford for what it really is: a farce ripe for cuckoldry.

Beside the farcical tone of various parts of the play, the traditional subjects of commercial trickery and sexual infidelity that are common to farce as a genre as well as to Heywood's play, there are also specific touchstones to the genre that shape and shift the tragedy.[16] Heywood's play is consistent with the Latin origin for the word "farce," *farcire,* "to stuff." It is a tragedy stuffed with comic bits that are meant to provoke uncomplicated laughter (unlike the reflective laughter that is the domain of comedy proper). Reflection and understanding in *A Woman Killed with Kindness* comes from the tragedy put forward in the play, but nonetheless laughter accompanies it. It is laughter that is quick, without complexity, like the response to a dirty joke, but laughter that nonetheless serves to reposition the meaning of the tragedy. The play, like farce, hinges on making the impossible commonplace, but the impossible in Heywood's play is not, for example, the improbable discovery of long lost siblings, an abbess who is really their mother and an old man who is really their father as in *The Comedy of Errors*. In *A Woman Killed with Kindness* making the impossible commonplace is inherent to the tragic depiction of a subject that is traditionally comic: bourgeois marriage. The grafting of an essentially comic subject onto tragedy creates a hybrid version of tragic improbabilities. This is most obviously seen in two parallel but related instances. Anne is Frankford's equal: she is educated, beautiful, and she admires him, he loves her and yet she cuckolds him; what seems improbable, even impossible, is the tragic supposition of the play. Similarly, Frankford "kills" his wife "with kindness." A conundrum, an impossible proposition and yet the play and many of its critics take this title with its impossible implications as if it were not only possible but perfectly natural. Finally, *A Woman Killed with Kindness* uses the farcical property of the gross exaggeration of character. This element, readily apparent in the character of the servants, particularly Nick, is also found when the main characters face critical moments of action in the play. When the they are forced into action they often act quickly, creating a kind of shorthand version of their character, a cartoon of their former more fully embodied selves.[17]

The first words in the play are: "Some music there!" called for by Sir Francis Acton, Anne's brother, to celebrate her marriage to Frankford. This auspicious beginning soon turns inauspicious when Charles, making a bawdy joke about the bride, says: "Yes, would she dance 'The Shaking of the Sheets'. / But that's the dance her husband means to lead her" (1.2–3). The "Shaking of the Sheets" is a double entendre, a bawdy reference to the wedding night and the name of a popular ballad referring to the dance of death (Scobie 5). As N. Loraux has noted, "No death of a woman takes place without involving the bed" (24). The linking of death and sex in this marriage is indeed an apt foreshadowing of Frankford's later realization at the end of the play that "A cold grave must be our nuptial bed" (17.124). More poignantly, of course, is that it is in bed where Anne dies. Again, we have a double entendre: her bed has always been a place where she might die (the sexual pun), and a place where she is starved to death. In other words, Anne's bed is a place where Frankford neglects her, a place where she is hungry, and a place where her hunger will ultimately kill her.

This reading is strengthened by several elements. In the largest sense of the play, it explains why Anne is seduced given her husband's love for her, his generosity, kindness, and gentility. But also, it explains much of the comedy that takes place at the wedding feast. The music that pervades the first two scenes of the play is extremely important. First it is the wedding music of the bourgeois household, music to which Frankford refuses to dance. He says that the bachelor, Sir Francis, may dance, but that "Marriage hath yoked my heels, pray then pardon me" (1.11). But this isn't quite right. A groom should dance at his own wedding and his refusal to do so intimates that he is lacking in skill, dexterity, manners, or perhaps that he is shy, or clumsy. He says that marriage prevents him from dancing by "yoking his heels." In other words, marriage stands to prevent him from doing the very thing marriage is supposed to legitimate, sexual relations between a man and a woman. This view is directly underscored in the next scene, where the servants with their own musicians play bawdy "rough music," in the vein of the rites of the charivari, music that serves to mock unequal or aberrant matches. Servants and assorted wenches who are called things like Jack Slime, Roger Brickbat, and Sisly Milkpail dance heartily, peasantlike, and their language is rife with sexual puns and innuendo. While Sir Francis mocks them, calling them "mill-horses" (1.85) who will make "The hall floor pecked and dinted like a millstone" (1.87) with their rough boots and heels, they dance exuberantly and boast their virility: "And though we may be country fellows, it may be in the way of dancing, we can do the horse-trick as well as servingmen" (2.13–15). Their dancing is in part a "downstairs" mockery of the truth "upstairs."

In the first scene of the play, much is made of Anne's beauty and accomplishments—but not by her husband. It is Sir Charles instead who says:

> Master Frankford
> You are a happy man, sir, and much joy
> Succeed your marriage mirth. You have a wife
> So qualified, and with such ornaments
> Both of mind and body. First, her birth
> Is noble, and her education such
> As might become the daughter of a prince,
> Her own tongue speaks all tongues, and her own hand
> Can teach all strings to speak in their best grace,
> From the shrill treble, to the hoarsest base.
> To end her many praises in one word,
> She is beauty and perfection's eldest daughter. . . . (1.12–23)

To this, Frankford merely replies something like, "If I didn't know you better, I'd be jealous."[18] But he himself does not praise Anne. She responds by demurring this lavish speech, saying that it is her husband's "sweet content" that to her is like "a flattering glass" (1.33). Her brother (a character reminiscent of Angelo in *Measure for Measure*) then continues her praises with:

> She doth become you like a well-made suit
> In which the tailor hath used all his art. . . .
>   She's no chain
> To tie your neck, and curb you to the yoke,
> But she's a chain of gold to adorn your neck. (1.59–60, 63–65)

Anne is seen as ornament, as precious, as art, but all these observations are made by a man other than her husband, who himself remains conspicuously silent. Perhaps he is gloating over his fortune, proud that his male friends admire his wife—perhaps he cannot express himself—but perhaps he does not fully appreciate the value of his bride.

In these descriptions it is also clear that Anne is a possession, that she really does not exist as her own subject. Her identity relies on her connection to her husband as ornament or chain or suit of clothes. She is tangential to others, an indication of which is that she never appears on stage alone. V. Comensoli has argued that Anne's fall comes from her vanity and further that she is "cowardly, untrustworthy, and lacking in 'intellectual resources' precisely because she is a woman" (79–80). Self-described as "want of wit" (11.112), Anne is vain, according to this view; when she pleads for mercy she says: "mark not my face / Nor hack me with your sword, but let me go / Perfect and undeformed to my tomb" (13.98–100). Here, it may be that Anne cannot bear to lose her beauty out of vanity. But it may also be that her pleas are a clue to why she commits adultery in the first place. By turning to Wendoll, Anne turns away from Frankford and in this sense her adultery may be as much an act of defiance as it is of desire. She is of course seduced, implying that she is taken over by the power of yet another man, but she describes her actions in terms that affect her soul. When she refuses Wendoll at first, she tells him that, "The love I bear my husband is as precious / As my soul's health" (6.139–40). Later this same passive soul, whose health is predicated entirely on her husband's love, begins to move. Confused, she says: "My soul is wandering and hath lost her way" (6.10), and finally when she is seduced she admits, "This maze I am in / I fear will prove the labyrinth of sin" (6.159–60). We are reminded of Michel Foucault's maxim that reverses the long held Christian view that the body is the prison of the soul. Foucault says to the contrary that "the soul is the prison of the body" (31). While Anne may be frail and vain, her actions immoral, her adultery is in part based on her ability to behave as her own agent, to act outside of her marriage, to be the subject of her own life—to be, in this sense, its hero. To return to the initial passage, when she asks Frankford not to harm her physically but to leave her "perfect and undeformed," it may be that she longs to preserve this newfound boundary of her self as subject. She does contemplate physical suffering later:

> O to redeem my honour
> I would have this hand cut off, these my breasts seared,
> Be racked and strappadoed, put to any torment.
> Nay, to whip but this scandal out, I would hazard
> The rich and dear redemption of my *soul.* (13.135–39; my emphasis)

Here her shame at what she has become, an adulterer, makes her contemplate a violent death, but it is her action outside her husband's power for which she stands to "hazard the redemption of [her] soul."[19] Adultery may deserve punishment in a domestic tragedy, but punishment for feminine independence may be the greater crime because it finally makes it impossible for a woman to remain as a member of a patriarchal household. In fact, her actions stand to disrupt the very principle on which such a household is founded (Belsey, passim). It is this silent crime, greater than the face-value of adultery, for which Anne is silently punished.[20] But her punishment is "kind," she is sent to live on her own, the mistress of her own "mansion." In this sense, Frankford's punishment truly fits the crime if the crime is one of defiance leading to individuation because Anne's punishment is the most extreme perversion of independence: exile.

In the end Anne dies as Frankford forgives her and "remarries" her on her deathbed. This remarriage is really quite extraordinary because now Frankford can have it both ways: he can marry Anne again and at the same time be assured that she won't live but a few moments longer. He reasserts his power and possession of her just as he lets her die, reestablishing the order in his household and preserving his honor simultaneously, as Elizabeth Bronfen has argued:

> Countless examples could be given to illustrate how the death of a woman helps to regenerate the order of society, to eliminate destructive forces or serves to reaggregate the protagonist into her or his community. A common pattern emerges even if the cultural values that are connected with the dead woman and debated in connection with her death vary. [. . .] The potential for change is shifted away from the self on to the signifier of the sacrificed body so as to be transferred into the existing order without fundamentally changing it. (219)

But Anne still retains something like heroism in death. She concludes the play begging pardon and forgiveness, but her final lines are telling: "Pardoned on earth, soul, thou in heaven art free. / Once more thy wife dies thus embracing thee" (17.123–24). Anne may be remorseful but while she embraces Frankford on earth, her soul is free and in heaven. Her "redemption," her heroic achievement, is her freedom, as Loraux tells us: "For women there is liberty in tragedy—liberty in death" (17).

After Anne is caught by Frankford with Wendoll, she speaks more. Her early utterances in the play pale by comparison. Now her language becomes increasingly expressive, substantial, and articulate. It is as if with her adultery, flawed and immoral as it may be, she has found a way to her voice. But a version of Anne's voice has existed in the play all along even though we do not hear it until almost the very end. The music of Anne's lute, learned and skilled, is the heroine's much admired talent. Nonetheless she never plays or sings even though Frankford later tells us how frequently and well she once did. Anne's lute is the one possession she leaves behind when she is banished. Nick finds it, "flung in a corner" (15.12) and to it Frankford makes his most impassioned confession of love for his wife:

> Her lute! O God, upon this instrument
> Her fingers have run quick division,
> Sweeter than that which now divides our hearts.
> These frets have made me pleasant, that have now
> Frets of my heartstrings made. . . .
> Oft hath she made this melancholy wood,
> Now mute and dumb for her disastrous chance,
> Speak sweetly many a note, sound many a strain
> To her own ravishing voice, which being well strung,
> What pleasant airs have they jointly sung.
> Post with it after her. Nothing's now left;
> Of her and hers I am at once bereft. (15.13–24)

A learned parallel to the "rough music" of the play, Anne's lute is related to her sexuality, as Nick later remarks under his breath to her, "Would that have been the worst instrument that e're you played on" (16.20–21).[21] Frankford says that the frets of the instrument are interchangeable like his own heartstrings. The lute is feminine in shape, an instrument to whose sound Anne would match "her own ravishing voice." The lute is left behind, a painful reminder of Anne's voice and her body in her husband's house. When the lute is returned to her she speaks to it saying that they "both are out of tune, both out of time" (16.19). In the fields, two miles from her new home, she plays it for the last time saying: "My lute shall groan; / It cannot weep, but shall lament my moan" (16.31–32). Wendoll, passing by this scene, sees and hears Anne's lament, whose power he likens to that of Orpheus. But here he is wrong. For while Anne's music may be as moving as the music made by Orpheus, she is really more like Eurydice whom he, like Wendoll and Frankford, leaves behind to suffer in hell.

Her song finished, Anne tells Nick that she is resolved: "Last night you saw me eat and drink my last" (16.65). Her death pact sealed, she orders her servants: "Go break this lute upon my coach's wheel, / That is the last music that I e'er shall make—" (16.72–73). Breaking the lute displaces the physical violence she avoids to her own body. Making music no more is her decision to commit suicide: starvation is silent.

While Anne's sorrow at the end of the play is poignant, Frankford's love for Anne is troubled from the outset. The day after the wedding, alone in his study (the same place he will go to contemplate Anne's punishment later in the play), Frankford is now, in Iago's words, "fast married" (1.2.11). In his musing on "the morning after," or sometime like it, he says the following to himself:

> How happy am I amongst other men
> That in my mean estate embrace content.
> That I am a gentleman and by my birth
> Companion with a king; a king's no more.
> I am possessed of many fair revenues,
> Sufficient to maintain a gentleman.
> Touching my mind I am studied in all arts;
> The riches of my thoughts and of my time
> Have been a good proficient. But the chief
> Of all felicities on this earth,
> I have a fair, a chaste and loving wife.
> Perfection all, all truth, all ornament.
> If man on earth truly happy be,
> Of these at once possessed, sure I am he. (4.1–14)

While the sentiment here is loving enough it is also a strange text for an aubade-like meditation. Frankford first lists his status as his estate: gentleman, equal to a king; then his revenue; then his education; and finally, his wife whom he praises for her fairness, chastity, and love. Anne is for the second time called "his ornament," and like his revenue, his happiness is his "possession." If we compare this response to that found in Shakespeare's great domestic tragedy, *Othello,* this new-married-man's praises pale by comparison.[22]

Following this commodified, gentrified reverie, Nick bursts in with news that a gentleman is here to see Frankford. The first thing Frankford asks is if his guest is "On horseback?" (4.16). Nick says he is and in fact that his horse is dirty, splashed with mud, "all spotted / And stained with splashing" (22–23). Wendoll arrives on his spotted horse, an apt description of his sins to come—Anne will later call herself "a spotted strumpet" (17.78).[23] Wendoll's horse is indeed like the woman he will seduce. He will trade this horse for one of Frankford's horses just as he will take his wife; both will be ridden and lost. In the second half of the play, Frankford, in a moment that recalls this scene, will leave his house on horseback in order to catch his wife with Wendoll. In keeping with the bawdy register of the play's puns on sexual inequity, Frankford's horse is a gelding (11.82) and a roan, a castrated stallion of mottled or spotted coloring.[24] Ironically Frankford goes out so that he can catch Anne and Wendoll at precisely that which he will would hate for them to be doing: cuckolding him—the humor here is underscored by his impotent and spotted horse.

It is likely that the pervasive references to horses, the "rough music" of the servants' dancing, are elements of the charivari that survive in the play. The opportunity for Anne's seduction first occurs when Frankford has gone out on his horse. The servant Jenkin tells Wendoll: "marry sir, her husband is riding out of town, and she went very lovingly to bring him on his way to horse" (6.63–64). Anne brings her husband to his horse; he will be a cuckold shortly, a prophetic gesture that humorously underwrites the coincidental moment that Frankford is away from home. Later the suspicious Frankford will watch Wendoll and Anne at cards, games full of bawdy double entendres, among them a game called "Lodam," from the Italian *scarica l'asino,* or load the ass (3.150).[25] At the end of the play, in keeping with those rituals of shaming associated with sexual crimes, among them adultery, Anne is "ridden in a cart." She is sent from Frankford's house to a mansion some seven miles away with all her possessions and a few servants in a carriage. The music that comes to accompany the riding is played by Anne on her lute. As we have seen, she serenades her own humiliation.[26]

In place of his more reserved attitude toward Anne, Frankford takes immediate and fond exception to Wendoll. In the absence of praise for his wife, his praise of Wendoll is lavish from the start, seemingly ill-merited given the brevity of their acquaintance and the fact that Wendoll's "possibilities [are] but mean" (4.64). But Frankford immediately offers him his hospitality: "Please you to use my table and my purse, they are all yours" (4.65). And then:

> Choose of my men which shall attend on you,
> And he is yours. I will allow you, sir,
> Your man, your gelding, and your table,
> All at my own charge. Be my companion. (4.69–72)

These displays of generosity culminate in Frankford's asking his wife: "Prithee Nan, / Use him with all thy loving'st courtesy" (4.79–80), to which Anne wisely responds: "As far as modesty may well extend, / It is my duty to receive your friend" (4.81–82). Why is it, we might wonder, that the newly married Frankford responds as he does to the bachelor, Wendoll, taking him into his household with such immediate trust and devotion? And further, we might wonder why it is that Wendoll seems to have what Anne does not: her husband's friendship and with it, his purse. He has what Anne wants: her husband's devotion and with it his economic power. She has some cause to be jealous and this in itself is motivation for adultery.[27]

We have already seen that eating is related to desire in Anne's suicide (Bryan, passim; Gutierrez, "Exorcism," passim) but food also functions as the currency of desire between men in the play. When Frankford first offers his hospitality to Wendoll he immediately invites him to dinner (4.83–84). Later, as Wendoll contemplates seducing Anne his guilt over Frankford's friendship is also expressed in terms of food:

> He cannot eat without me,
> Nor laugh without me; I am to his body
> As necessary as his digestion,
> And equally make him whole or sick. (6.40–43)

Then when Anne meets Wendoll she tells him that her husband is away but that he asks Wendoll in his absence to "keep his table, use his servants / And be a present Frankford in his absence" (6.77–78). Frankford offers Wendoll the possibility of impersonating him, at his table, with his servants, and by implication, with his wife (DiGangi 50). Later, when they are left alone again, Wendoll pretends he and Anne are going to her room to dine privately: "My pleasure is / We will not sup abroad so publicly, / But in your private chamber, Mistress Frankford" (11.90–92).[28] The implications of his desires are not lost on the servants. Jenkin nonetheless hopes for the best, saying, "and if they do sup together, pray they do not lie together" (12.12–13). The meaning of this thematic register was clearly understood by Claude Lévi-Strauss who notes a:

> very profound analogy which people throughout the world seem to find between copulation and eating. In a very large number of languages they are even called by the same term. In Yoruba, "to eat" and "to marry" are expressed by a single verb, the general sense of which is "to win, to acquire," a usage which has its parallel in French [and also in English], where the verb, "consummer," [to consummate] applies both to marriage and to meals. (105)

The images of eating and food, as we have already seen, transcend gender and class in this play. Nick, the servant who comes to replace Wendoll in Frankford's trust, acts to destroy his master's marriage by claiming, as Iago does, "I love you better than your wife" (8.43).[29] Nick, whose name variously means to cheat, to steal, to gamble, to deny, the precise mark (as in the nick of time), and the devil (as in St. Nick), is also affected by appetite when it comes to dealing with his master. When he first contemplates telling Frankford about his wife's antics, he says: "I cannot eat, but had I Wendoll's heart, / I would eat that" (8.17–18). Frankford comes in, the stage directions tell us, "brushing crumbs from his clothes with a napkin and newly risen from dinner" (8.23), and accuses Nick of disrupting his meal because he wants an advance on his salary, "Nicklas, you want money, / And unthrift-like you would eat into your wages" (8.29–30). After Nick tells his master about his wife's adultery, he closes the scene with his appetite restored: "And now that I have eased my stomach, / I will go fill my stomach" (8.96–97). One is reminded of well-known homosocial gatherings founded on exclusive sumptuary regulation—The Symposium, The Last Supper, the Super Bowl Party, High Table—attempts to create alternative, fully patriarchal and fraternal relations in the domestic sphere predicated on the exclusion of women. This, if nothing else, is a strange backdrop to a play whose didactic subject is marriage.

In the same vein, *A Woman Killed* is strangely full of confessions of male affection and admiration—and curiously thin on expressions of devotion by men to women despite its purported subject being the value of marriage. One of the most poignant examples of this occurs in the subplot of the play. There Susan is forced by her brother to offer herself to their enemy, Acton (who coincidentally is Anne's brother), in place of a debt he owes him of five hundred pounds. She will, he tells her, "In one rich gift pay back all my debt" (10.124). The scene between brother and sister is rife with the language of incest and prostitution. Charles like a pimp courts his sister for Acton:

> Nor do I woo you in a brother's name,
> But in a stranger's. Shall I die in debt
> To Acton, my grand foe, and you still wear
> The precious jewel he holds so dear? (14.50–53)

He dresses her specially for meeting Acton, twice referred to as having her "tricked up" (14.1 and 84). Susan, like Anne, offers to suffer physical mutilation rather than to be sold to Acton:

> Will Charles
> Cut off my hands, and send them Acton?
> Rip up my breast, and with my bleeding heart
> Present him as a token. (14.55–58)

She even offers to use a knife "to slice out my life" (14.85). But Susan ultimately succumbs to her brother's wishes, and while Acton does not prove either her seducer or rapist, he marries her: her complete surrender is implicit in the acquiescence to the match. She says, "I will yield to fate / And learn to love where till now I did hate" (14.147–48).

What is interesting about all this is Charles' reaction to Acton. When Acton proposes to marry, instead of use, his sister, he makes the following confession of his love for him:

> With what enchantment you have charmed my soul,
> And made me rich even in those very words.
> I pay no debt but am indebted more;
> Rich in your love I never can be poor. (14.149–52)

Susan's function has been to unite former male enemies. Her fate, despite her brother's enthusiasm, is grim. She says very little in the play from here on. Significantly, at Anne's deathbed, she asks the dying woman, her sister-in-law after all, "How is it with you?" (17.112). She might well ask herself the same question because Anne's fate is her mirror.[30] In order for these men to love each other, to forget harm done and establish kinship, they exchange women between them: Charles and Acton fight and in order to reestablish peace, Charles must offer his sister to his enemy. The result is reestablished love between the two men. The subplot is a direct inversion of the Wendoll/Frankford plot where Frankford all but offers his wife to his friend and when he takes her, she is punished. Here a man is punished but his crime of debt is absorbed and displaced onto his sister's sexual value. Kinship is established between men through kindness, their generosity to each other, a generosity that frequently takes the form of money and women. But in the play, money is finally the signifier of a more precious currency: in both plots, it is the women who pay the real price of patriarchy.[31]

And here finally the ironic meaning of the play's title comes full circle. "Kind-ness" means essentially two things in the play: goodness and kindness as in kinship, Hamlet's "a little less than kin and more than kind" (Ure, passim). But kinship/kindness does not seem to refer to the play's subject, domestic relations between husband and wife, even brother and sister; rather its emphasis is on kind-ness as in sameness, the relations between the same kind, relations between men whose bonds are stronger between each other, whose bonds threaten to outstrip those between themselves and their wives or sisters. In this sense, Anne is killed with kindness: because she is a woman, she is not the same "kind" as Frankford or Wendoll. What Heywood seems to have written is a critique of marriage predicated on patriarchy.[32] If marriage, as the Tudor apologists argued, is the nucleus of state, of religion, and of the future, then something, at least in this play, is deeply wrong when men's power is greater, as it must be, than women's. Because when this happens, as in Heywood's version, the bonds between men stand in direct conflict with the fundamental basis of marriage.

In closing the play's final couplet echoes the cruel and ironic riddle of the play's title. The last lines of the play are Frankford's description of the epitaph he will place on Anne's "marble tomb" (17.138): "In golden letters shall these words be filled: / Here lies she whom her husband's kindness killed" (17.139–40). What Frankford describes is the creation of a monument to memorialize his "kindness," not Anne's life or death, his love for her, or even her repentance. Her grave, like her life, will be his "ornament" (1.15). As the gold letters engraved in marble will forever reiterate, he was kind and she seems never to have existed. His words mark and interpret her end; set in stone, they nonetheless reveal how anxious he is to establish his control over his wife even after death. Anne's heroism in the play, in contrast to her husband's marked "kindness," is that she finds (tragically but truly) a way out. Unlike Hermione she will have no resurrection from stone, but ultimately she evades the world in which her husband rules. She does so incrementally—dancing, playing a lute, losing her soul to Wendoll, and finally starving herself to death. In the end, it is tragedy that liberates her. Ironically therefore, it is not only Frankford who kills her with kindness, but Anne herself. Her end, her refusal to eat or drink, is an action of most tragic heroism, at once passive, courageous, desperate, premeditated, silent, and most of all, misunderstood. By the only means at her disposal, Anne kills herself and in doing so she defies her husband's epitaph. Despite everything else, her death reveals that she (and not her husband) controlled, if nothing else, how her life would end.

Notes

1. All quotations are taken from Thomas Heywood, *A Woman Killed with Kindness,* New Mermaid Edition (London: A. & C. Black, 1985). The editor, Brian Scobie, may have made this unattributed comment. There are various arguments that defend the play on grounds that it is both instructive and cautionary. L. Bromley, for example, argues that, "Heywood intended to dramatize a code of gentlemanly behavior for an emerging middle-class audience eager for guidance in the business of living" (260). M. Doran sees Frankford's punishment as enacting what would be expected of a rational and constant husband (143); N. Gutierrez ("The Irresolution of Melodrama") sees Frankford as "able to control his grief and passion with reason," although she judges the oppressive treatment of women by patriarchy and not "Frankford's self-restraint and non-violence . . . unusual responses to a wife's infidelity," as undercutting the resolution at the end of the play (277).

2. As D. Atkinson has shown, the proverb, "to kill with kindness," prior to Heywood's play, was usually given as a warning against overfond indulgence. Atkinson is one of the few who suggests that Frankford's interpretation of this phrase contains "more than a hint of cruelty" (23). G. Herndl also detects cruelty in Frankford's punishment (passim).

3. While I hope to show that the subplot is vital to the meaning of the larger play, many critics have regarded it as weak, unrelated, and highly problematic. Among the most famous proponents of this position were T. S. Eliot, "Thomas Heywood," *TLS*, 30 July 1931; William Hazlitt, *Lectures on the Dramatic Literature in the Age of Elizabeth* (1818); A. C. Swinburne, *The Age of Shakespeare* (1908). More recently, there have also been similar arguments made by Arthur Brown and Freda Townsend.

4. See Wendoll's final speech in the play (16.125–37).

5. As N. Gutierrez has shown ("Philomela strikes back"), while punishment for witchcraft might include physical violation and mutilation, the typical punishment of the ecclesiastical courts for adultery was rather lenient, normally enacted as a public display of shame in which the guilty party would wear a white sheet in a prominent place in the church or churchyard, a practice that was nonetheless difficult to enforce. As the century wore on, tighter controls and punishments were sought by civic institutions so that by Parliament's Act of 1650 severe penalties including death were prescribed for crimes of adultery and incest (Gutierrez 429–43; Atkinson 19–20).

6. In her study of the films of Alfred Hitchcock, Tania Modleski writes an analysis of the heroine of the film, *Notorious* (1946), who is "punished" for her sexual notoriety by the various men in the play, culminating in her slow poisoning in bed. Modleski notes that the heroine, "Alicia," is punished not only for her erotic worldliness but because she uses her sexuality in order to gain knowledge and power. By the end of the film, she is "rescued" from near death, a state in which she, like the starving and presumably emaciated Anne, emerges desexualized, in Modleski's words, "etherealized and spiritualized until she becomes practically bodiless" (61). See also Loraux, *Façons Tragiques,* passim.

7. Comensoli's longer argument is particularly interesting because it synthesizes the medieval dramatic inheritance of the play with later codes of marital conduct fashioned by the Tudor apologists.

8. S. Cerasano's unpublished dissertation on the First Fortune Playhouse, the first and most important popular theater of its day (1600–21), discusses the complex commercial and ideological arrangements between the popular theater and its audience. See also Kathleen E. McLuskie, *Dekker and Heywood* (passim) and Louis B. Wright 638.

9. Hallet Smith sees the play in terms of the figure of the Elizabethan fallen woman while P. Meyer Spacks argues that the play is an exposé of human, as opposed to feminine, frailty and further that all the characters (save Nick)

are enmeshed in a world of appearances from which they cannot extricate themselves.

10. Anne's tragedy might be read as the tale of Griseldis backward. Griseldis begins a poor and landless maid, marries the rich nobleman, has children, is tested, and ultimately she is restored to her rightful place in the marriage and court. Anne is wealthy, marries an equal, she has children, she commits adultery, she is exposed, and she is exiled from her place in the household, from her children and her husband.

11. T. S. Eliot began the generic debate in his influential piece on the play; he says that, "Heywood's is a drama of common life, not, in the highest sense, tragedy at all" (109). Since then, many scholars have thought it important to argue whether or not Heywood's play is indeed a tragedy, see for example David Cook as well as N. Gutierrez ("Melodrama"). Many critics view the play, as we have already seen, as various permutations of homiletic, domestic, didactic, prescriptive, not to mention popular, drama.

12. There are two other dramatic predecessors in which comic depictions of adultery exist. There is the N-Town *Woman Taken in Adultery,* in which Christ asks the audience to remember mercy and forgiveness: "Whoso aske mercy, he xal haue grace" (l.38), and further says that anyone truly contrite like the woman caught in adultery, is "better loue[d]" than all other sinners (ll. 289, 291). [*The N-Town Play: Cotton MS Vespasian D.8.* Ed. Stephen Spector. 2 vols. EETS, s.s. 11–12 (Oxford: Oxford UP, 1991)]. There is also the Tudor piece by John Heywood, *Johan, Johan* (printed in 1533), in which adultery is both unrepentant and unpunished. [John Heywood, *Johan, Johan.* In *The Plays of John Heywood.* Ed. Richard Axton and Peter Happé (Cambridge: D.S. Brewer, 1991)]. See H. Norland on this play and its relation to French and English farce.

13. The prominence of the crisis in the larger sense is suggested by the title of a now well-known collection of essays edited by Trevor Aston. See also Comensoli 20–26.

14. Shakespeare, for example, includes only two titles with women named in them before 1600: *The Taming of the Shrew* (1593–94) and *The Merry Wives of Windsor* (1597, revised 1600–1601) though he did write *Venus and Adonis* (1592–93) and *The Rape of Lucrece* (1593–94). The "shared" title, *Romeo and Juliet* (1595–96) is the only one before 1600, followed then by *Troilus and Cressida* (1601–2) and *Antony and Cleopatra* (1606–7). The discussion of a general trend in an author's work leaves one open to objections on specific cases that are justifiable. Nonetheless I would suggest that while women of course figure prominently in Shakespeare's plays throughout his career, he increasingly includes and explores the subject of women, drawing them to the forefront of the plays as he approaches the romances. Before 1600 (to name a few) we have Tamora and Lavinia; Kate and Bianca; Juliet; Helena, Hermia, and Titania; Portia; and Beatrice. In 1599 Calphurnia and Brutus's Portia along with Rosalind usher in the great heroines of Shakespeare including: Ophelia and Gertrude; Viola and Rosalind; Cressida; Helena; Isabella;

Desdemona; Cordelia, Goneril, and Regan; Lady Macbeth; Cleopatra; and Volumnia, culminating with the many and various heroines of the romances. Indeed, it might be argued that Shakespeare writes "the great tragedies" after 1600 and therefore better or more plentiful female subjects might occur more naturally there. Nonetheless, before 1600, Shakespeare had already written *The Comedy of Errors; Richard II* and *Richard III; Henry IV, I and II; Titus Andronicus;* and *Love's Labors Lost,* all plays in which men are very much the subject and women, while they are important in psychological and narrative terms, are not, it might be argued, themselves subjects. When we compare Anne (*Richard III*) to Desdemona, or Titania to Hermione, for example, this general but important distinction between heroines emerges. There are those who stand at the periphery of the play and those who at times are its subject.

15. I am indebted to S. Longstaffe for this observation.

16. Farce determines some of the structure of this play because it is in farce that adultery is not only conventional but light, frivolous, comic, even harmless. What follows is based on the definition of "farce" in the *Princeton Encyclopedia of Poetics and Poetry,* 8th edition, 1990.

17. Anne, Wendoll, Frankford, Acton, Susan, and Charles all seem to have varying levels of self-understanding, for example, and yet each one acts quickly, desperately, "out of character" we might say in a shorthand version of their more complex selves at work at the same time as their less complex selves. For example, Acton behaves as a villain toward Charles, but in a quick turn of events becomes the virtuous husband. Susan is ready to mutilate herself, but then decides in a few words that she will marry her enemy and learn to love him. Neither Anne nor Wendoll wants to commit adultery because of their affection for Frankford; they both spend some time on their deliberations but when each does act it is swiftly and irrationally. Charles is a model of gentlemanly behavior but he acts suddenly, rashly, and kills three of Acton's men, and so forth.

18. The lines are: "But that I should know your virtues and chaste thoughts, / I should be jealous of your praise, Sir Charles" (1.25–26).

19. Anne's description of her seduction in relation to her soul finds an apt parallel in the writings and experiences of medieval female mystics such as Hadewijch of Antwerpen or Beatrice of Nazareth. There is a long tradition of feminine resistance in the work of female mystics (including more well-known names such as Teresa of Ávila) who also use the figure of the wandering and transfigured soul (a feminine noun) and its journey to love, "minne" (also a feminine noun) to mystical/erotic union with the Christ in order to legitimate their teaching and writing on matters ecclesiastical. The mystical experience is essentially adulterous because it concerns the erotic as well as spiritual union of a professed virgin, "the bride of Christ," with Christ (E. Petroff, passim; T. de Vroom, "Beatrijs of Nazareth," passim). In the same vein, the French political theorist, Malby (*De la législation, Oeuvres complètes, IX,* 1798) would, a few centuries later, agree with Frankford: "Punishment, if I may so put it, should strike the soul rather than the body"

(qtd. in Foucault, *Discipline and Punish* 16). It is, of course, precisely "her soul" that Frankford wishes "to torment" by "kill[ing her] with kindness" (13.156–57).

20. Here is one of the many echoes of the play to *Othello* (1603–4). Desdemona, also murdered in her bed, is not punished for the crime of adultery but for loving Othello too much and he her (cf. Greenblatt [*Renaissance Self-Fashioning*], Cavell, and so on), or, as P. Berry (*Shakespeare's Feminine Endings*) has shown, she is killed (as Anne is killed) because she represents the power of "the opacity of the sexualized female body" (101). Further, as in *Othello,* it is through the linking of men against women in this play (Frankford/Wendoll/Nick; Othello/Cassio/Iago; Anne/Susan; Desdemona/Emilia, and so on) that tragedy is plotted and carried out.

21. For a different analysis of the use of music in the play see Carey.

22. For example: "she lov'd me for the dangers I had pass'd, / And I lov'd her that she did pity them" (1.3.168–69) and: "I will deny thee nothing. . . . / Perdition catch my soul / But I do love thee! and when I love thee not, / Chaos is come again" (3.2.83, 90–92).

23. On discovering his wife in the arms of Wendoll, Frankford exclaims, " . . . that I might take her / As spotless as an angel in my arms" (13.63–64). Later, before her children, Frankford says that Anne is "The blemish of my house" (13.119), that she has "charactered" her infants with "shame" (13.123), and he refers again to her body as "spotted" (13.125).

24. Wendoll's horse is a sorrel, or chestnut in color, and this horse that Frankford gives him is also a gelding.

25. I am grateful to Roberta Mullini for telling me that this is a Neapolitan card game, still played today, whose object is to rid oneself of the card with the ass on it. The card game in the play is rife with bawdy puns and unknown to Anne or Wendoll, Frankford is onto them all.

26. The playing of the lute by a woman in the Renaissance seems to have been uncommon given the iconographic and literary evidence. In this respect, Anne's lute again underscores her remarkable and, perhaps, defiant nature. Iconographic depictions of women playing lutes are rare before the late seventeenth century (as opposed to the early and commonplace depictions of women playing virginals, for example). The only "literary" and female lute player that comes to mind in this period is Bianca in *Taming of the Shrew* whose lute, which she never plays, becomes an excuse for the pedant, Hortensio, disguised as a music teacher to try and win her (*T. S.* 3.1). There is also the contemporaneous lute song by Thomas Campion (1567–1620), "When to her lute Corinna Sings," whose lyrics, also written by Campion, are uncannily parallel to Heywood's depiction of Anne:

> When to her lute Corinna sings,
> Her voice revives the leaden strings,
> And doth in highest notes appear
> As any challeng'd echo clear.

But when she doth of mourning speak,
Ev'n with her sighs, her sighs
Her sighs the strings do break,
The strings do break.

And as her lute doth live or die;
Led by her passion, so must I.
For when of pleasure she doth sing,
My thoughts enjoy a sudden spring.

But if she doth of sorrow speak,
Ev'n from my heart, my heart
My heart the strings do break,
The strings do break.

Since no text or directions from Heywood accompany this serenade it would be interesting to consider how it might be performed. Anne's performance could greatly effect the way in which her character is read. Her heroism, our sympathy, her skill, and her voice, not to mention the text, length, or quality of the piece she might play, all would contribute to an audience's perception of what has happened in the play. I am grateful to Francis Guinle for suggesting the further exploration of this topic.

27. As J. Dusinberre eloquently observes: "In some ways the Elizabethan tragedy of adultery is the woman's version of the revenge tragedy. Adultery is a woman's only weapon of vengeance, not only for the particular wrongs of a husband, but for the helplessness of women in a world where action is strength" (303). While I think Anne's adultery is not consciously motivated by revenge but by a desire, however confused, to assert her own identity, the effect on Frankford (and to some extent the other men in the play, especially Nick and Acton) is that her action craves retribution and punishment. It is her adultery, or rather her cuckoldry of her husband, that results in the assertion of patriarchal retribution throughout the play. Again, as Dusinberre has argued in her comments on *Othello:* "The adulteress, taking the initiative in illicit sexual activity, forces on her husband the passivity of the cuckold. The adulterous woman adopts a male role; her femininity no longer stands in the way of physical violence. Similarly, the cuckold can only recover respect through the *violent* re-establishment of his manhood" (302, my emphasis). This argument underscores the assertion of maleness at the end of *A Woman Killed* that is not only evident in *Othello,* but also in many other plays "about" adultery. Compare, for example, the actions of Leontes toward Hermione in *The Winter's Tale;* of Claudio toward Hero in *Much Ado About Nothing;* Titus and Saturninus toward Lavinia and Tamora in *Titus Andronicus* as well as the violence of masculine reassertion in plays like *The Duchess of Malfi, The White Devil,* or *The Maid's Tragedy.* In the same vein, Hamlet's

> "adulterous" mother is reflected in his accusations of Ophelia, the woman on whom his (unintentional?) revenge is the most complete, to whom he most directly can assert his manhood.

28. He reiterates this desire a few lines later: "Come, Nan, I prithee let us sup within" (11.102).

29. Iago, when he first arouses Othello's suspicions, says, for example: "—but I am much to blame; / I humbly do beseech you of your pardon / For too much loving you" (3.3.211–13).

30. Strengthening the interchangebility of the Anne/Susan plots is Canuteson's observation that "the matter of the expensive 'back veluett' gown which Anne would have worn from scene xvi to the end of the play [is] in contrast with Susan's white wedding dress—probably the same white dress that Anne wore in the first scene" (125).

31. We are reminded of Hermione's proclamation that her husband's accusations of adultery are his fantasies, which she is made to live out and be punished for, even with her life (and those of her son and daughter): "My life stands at the level of your dreams, / Which I'll lay down" (*The Winter's Tale* 3.2.81–82).

32. Heywood's own comments in the *Apology for Actors* show that he saw the moral and didactic power of theater to "mold the harts of the spectators" (*Apology*, sigs. B5v, G1). In the same vein, he says that all drama, "Tragedy, History, Comedy, Morall or Pastorall," can "either animat[e] men to noble attempts, or attach the conscience of the spectators" (*Apology*, sig. F4). In keeping with his didactic interest in theater, Heywood would write a *History of Women* in 1624 as well as his *Exemplary Lives and Memorable Acts of Nine of the Most Worthy Women of the World* (1640), both works that may be seen as sympathetic defenses of women.

"As If a Man Should Spit against the Wind"

Martin Orkin

Bosola's cry just before his death at the conclusion of *The Duchess of Malfi*, "In what a shadow, or deep pit of darkness, / Doth womanish and fearful mankind live!" (5.5.101–2), may postulate, within misogynist and patriarchal parameters, a "mankind" not only afraid but rendered effeminate by epistemological and ontological opacity. However it simultaneously at least admits, perhaps unusually so in the context of conventional use of the generic term, the glimpse of two genders rather than one. The coordinating conjunction "and" implicitly prompts the adjectival "womanish" toward the substantive "woman" so that the phrase "womanish and fearful mankind" seems informed also with the admission that if "mankind" is "womanish" it is also born of woman. Concomitantly the "womanish" section of [hu]mankind, too, is subject to existential uncertainty/suffering. That such a potential dismantling of the masculinist containment evident in the more overt meaning of the line is present may well be partly an effect of the murdered Duchess's persisting influence in act 5, but the accompanying semantic torsion suggests, too, Webster's attempt to think beyond the patriarchal paradigm in his endeavor, as the titles of both his major plays hint, to present female heroes.

Another of the ways in which this project might manifest itself in his tragedies occurs when Monticelso utters his well known denunciation of Vittoria in *The White Devil:*

> Shall I expound whore to you? sure I shall;
> I'll give their perfect character. They are, first,
> Sweet-meats which rot the eater; in man's nostril
> Poisoned perfumes. They are coz'ning alchemy,
> Shipwrecks in calmest weather. What are whores?
> Cold Russian winters, that appear so barren
> As if that nature had forgot the spring.

> They are the true material fire of hell,
> Worse than those tributes i'th'Low Countries paid,
> Exactions upon meat, drink, garments, sleep—
> Ay, even on man's perdition, his sin.
> They are those brittle evidences of law
> Which forfeit all a wretched man's estate
> For leaving out one syllable. What are whores?
> They are those flattering bells have all one tune,
> At weddings and at funerals; your rich whores
> Are only treasuries by extortion filled,
> And emptied by cursed riot. They are worse,
> Worse than dead bodies, which are begg'd at gallows
> And wrought upon by surgeons, to teach man
> Wherein he is imperfect. What's a whore?
> She's like the guilty counterfeited coin
> Which whosoe'er first stamps it brings in trouble
> All that receive it. (3.2.78–101)

The misogyny in these lines has often been acknowledged. The fact that it is voiced by one of Vittoria's accusers, himself morally equivocal, seems strongly to argue Webster's own disparagement of dominant patriarchy. Equally important, however, Monticelso tropes the unruliness of women by means of imagery that comes from or represents his male world and its institutions. In effect he interpellates the feminine by marking Vittoria's (woman's) body with images that provide repeated evidence of the masculine world and/or male unruliness: "coz'ning alchemy," the hazards of navigation, harsh "tributes" and "exactions" leveled in the process of taxation, "brittle evidences of law / Which forfeit all a wretched man's estate / For leaving out one syllable," "treasuries by extortion fill'd / And emptied by cursed riot," "dead bodies begg'd at gallows" in the course of the (illicit) practices of surgeons, "the guilty counterfeited coin / Which wheresoe'er first stamps it brings in trouble / All that receive it." Here again, despite the simultaneous attempt to hide one gender by the well-known male habit of displacement, two genders—in the semantic torsions producing meaning—emerge as under scrutiny.

Such scrutiny of not one but two genders seems to have been overlooked in critical discussion. Traditional critics of Webster were hardly interested in gender at all. In their rendition of a dark and excessive Webster—captured best perhaps in T. S. Eliot's dramatist, "much possessed by death" who "saw the skull beneath the skin" ("Whispers of Immortality," quoted in Hunter and Hunter 111)—the playwright's probing of gender and gender relationships remained unexplored. The predilection to diagnose only a generalized and therefore obscurantist "morbidity" or "obsession" with violence and decay lives on—most recently in the film *Shakespeare in Love,* in the joke that presents Webster to the audience as an adolescent who loves rats.

Feminist criticism has helped to correct such evasions by exploring problematics in Webster's representations of woman as well as their significance in the works. For example, Dympna Callaghan argues that Webster's female protagonists destabilize Aristotelian paradigms of tragedy, so that "There is no need for a female hero nor should feminists try to create a new critical paradigm. . . . Heroes are merely the chief characters of the plays . . . tragic action is . . . 'a particular kind of heterosexual dilemma,' leading to mortal ends unmitigated by transcendence or apotheosis" (68). She focuses on "the complex nature of woman's subordination produced by the ideological configuration of woman herself" (172). Mary Beth Rose places the Duchess in the context of seventeenth-century discourse about marriage to maintain that Webster presents the "career of a female hero whose private life subverts the established order" (166). But neither in eschewing a "heroic" role (Aristotelian or otherwise) nor in identifying it does either critic, or indeed others I have encountered, explore as well Webster's concurrent scrutiny of masculinity evident in the plays and how this may affect readings of the position of the women in the texts. When Webster writes in his dedication to his patron in *The Duchess of Malfi* that "I do not altogether look up at your *title,* the ancientest *nobility* being but a *relic* of time past, and the truest *honour* indeed being for a man to confer *honour* on himself, which your *learning* strives to propagate and shall make you arrive at the *dignity* of a great example" (2), he has his eyes clearly on honorable masculine praxis but also on, by implication, those lapses in others from the standards of male authority that he claims for his exemplar. I will attempt in this essay, primarily by an examination of *The White Devil,* to argue that Webster, against the silence about male unruliness that is usually an effect of hegemonic patriarchy, works to articulate evidence of such lapses and to expose the problem of masculine disorder. It is within the context of his presentation of disruptive male behavior, which undoes the patriarchal master narrative, that the stand taken by his women gains particular power. They emerge as tragic spokespersons in the battle, confronting, identifying, and opposing, as they do, male authority in its aspect of injustice and/or unruliness. Given the hegemonic pressures within which these women exist, and their persecution or destruction by the very male violence and disorder they attempt to confront, their acts of articulation and the resistance it implies are in this sense especially heroic.

I

Kathleen McLuskie and Felicity Dunsworth argue that by the time Webster was writing, Jacobean theater depended on a paying theater public ("Patronage and the Economics of Theatre" 426). From this point of view Webster's presentation of the adulterous woman in *The White Devil* and of the lusty widow in *The Duchess of Malfi* may be evidence of the commodification of representations of "fallen" woman. But McLuskie also observes that, although dramatists complained of the "detrimental effects on their art" of a more commercial theater, "an appeal to theatrical pleasures was not as incompatible with political ideals as the opponents of an exclusive high culture would have claimed" ("'When the bad bleed,'" in Zunder and Trill 70). Webster's complaints about his first audiences at *The White Devil* underline his sense that more than commercial exploitation was at stake.

In the case of *The White Devil*, it is true that certain elements in the presentation of Vittoria Corombona confirm presentation of a patriarchal stereotype. For example, as Trussler remarks, "Vittoria Corombona is generally thought to be the 'white devil' referred to in the play's title" (xxviii). And it is worth noting that its title page dated 1612 reads "THE WHITE DIVEL, OR, The Tragedy of *Paulo Giordano Ursini*, Duke of *Brachiano*, with The Life and Death of Vittoria Corombona the famous Venetian Curtizan." The juxtaposition of the "tragedy" of the Duke of Brachiano with the "Life and Death" of a "famous Venetian Curtizan" may also contribute to the impression of or invite expectation of a demonic and disruptively devilish female protagonist. The association of Vittoria with the title of the play appears underlined in Flamineo's interpretation of the tale of her dream as the work of an "excellent devil" (1.2.257) who teaches the Duke to murder "his Duchess and her husband" (1.2.259) and during the arraignment of Vittoria, in Monticelso's accusation "You know what whore is, next the devil / Adult'ry, / Enters the devil, Murder" (3.2.108–9) as well as in his later remark, "If the devil / Did ever take good shape behold his picture" (3.2.216–17).

It is true also that Vittoria's dream narrative in act 1 may well provoke the men around her (although it is they who contemplate and then execute murder). In act 2—in what is regarded as a disjunctive moment (a point to which I will return below)—Isabella briefly voices her desire for violent revenge against Vittoria (2.1.246–51). But while she is frequently the object of male scrutiny and blame during this act, Vittoria herself is absent. The subsequent discontinuity in her presentation as to some extent the victim of male aggression, from when she reappears in act 3 onward, is well discussed, although here some of her lies most certainly develop the resonance of the unruly woman. In act 5 too, there are incidents of feminine violence. Cornelia momentarily assaults Zanche. Zanche plans to rob her mistress, but—also disjunctively—later stands with her against Flamineo's attempt to murder them both. In the penultimate moments of the scene, Vittoria, in the attempt to save their two lives, shoots Flamineo (at his suggestion) and in their anger both women trample on the man who has tried to murder them.

Such elements in Webster's representation of woman in *The White Devil* do suggest his putative exploitation of their marketability as predictably troublesome counters within the patriarchal exchange system. And from this point of view the deaths of most of them, like the punishment and death of the Duchess of Malfi, would seem to provide modes of containment for the various unrulinesses they have exhibited. But unpleasant as such apparently conventional positionings of women or instances of female violence—particularly the episode that concludes *The White Devil*—may be, these hardly compare in the play with the extent to which Webster explores throughout episodes of male violence: the plots they hatch, their verbal assaults, their repeated resort to poison, cruelty, and murderous kinds of verbal as well as physical violence. It is especially in this context that Webster's women and their active engagement with structures of patriarchy need also to be seen.

II

If Webster plays in *The White Devil*—somewhat equivocally from a twentieth-century perspective—with the colors "white" and "black" and the word "devil," not only in the title but also in the play itself, there is strong evidence that this intersects as well with play involving stereotypes of "masculinity" and "femininity." After Vittoria's trial, in contrast to the more conventional attributions of the word "devil" to the body of woman that I have just noted, the word "devil" is attached increasingly to men in the play. To cite only a few of these instances, Monticelso gives Francisco his "black" book in which "lurk / The names of many [male] devils" (4.1.35–36), Flamineo responding to Brachiano's question "Do you know me?" observes, "O my lord! Methodically / As in this world there are degrees of evils; / So in this world there are degrees of devils" (4.2.57–60), Monticelso asks Lodovico "What devil was that you were raising when you were pardoned by the Duke of Florence?" and act 4 ends with the pseudo-sententious "There's but three Furies found in spacious hell; / But in a great man's breast three thousand dwell" (4.3.152–53).

Pointed identification of male "devilry" with its concomitant recurring inversion of gender stereotypes is evident throughout the play. Thus, although Webster shows both Lodovico and Flamineo sporadically citing women in one or other way as origin of disruption in act 1, the personal corruption of the men is simultaneously foregrounded. Lodovico's opening words blame his banishment on the "whore" fortune, but scene 1 presents a catalogue of his personal debauchery, excess, and crime, as well as that of the noblemen who have followed him, his amoral attitude to his victims (he refers to his murders as mere "flea-bitings" 1.1.32), and the viciousness of his desire for revenge— see "O I pray for them. / The violent thunder is adored by those / Are pashed in pieces by it" (1.1.10–12); "I'll make Italian cut-works in their guts / If ever I return" (50–52). Again, in the first of several inversions of patriarchal stereotypes in the play, Lodovico announces Webster's *male* protagonist as originator of sexual impropriety, with the female presented only as target *for* sexual corruption—Brachiano, "by close panderism" seeks to "prostitute / The honor of Vittoria Corombona" (1.1.41–42).

Flamineo, too, treats woman intermittently throughout act 1 as the receptacle of blame, describing his and Brachiano's conspiracy of seduction by troping "policy" as feminine (1.2.353–55) in the same way indeed that Lodovico earlier attempts to feminize the wolf as representative of predacity (1.1.8–9). At the beginning of 1.2, to persuade Brachiano to seduce his sister, Flamineo talks of "the superfices of lust most women have" (1.2.18–19); later he tells Brachiano "women are like curs'd dogs, civility keeps them tied all daytime, but they are let loose at midnight; then they do most good or most mischief" (1.2.199–202). It may be true that Vittoria is shown in this scene to be a willing accomplice in the proposed seduction but, his representation of women notwithstanding, the main portrait of deceit and corruption is to be found in the behavior and language of Flamineo himself, as he interacts with two husbands, one on the brink of adultery and the other, cuckoldry. By feeding the adulterous intent of the one and manipulating and mocking the impotence of the other it is he, rather than—as he claims by implication—Vittoria, who is shown throughout the scene to be working to "let loose" the dogs of illicit desire.

Webster's inversion of conventional presentations of woman as the origin of misrule despite what men may say about them reaches a fine point of almost protoheroic intensity, in its challenge to patriarchal narrative, with the entrance of Cornelia in this scene: it is the woman who becomes the mouthpiece of sexual control and morality. Although Flamineo receives Cornelia's denunciation of Brachiano's relationship with her daughter as the words of a "fury" (1.2.271) and Brachiano mutters "Fie, fie, the woman's mad" (1.2.298), Cornelia herself speaks up for (Christian) monogamy. The situation thus presents a woman reprimanding a man for *his* sexual transgression. In the context, moreover, of an economy of misogyny, the focus in part of her language upon male depravity, defective authority, and deceit is significantly wide ranging. Thus, while some of her judgments are directed at her daughter, she also condemns "my son the pandar" (1.2.218), compares Brachiano's visit to Vittoria to "mildew on a flower" (1.2.273), calls him "adulterous Duke" (1.2.285), admonishes "The lives of princes should like dials move / Whose regular example is so strong, / They make the times by them go right or wrong" (1.2.288–90) and curses her daughter by comparing her act to that of archetypal male treachery: "Be thy act Judas-like, betray in kissing" (1.2.299).

Cornelia's subsequent comment to her son, "What? Because we are poor / Shall we be vicious?" (1.2.315–16) precipitates Flamineo's extended identification, in turn, of an exploitative system involving service, exploitation, and false reward—a system populated and controlled of course by men. His bitterness about a father "who proved himself a gentleman" (1.2.318) by social and familial irresponsibility, "sold all's land, and like a fortunate fellow, / Died ere the money was spent" (1.2.319–20) develops, perhaps inadvertently on his part, the concern with *masculine* irresponsibility initiated by his mother, while his satire about what is in effect a male world ends by foregrounding, significantly, male sexual unruliness. He has returned, he tells his mother, from his service at the Duke's court "more courteous, more lecherous by far" (1.2.327):

> Nature is very pitiful to whores
> To give them but few children, yet those children
> Plurality of fathers; they are sure
> They shall not want. Go, go,
> Complain unto my great lord cardinal,
> Yet may be he will justify the act.
> Lycurgus wond'red much men would provide
> Good stallions for their mares, and yet would suffer
> Their fair wives to be barren. (1.2.337–45)

III

Although, as I have noted, the men in Webster's play often attempt to locate the origins of sexual unruliness in the woman's body, Flamineo's language here foregrounds masculine sexual excess and impropriety. It may be true that patriarchy—interpellating male bodies that are at the same time inconsistent, unfixed, and fluctuating sites of potentially transgressive, disruptive, and unpredictable desire—attempts to construct, in the face of "woman's" putative sexual unreliability, "heterosexist masculinity" as unitary, fixed, and stable. But, as in the case of Flamineo's comments elsewhere in *The White Devil,* recognition of male promiscuity, specifically in passages of bawdy, interrupts the patriarchal narrative as well.

The explicit sexual references and puns that this bawdy brings with it relate in the play to evidence of "malfunctioning" or promiscuous modes of male sexuality that lie beyond the parameters of conventionally structured "unitary" patriarchal sexuality. Such intrusions confirm that in this respect, too, Webster's text acknowledges that (heterosexual) adultery, uncontrollability, and sexual transgression involve two genders.

Thus in acts 1 and 2 the project of Vittoria's seduction is located within bawdy that reflects anxiety about masculine impotence as well as illicit masculine sexual virility and cuckoldry. Flamineo's encouragement firstly of Brachiano as well as his subsequent encounter with Camillo both work partly through the implicit contrast between the prospective adulterer's virility and the legitimate husband's impotence. Thus, "cold in the liver" (1.2.28) [supposed to be the seat of the passions], Camillo has, according to Flamineo, "by the confession of his doctor" (1.2.29–30), shed more hairs—in the course of the treatment of venereal disease—than pikesmen or swordsmen have knocked plumes from the helmets of duelists. Like "Irish" gamblers, having lost all else, he will even venture "all downward" [his testicles] (2.1.30–32), which again, being impotent, will be no loss. The fact that his "back is shrunk into his breeches" (1.2.33–34) further signifies Camillo's lack of virility. Such bawdy brings illicit/diseased/impotent male sexuality clearly into view.

When Camillo himself enters at 1.2.46, Flamineo, again by means of bawdy, taunts him with images of his rival's virility and desire to "lie" with Vittoria, as well as with images of impotence and cuckoldry. Using the metaphor of two ships, Flamineo plays with crude sexual puns to underline Camillo's sexual ineptitude. He asks him if he is "travelling/travailing" to bed to his "kind wife" (1.2.52) and, to Camillo's reply that he travels rather farther north to "a colder clime . . . / I do not well remember, I protest, / When I last lay with her" (1.2.53–56), Flamineo's rejoinder is quick: "Strange you should lose your count [cunt]" (1.2.57). This precipitates further explicit sexual puns that on the one hand denote the compelling nature of (unrestrainable) physical desire, a pleasure from which, on the other hand, Camillo's inability to fill his wife's "flaw," his implied need for "provocative electuaries [lust-inciting aphrodisiacs]" (1.2.96), the suggestion that he is castrated, and reference to his testicles as "false stone" (1.2.143), all disqualify him. The specters of compulsive desire for (illicit) sexual virility and fear and panic attending its loss or absence thus foreground the disturbing vagaries attendant on the male desire. Moreover, a further series of puns accents its treacherous competitiveness. When Flamineo uses a series of bowling metaphors to describe Brachiano's erotic designs on Vittoria, the evocation of Brachiano's putative virility repeatedly prompts fear of cuckoldry in (the impotent) Camillo, which Flamineo relentlessly exacerbates: "I do commit you to your pitiful pillow / Stuff'd with horn-shavings" (1.2.76–77) and "take the height of your own horns with a Jacob's staff after they are up" (1.2.93–94). Moreover, Camillo's cuckoldry-anxiety is fired again at the end of act 2 by Francisco and Monticelso when they taunt Camillo, "'tis given out / You are a cuckold" (2.1.330–31), advise him to "Go change the air for shame; see if your absence / Will blast your cornucopia [horn of plenty]" (2.1.358–59), and, to his fear that "Ere I return the stag's horns may be sprouted, / Greater than these are shed," Francisco promises, "I'll be your ranger" (2.1.363–65).

While it is perhaps to be expected that, in accordance with the well-recognized misogyny of this culture, such bawdy would include joking reference to the female genitals, it is significant that the male genitals are repeatedly brought into view as well. This is especially the case in the sequences when Flamineo, and later Francisco and Monticelso, taunt Camillo with the specter of cuckoldry. Adultery as well as the horns of cuckoldry are, of course, themselves both evocative of the wandering, unruly, transgressive penis. Just before the trial scene, Flamineo has a bawdy exchange with the Lawyer, in which, to the Lawyer's jest, "methinks none should sit upon thy sister but old whore-masters," he replies, "Or cuckolds, for your cuckold is your most terrible tickler of lechery" (3.1.12–15). We may recall here that the word "lecher" is defined in the *Oxford English Dictionary* as "a man immoderately given to sexual indulgence; a lewd or grossly unchaste man, debauchee" with the first meaning dated ca.1175. Often the bawdy about cuckoldry implies not only the image of the penis, as when Monticelso says of Camillo "Plenty of horns hath made him poor of horns" (2.1.329) or when, in his tale of Phoebus, Francisco narrates how a petition was brought to Jupiter "That Phoebus might be gelded, for if now / When there was but one sun, so many men / Were like to perish by his violent heat, / What should they do if he were married / And should beget more, and those children / Make fireworks like their father?" (2.1.348–53) but also recognition of the sexual diseases often consequent upon male promiscuity, already glimpsed in act 1 in Flamineo's initial remarks about Camillo to Brachiano. More in line with conventional recognitions of misogyny, the sharpness of the initial encounter between Brachiano, Francisco, and Monticelso includes Francisco's telling attempt to feminize what is his brother-in-law's lechery, but, after a further exchange of threats, to Brachiano's promise of "gunpowder in thy nostrils" he responds "Better that / Than change perfumes for plasters" (2.1.75–76), imagery that, with the plaster, points specifically to (male) obsessional fear of the diseased penis, which unrestrained sexual license causes. The ensuing argument returns again and again to the image of the diseased penis: in Francisco's observation that the Tiber's "wild ducks" [prostitutes] revealed to "each prowling passenger" lead to "moulting time" [not only the loss of bird's feathers but the loss of bodily hair caused by venereal disease] and "a tale of a tub" [not only a cock-and-bull story but the use of hot baths in the attempt to cure the disease] (2.1.88–92).

Such humor posits the male body as grotesque and male sexuality and desire as viciously competitive, prone to transgression and treachery, informed as well by multiple anxieties concerning performance, virility, impotence/failure, betrayal, and disease. Although patriarchy attempts to locate errant and dangerous sexual motility in the woman's body, such motility is in these jokes repeatedly assigned to the bodies of men. And on one or two occasions, awareness of masculine uncontrollability merges interestingly with punitive desires resonating penetration, humiliation, or disruption of what simultaneously emerges in such bawdy as the more vulnerable and less fixed male body. During the trial scene Brachiano threatens Francisco and Monticelso, "the sword you frame of such an excellent temper, / I'll sheathe in your own bowels" (3.2.166–67); earlier, Flamineo, seeing Francisco and Monticelso whispering, promises Brachiano: "I will compound a medicine out of their two heads, stronger than garlic, deadlier than stibium; the catharides which are scarce seen to stick upon the flesh when they work to the heart, shall not do it with more silence or invisible cunning" (2.1.284–87), and, a moment after making this promise, introduces the doctor who

> will shoot pills into a man's guts, shall make them have more ventages than a cornet or a lamprey; he will poison a kiss, and was once minded, for his masterpiece, because Ireland breeds no poison, to have prepared a deadly vapour in a Spaniard's fart that should have poison'd all Dublin. . . . O thou abhominable loathsome gargarism, that will fetch up lungs, lights, heart and liver by scruples. (2.1.229–311)

Such language also hovers on the brink of recognition that the male body itself may be grotesque, origin of sexual as well as political disease and corruption, suitable target therefore for punishments that have appropriately momentary sexual and sadistic overtones.

The moments in the play when the use of bawdy reveals profound masculine anxieties about male sexual unruliness are, in a patriarchal culture, for obvious reasons, infrequent. They appear in the text as almost involuntary, sudden eruptions that threaten to undo the misogynist project. As I have noted, it is more usually the woman who is the receptacle of blame. Indeed, a nice example of the way in which rarely addressed male unruliness, with which *women* have to contend, is merged back always into the focus upon the feminine as origin of disruption—a habit of thinking that informs, I began briefly by hinting, at least some Webster criticism as well—may be found in *The Body in Parts: Fantasies of Corporeality in Early Modern Europe*. David Hillman and Carla Mazzio observe in their introduction that "the most notably absent sexual organ in this volume is the penis" (xx). This is staggering in a book concerned with representation of the body (during any period), when set against—to go no further—the experience of every pubescent teenage and adult male, who has daily experience not only of the use of this part of the body, but more important in this context, of its unpredictability and uncontrollability.

However, Hillman and Mazzio's volume is not entirely free of reference to the unruly penis. In her chapter entitled "Sins of the Tongue" Carla

Mazzio writes that in many poems "the tongue was often upbraided for thwarting its owner's mastery" and that "involuntary motions attributed to this significant other might lead some to consider the isomorphic relations between the tongue and the penis, that other bodily member with an apparent will of its own" (58–59). She then quotes John Bulwer, who writes that the relation between "the Egresse of the Tongue out of the mouth and of *Priapisme* is a thing of very subtile Speculation":

> [T]he action in kissing, which some beastly Leachers use when their veins are inflate with lust would enduce one to think that there were some analogy between the extension of the two unruly members. The difference between the erection of both parts is that the viril member is not only encreased in length but in thickness and compasse: but the Tongue onely in length being not increased in all the dimensions of its body when it goes out of the mouth. (Hillman and Mazzio 59)

Mazzio adds that "as associations between the tongue and the penis became more explicit in the sixteenth and seventeenth centuries, so too did the imagined relationship between rhetorical and sexual performance" (59). But she also points out that

> If the tongue is in some sense *virile* (meaning both manly and hard), it is also often imagined as its opposite, *Mueller* (meaning both womanly and soft). The fact that one of the first early modern medical descriptions of the clitoris not only imagined it as part of woman's "shameful member" . . . but as "a little tongue" . . . problematizes the gendering of the tongue (or speech itself) as "phallic." (60)

And although she notes, during her comments on "the spectacular corporeality of the revenge drama of Elizabethan and Jacobean England" (62) phallic resonances in, for example, the signification of the tongue as possible "locus of exteriority, the site where the self was performed" (63), when her discussion turns to seventeenth-century focus on the praising and blaming of this body part, the attention to phallic associations that she has been discovering appears interestingly in the literature to diminish. Mazzio then argues that "the fetishization of the organ of speech in discourses about discourse is perhaps nowhere more explicitly thematized than in Thomas Tomkis's *Lingua, or the Combat of the Tongue and the Five Senses for Superiority* (1607)" (65). And in this representative text, to which she turns in order to address the "spectre of monstrous orality" that "haunts a range of early modern texts," although she points out that Lingua is "explicitly fashioned after her non-gendered ancestors" (68), even the rebellious (independent) and interrogative tongue—only, after all, the mildest and most indirect of penis substitutes—which is "the site upon which anxieties about language, agency and the articulation of selves are powerfully cathected" (68) now proves to be inescapably and perhaps inevitably, feminized.

IV

The seminal work of scholars such as Eve Kosofsky Sedgwick over a decade ago has delineated multiple ways in which, in patriarchy, relations between men and women seem always to be an effect of various kinds of male bonding. Sedgwick mentions for instance Girard's notion of triangular relationships in which "in any erotic rivalry the bond that links the two rivals is as intense and potent as the bond that links either of the rivals to the beloved" (21). Citing Heidi Hartman's definition of patriarchy as "relationships between men, which have a material base, and which, though hierarchical, establish or create independence and solidarity among men that enable them to dominate women" (3), Sedgwick also argues that

> in making the power relationships between men and women appear to be dependent on the power relationships between men and men, [this definition] suggests that large-scale social structures are congruent with the male-male-female erotic triangles described most forcefully by Girard and articulated most thoughtfully by others. We can go further than that, to say that in any male-dominated society, there is a special relationship between male homosocial (*including* homosexual) desire and the structures for maintaining and transmitting patriarchal power. (25)

She relates this, finally, to Gayle Rubin's contention that "patriarchal homosexuality can best be discussed in terms of one or another form of the traffic in women: it is the use of women as exchangeable, perhaps symbolic, property for the primary purpose of cementing the bonds of men with men" (26).

It is of course significant—though, in view of our knowledge of seventeenth-century misogyny, hardly surprising—that feminist formulations that reveal women to be tokens within male patriarchal economies are as applicable to Webster. Act 1 of *The White Devil* presents Vittoria at least partly as counter in the transactions between the men around her: the powerful Lord Brachiano who desires her, the husband whose gullibility, impotence, and folly renders her ever more vulnerable and the brother, who measures her primarily as means to self-advancement with the man who desires his sister. In act 2, Isabella is presented to us in ways that show that she too, in the endeavor to save her marriage, is largely a counter in the transactions between the men of her family and her husband. On the one hand, Francisco's and Monticelso's anger is based on the offence to family honor that Brachiano's behavior has produced. Their motive for reconciliation emerges clearly when Isabella articulates anger (albeit allegedly pretended anger) against Brachiano; they reprimand her as compared to "other women, [who] with . . . patience / . . . suffer these slight wrongs" (2.1.240–41). Hostility to Isabella's adulterous suitor has primacy over Isabella herself—Francisco and Monticelso coldly endanger her further by providing a commission for Camillo, whom they anyway despise, purely in order to trap Brachiano. On the other hand, patriarchal familial rivalry is as important to Brachiano. He reprimands Isabella because, instead of submission, she has had "the trick of impudent baseness to complain / Unto [her] kindred" (2.1.173–74). He repeatedly articulates hostility toward these men not only to Isabella—"I scorn him / Like a shav'd Pollack" (2.1.183–84)—but directly to them as well: "Uncivil sir there's hemlock in thy breath . . . were she whore of mine / All thy loud cannons, and thy borrowed Switzers . . . durst not supplant her" (2.1.59–63). Despite this, and individually for whatever malign reasons, the men preserve a public show of reconciliation. In the face of Isabella's apparent anger, patriarchal solidarity takes priority: just before Isabella exits, Brachiano says to Francisco "'Twere best to let her have her humour," to which he replies, "To see her come / To my lord cardinal for a dispensation / Of her rash vow will beget excellent laughter" (2.1.272–76).

It is true that while such interactions between men exclude or present the importance of women as secondary, the word "homosocial" may not always be the best to describe their relations. These are fluctuating, often even openly hostile. Flamineo has a fractious and problematic interaction with the lord he follows, exemplified in his frustrated cynicism on the topic of service and reward. The deceit that underlies dealings between Monticelso and Francisco never admits the kind of male bonding that so interests Quentin Tarantino, for example, in the contemporary film *Pulp Fiction*—which offers a "postmodern" feast of male unruliness—in his representation of the alliances between his men of violence. And the struggle over patriarchal family honor between them and Brachiano is hugely antagonistic and competitive. Evidence of the particularly deceptive, amoral, and murderous nature of such dealings amongst the men in the play, includes, after the trial of Vittoria, the detail of Flamineo's language in 3.3 and later, which points obsessively to corruption in masculine institutional and social life, the murderous duplicity of Lodovico and Francisco, with Monticelso's hypocritical help in acts 4 and 5, the excess of poisoning, torture, and killing of Brachiano, the behavior of Flamineo to his brother, and the extended use of disguise and deception. Nevertheless, in all these cases, women remain largely isolated from the interactions between these men. In this they have validity only as objects of desire, origins of disruption, targets for punishment. I argue that it is especially in this context significant that, when the opportunity arises, they resist this positioning.

V

Before addressing this directly, however, I want to turn from the violence and disorder that characterizes dealings between Webster's men, as well as representations of their sexuality, to the intersections between "race" and sexuality in *The White Devil* that probe further the insecurities and mechanisms that lie behind the illusory unity and wholeness that patriarchal masculinity implies for itself. Here, assertive "white" masculinity appears, in "heterosexual" configurations, unable to include the "black" body. It may be true that, in this, Webster's play with the colors "black" and "white" and with the word "devil" may be said to derive from religious and patristic discourse, but, with the burden of the intervening centuries between the seventeenth century and our own, it is impossible not to regard it as at least potentially tainted too by the incipient racism that encounters with cultural difference engendered by early colonialism precipitated. Here, the element of displacement that racism, like misogyny, often entails, emerges clearly.

Thus Ann Rosalind Jones argues that in *The White Devil* Webster draws on "stereotypes of the hyper-civilized Italian, the savage Irish, and the 'Ethnicke' Moor" to provide his English audience with complex pleasures (251–62). As one example she cites Francisco's plan, adopting "the exploitative familiarity of the ethnologist temporarily gone native" to cut off the head of his sister's killer as fiercely as the Irish decapitate one another, when he says "Brachiano, I am now fit for thy encounter. / Like the wild Irish I'll ne'er think thee dead / Till I can play at football with thy head" (4.1.136–38). In addition to Jones' points about the use of the Irish in these lines, we may foreground mention of the obvious fact of displacement: it is Francisco's own violence here, and his own violent image of playing football with the severed head of a human body that he simultaneously suggests, originates not so much in himself as in the Irish.

The racism suggested by the treatment of Zanche in act 5 offers another important instance of displacement, involving interestingly, a female as well as a male member of Brachiano's court. Ania Loomba points out how, throughout *The White Devil*, "'blackness' is a signifier for various forms of socially unacceptable behavior" (27). She shows also how in the trial of Vittoria, "overlaps between the construction of women and cultural outsiders . . . are similarly evident in the process of 'naming' Vittoria" (28). In act 5, Cornelia and Marcello live at Brachiano's court despite the fact that they have adapted a morally critical stance toward Vittoria's involvement with him. Moreover, within some hundred lines of the same scene, both of them are shown to display excessive hostility toward Zanche, appearing to displace their moral judgments of the behavior of Brachiano, Flamineo, and Vittoria onto her. Marcello characterizes Flamineo's relationship to "this devil" (5.1.86) as his "shame" (5.1.91) and Cornelia actually strikes her on stage, declaring "Is this your perch haggard: Fly to th'stews" (5.1.186). The focus of such antagonism, particularly on the part of Cornelia, against someone who until this moment has been an entirely minor character, in references that position her as "devil" or "wanton woman" belonging in a brothel, suggest her convenience for them, in terms of race, class, and gender, as a receptacle for blame.

More important, so far as Zanche's relationships to the men around her are concerned, it is they not she who emerge as changeable and untrustworthy. Both of the white men with whom she deals are theoretically erotically involved with her but both are shown to have at the same time no interest in her body. Although Flamineo appears to have had some relation with her before the play begins, his stance toward her during the play is one of contempt and dismissal—"I do love her, just as a man holds a wolf by the ears" (5.1.154–55). Francisco's treatment of her when disguised as a Moor manifests ruthless and cynical manipulation of her cultural isolation and the desire for him that this isolation prompts in her. In an age of incipient colonialism, the disguised white male in this situation emerges as archetypal representative of treachery, unreliability, and betrayal.

Displacement as a noticeably male means of escaping or avoiding internal violence and contradiction is of course applied repeatedly throughout *The White Devil* where women are concerned. I have already noted some instances of this early in the play. In acts 4 and 5, in the midst of the sustained representation of male unruliness, men continually attempt to displace their propensity for violence and disorder onto woman. Thus Flamineo who, throughout the drama, has played the major part in helping Brachiano to seduce his sister, who murders her husband and who tries in act 5 to trick her into committing suicide, cries "O men / That lie on your death-beds, and are haunted with howling wives, ne'er trust them" (5.6.154–56). In act 4 Francisco, embroiling himself in illicit violence and conspiracy, interpellates woman as origin of the deception his own practice exemplifies: "I know / Treason, like spiders weaving nets for flies, / By her foul work is found, and in it dies" (4.1.26–28).

VI

The habitual frequency of such and many other attempts at displacement suggests not only the male insecurity that lies behind repeated attempts to demonize a convenient other in order to emerge as unified and homogeneous, but also the frustrating inadequacy of the manoeuvre itself, which never suffices. Such frustrations may account too for the viciousness with which the men in Webster's texts react to evidence of that which lies beyond their hegemonic claims. The inevitable gaps between the discourse of patriarchy about what constitutes "masculinity" as well as "femininity" and that which it attempts to contain and define, are, as I have been trying to argue, a central concern in Webster, either inevitably present in his texts as they unfold—as they must be in the culture from which the texts come—or actively foregrounded by him. In such contexts, it is Webster's women who are not only most bravely eloquent about these gaps, but who, in the specific course of challenging men over them, are destroyed by proponents of the very symbolic system they expose.

I have already briefly noted how, in acts 1 and 2, both Cornelia and Isabella attempt specifically to invert processes of misogyny and to name, instead, male unruliness. In the case of Isabella, particularly, her repeated attempts at honest articulation are in themselves acts of heroic defiance in the face of the kinds of hegemonic patriarchy evident in the play. As Cornelia does with Flamineo, in her active criticism of Brachiano, she attempts to reform him. This itself also inverts the patriarchal stereotype of female unruliness. Her courage in so doing is intensified by the predicament in which she is placed—doubly incarcerated as she is by patriarchy. Her extraordinary submissiveness, after her husband has rejected her, in taking up his script—she literally echoes his lines in her public enactment of a rejection of him—may be an attempt to keep the peace between her husband and her brother. And it underlines the homosocial nature of her fetters: preservation of male familial bonds appears more important even to her than the betrayal she has suffered. Nevertheless, although in the name of this homosocial system, she takes the chance also to express the real anger she must in part inwardly be feeling. The text foregrounds the courage of her attempts at articulation in the face of the odds against her: it is the very brother who claims to be defending her who reprimands her, reminding her of the patriarchal code of submission (in this case to male promiscuity) to which she ought to conform. Her concluding utterance thus protests to the audience awareness of herself as subordinated and objectified counter in decadent male dealing: "Unkindness do thy office, poor heart break, / Those are the killing griefs which dare not speak" (2.1.277–78).

Masculine disruption and violence as well as the strategies of displacement and denial in patriarchal narrative, everywhere evident in the play, frames also the presentation of Vittoria in acts 3, 4, and 5. Indeed one of the reasons for the shift in the audience's perception of Vittoria in the trial scene lies in the sustained interest that Webster displays, before her appearance, in the corruption of Flamineo and Brachiano, and the viciousness of the patriarchal structures within which, as act 2 shows clearly, women are situated.

The trial of Vittoria is itself notoriously full of misogyny and it also fore-grounds the extent to which men deal with one another in ways that oper-ate independently of women: for example, Brachiano's gender and class immunity throughout a trial in which he is as involved as Vittoria is under-lined by his presence as independent and untouched observer.

But it is Vittoria's eloquence, in the context of all this, that emerges, as in the case of Cornelia and Isabella, as heroic, an almost superhuman attempt to identify, against the charge of female unruliness, corrupt and decadent male authority, evidence of masculine disorder. Thus she objects to the lawyer's use of Latin and to his rhetoric as obscurantist, questions the propri-ety of a cardinal playing a lawyer, suggests that the "uncivil Tartar" offers bet-ter justice than "this Christian court" (3.2.128–29) and points out the devious hypocrisy of her male antagonists: "If you be my accuser / Pray cease to be my judge" (3.2.225–26). In her appeal to the ambassadors she makes it clear that it is misogyny that disempowers her: "my modesty / And woman-hood I tender; but withal / So entangled in a cursed accusation / That my de-fence of force like Perseus, / Must personate masculine virtue" (3.2.132–36) and she describes her sentence with the archetypal image of male sexual un-controllability and violence: "A rape, a rape!" (3.2.273). She articulates liter-ally her desire to redirect the constructions of unruliness directed at her back toward her male accusers: "For your names / Of whore and murd'ress, they proceed from you, / As if a man should spit against the wind, / The filth re-turns in's face" (3.2.148–51). Casting such accusations back at her accuser, she repeatedly proposes femininity as dignified and innocent, if powerless, al-ternative to corrupt male power:

> That the last day of judgement may so find you
> And leave you the same devil you were before.
> Instruct me some good horseleech to speak treason,
> For since you cannot take my life for deeds,
> Take it for words. O woman's poor revenge
> Which dwells but in the tongue! I will not weep
> No I do scorn to call up one poor tear
> To fawn on your injustice. (3.2.279–86)

Again, in act 4, when Brachiano falls into Francisco's misogynist trap and, in stereotypically patriarchal fashion, chooses instantly to believe his letter about her "treachery," Vittoria inverts his accusations by accusing *him* of *mas-culine* duplicity as well as lechery when she asks, "What have I gained by thee but infamy? . . . Go, go brag / How many ladies you have undone, like me" (4.2.107, 118–19), a charge that she later generalizes in her exclamatory "O ye dissembling men!" (4.2.182). Here, the fact that Brachiano's dependence on patriarchal stereotypes is prompted by the deceptions of another male, Francisco, only serves to underline the fact of masculine unreliability and duplicity that males simultaneously attempt by means of misogyny to displace. Set beside all this, Flamineo's cry at the end of act 5, " . . . Trust a woman?— Never, never. Bracciano be my precedent: we lay our souls to pawn to the devil for a little pleasure and the devil makes the bill of sale. That ever man should marry!" (5.6.160–63), as well as pronouncements such as "Man may his fate foresee, but not prevent" (5.6.180) sound resoundingly hollow.

Vittoria's eloquence, it is worth adding, may provide a momentary instance in the production in the sixteenth and seventeenth century of a feminized and rebellious tongue, which, I noted earlier, Carla Mazzio so helpfully traces. But, notwithstanding any patriarchal project of categorization putatively under way, Vittoria's verbal acuity and potency simultaneously resonate, far more powerfully, the very gender parallels, ambiguities, and confusions that attempt to represent the image of the tongue they themselves, often inadvertently, reveal.

VII

Webster's plays, in this argument, present fluctuating struggles in which the attempt by men to displace their own unruliness continually comes unstuck, while women sporadically actively struggle, in their articulations against them, heroically, to relocate the accusations directed at them—as "origins" of disruption—in the male body. It can perhaps be argued that the Duchess of Malfi provides an even more intense realization and concentration into one figure of the battle of Webster's three earlier woman heroes. While this concentration may partly be responsible for the fact that it has been difficult for critics in practice not to recognize and explore the stature of the titular hero in the play, it is important in assessing her significance, as well as in the case of *The Duchess of Malfi* as a whole, too, to recognize the centrality of Webster's focus not only on the interaction between two genders but, more especially, on evidence of the often murderously perplexed adulteration of the dominant one. The linguistic texture and situation of male decadence, unruliness, and corruption that Bosola identifies, for example—in the functioning of the social order, or the system of service and reward—and to which Antonio in his description of male authority at Malfi (as compared with the French court) gives voice, provides the context within which a woman who seeks, in such terrain, survival, attempts to disregard corrupt masculine authority and to enact or realize feminine desire. She seeks this, again, within the confines of early modern Christian versions of heterosexual, monogamous, and unadulterous marriage—a motive conventionally annexed by or ascribed to males. This kind of desire and its attempt at institutional realization and implementation, in turn, contrasts with, in the play's bawdy, and more especially in the fevered and murderous sexual disarray demonstrated in both the behavior of Ferdinand and the Cardinal, evidence of a masculinity quite different from that posited in the narratives of patriarchy. It is set, also, against the unruliness of male authority evident not only in the rule of the brothers but also brought to a point of eloquent excess in the asylum scenes of act 4.

Lena Cowen Orlin in *Private Matters and Public Culture in Post-Reformation England* indicates that her interest is in the way early modern texts

> explore the nature of women, acknowledge ambiguities in the inscription of domestic rule, test the practical application of abstract philosophies of rule and order, register the competing pulls of political and economic interests in the household, expose the obsolescence of received ideas of virtue and ideals of friendship and benefice and eventually discover that masculine authority can be an unwelcome burden. (13)

This essay is attempting to argue, albeit in a far more preliminary if, hopefully, analogous way, that our understanding of gender relations in these texts depends partly, in addition to what has already been done, on the extent to which we are prepared to analyze, deconstruct, and dissect detailed evidence in texts of unruly masculinity that, in turn, give the lie to patriarchal narrative. This is not in order to deny the perniciousness of its effects. It is to recognize that attempts at gender structuration, whatever they might be, whenever or wherever they might be located, involve two genders and that, at least in the terms I have tried to argue, patriarchal narrative misrepresents both. If such assertions have any value, then, it may also be true that Webster, albeit only tentatively, appears to anticipate this project, both in the critiques of patriarchy he attempts to offer, and in the extraordinary female heroes who, in his texts, actively resist.

Queen of Apricots

The Duchess of Malfi, Hero of Desire

Linda Woodbridge

> Nature, that framed us of four elements
> Warring within our breasts for regiment,
> Doth teach us all to have aspiring minds.
>
> —*Tamburlaine*

> "Does not our lives consist of the four elements?"
> "Faith, so they say, but I think it rather consists of eating and drinking."
>
> —*Twelfth Night*

The dogged sexiness of the Duchess of Malfi—not to mention her ravenous cravings in pregnancy—has troubled and intrigued audiences and readers for going on four centuries now. Some argue that sexuality per se is not among the play's central issues: Frank Whigham reads Ferdinand's sexual hysteria as a smokescreen masking his real anxieties as "a threatened aristocrat, frightened by the contamination of his ascriptive social rank and obsessively preoccupied with its defense; . . . Ferdinand's incestuous inclination toward his sister is a *social posture,* of hysterical compensation—a desperate expression of the desire to evade degrading association with inferiors" (169).[1] Others find bodily sexuality of less interest than the play's tapping into the new discourse of companionate marriage and valorization of private life—even the invention of the nuclear family (see Jankowski 226–30; Pechter 102); for Whigham, the Duchess is a hero of modernity in opposing class strictures and championing private life ("a cultural voyager, she arrogates to herself a new role, that of female hero, going knowingly to colonize a new realm of privacy" [172]). A few readers do focus on bodily sexuality: several find the Duchess's sexuality wholesome and joyful. Theodora Jankowski celebrates her as "a woman who thoroughly enjoys her sexuality" (235); Christina Luckyj finds her wooing of Antonio "profound and convincing precisely because it is not 'chaste,' . . . The Duchess is a woman of sexual energy, . . . [of] intense sexuality" (77); Edward Pechter is moved by the "tenderness" of the bedchamber scene, "the continued sexual delight the Duchess and Antonio take in each other, apparently unabated over the years. . . . The scene is suffused with a sense of fulfilled desire" (100). But many more critics stress that the Duchess's sexuality is represented in the play as ruinous, and attribute this to misogyny, to a double standard of sexual morality for men and women, or to the residue of a medieval Catholic suspicion of sexuality in general; whether these unlovely attitudes belong to the Cardinal and Ferdinand or to Webster himself (and his culture) remains subject to dispute. Dympna Callaghan reads the Duchess's sexuality in light of a generalization she makes about Renaissance attitudes toward female sexuality: "Voracious female sexual desire was posited as the most conspicuous sign of gender difference, and was treated both as a disease and as a monstrous abnormality" (140). Lisa Jardine declares, "Lower in her sexual drive than 'a beast that wants discourse of reason,' the Duchess of Malfi, like Hamlet's mother, steps out of the path of duty and marries for lust" (*Still Harping on Daughters* 71). Lori Haslem reads in the "apricot scene" widespread disgust with female sexuality: "the gestating woman becomes associated with a patient who has overindulged appetites for the wrong foods, and childbirth itself becomes associated with the purging of an ailing or overtaxed digestive tract" (439). My sympathies are with those who read the play as celebrating rather than damning the Duchess's sexuality; but so complex is Renaissance sexuality that we need to shed considerably more light on the topic before we can declare the Duchess what I think she is: a hero of desire.

By "hero of desire," I mean that she is a champion of desire, defending desire as wholesome and taking risks knowingly to pursue desire as something she believes in and is not ashamed of. "Why might not I marry?" she demands forthrightly. "I have not gone about in this to create / Any new world or custom. . . . Why should . . . I . . . / Be cased up, like a holy relic? I have youth / And a little beauty" (3.2.107–9). But I also mean that in dying for her desire, the Duchess dies as a tragic hero. That she dies for her assertive sexuality doesn't necessarily mean the play is against it; it means that she occupies the subject position of the tragic hero, which does tend to be fatal. Those who think Webster damns the Duchess for her sexuality, as Luckyj notes, "reduce the status of the play as tragedy" and "come perilously close to reading the play as a cautionary tale" (78). Structurally, the Duchess occupies the position of hero and her brothers (and secondarily Bosola) the position of her antagonists; that *all* the harsh comments on female sexuality in the play emanate from the antagonists would seem to discredit such sentiments, and as Harriett Hawkins puts it, "To argue that the Duchess deserved torture and death because she chose to marry the man she loved and to bear his children is, in effect, to join forces with her tyrannical brothers" (29). Or to join forces with Bosola—many a critic accepts the views on female sexuality of this spy and murderer; for example, Callaghan traces Renaissance sexual ideas by noting that "Bosola posits that female desire must always be countered by restraint" (143).[2] Of course, tragic heroes are not always morally good nor their opponents morally evil or ideologically misguided: Renaissance drama offers such villains-as-heroes as the Macbeths, with harsh comments against them provided by antagonists who have moral right on their side. But that seems not the case here. Throughout the play, the Duchess is marked as the object of our empathy—in the warmth of her humanity, in the attractive intimacy of the loving bedchamber scene, in the courage and dignity with which she faces death. And throughout the play, the attitudes and behavior of the three antagonists are marked as vicious, destructive, and antisocial. (The very fact that her antagonists outnumber her three to one creates sympathy for the Duchess. Even Hamlet and Othello face only one antagonist each.)

But how important is sexuality in the scheme of things? Despite the best efforts of Freudians, feminists, and queer theorists, there has been a lot of downgrading of sexuality going around, during the last couple of decades of Renaissance literary criticism. Arthur Marotti's classic essay "'Love is Not Love': Elizabethan Sonnet Sequences and the Social Order" argues that what appears to be strong sexual attraction by sonnet speakers toward sonnet mistresses is actually a displacement of male courtiers' desire for career advancement at court, and the seeming sexual frustration voiced in love sonnets is actually a displacement of the frustration male courtiers encountered while trying to get on in a court presided over by a female monarch. Louis Montrose writes of "an encoding principle that is undoubtedly operative in much of Elizabethan literature: amorous motives displace or subsume forms of desire, frustration, and resentment other than the merely sexual" ("Of Gentlemen" 440), a maneuver that dismisses everything in life but politics and public striving, erasing or translating much Renaissance literature too—the loves of Romeo and Juliet, Othello and Desdemona, the Duchess of Malfi and Antonio, Rosalind and Celia must be politics in disguise; the "merely sexual" is not important enough to be a subject of literature. Montrose generalizes about the sexual attitudes of the day: "In a Reformation society whose ideology reinforces strict control by personal, political, academic, and ecclesiastical fathers, sexual passion and love poetry signify waste and idleness, a dangerous lack of bodily and spiritual self-definition, a potential threat of insubordination and rebellion" ("Perfecte Paterne" 36). Montrose seems to think love was so revolting a topic that love poetry wouldn't have been published at all had not authors masked its pornographic potential by ascribing to it proper—that is, political—motives: "Royal encomium provides an allowable occasion for the cultivation of love poetry" ("Perfecte Paterne" 40). As Frank Whigham revealingly shows, sometimes this critical flight from sexuality has been honorably motivated as an attempt to avoid sexism when writing about women: "The Duchess [of Malfi]'s actions should be seen not as erotic (a common male reduction of women's issues) but as political" (184). But I think this well-meaning gesture is misguided. Why can't her actions be *both* erotic and political? When we as feminists declare that the personal is political, we mean that any person's private life is subject to constraints that operate in the gendered realm of power politics—"sexual politics," as Kate Millett called it; we do *not* mean that sexuality can simply be subsumed under the rubric "political," or that sexuality is inevitably of negligible importance compared with court politics or the strivings of careerist ambition. In the laudable quest not to reduce women to sex objects, to merely sexual beings, we should be wary of shying away from female sexuality to the extent that we erect new taboos around it, or fall into the trap of viewing only nonsexual women as "good." Sex was once something you shouldn't talk about in front of children. To make it something you shouldn't talk about in front of feminists isn't doing us any favors.

But what if sexual desire in *The Duchess of Malfi* after all *is* just a smokescreen or a displacement of some other urge? Maybe the brothers' opposition to the Duchess is, say, pure misogyny, or male supremacy expressed in resentment of her independence? (Independent women were often smeared as lecherous, called "impudent," which meant both sexually shameless and aggressive.) Suppose, that like those wishing to impeach President Clinton, the brothers considered a range of ways to "get" the offender, and when nothing else worked (Whitewater, Filegate, Travelgate) they attacked the President/Duchess where they were known to have a weakness—their fondness for sex. What if opposition to the Duchess's sexuality were just an alibi, masking some darker purpose? The problem is that the evidence is sparse, and ambiguous. For example, late in the play Ferdinand rather wildly lights on an economic explanation for persecuting the Duchess: "I had a hope, / Had she continued widow, to have gained / An infinite mass of treasure by her death" (4.2.281–84). Do we believe this? It is so hastily tacked on as to look like Coleridgean "motive-hunting," and we could just as easily interpret *this* as the smokescreen, masking more sexual motives, rather than the other way around. Since no other persuasive motive is on offer, we are

1

thrown back onto what Ferdinand has said all along—he is against the Duchess's indulging her sexuality, and because she does indulge it, he has her killed.

Suppose, then, that we do foreground bodily sexuality in this play. What available discourses about sex might the play have activated? Dozens, maybe hundreds! Patristic misogyny, adulation of celibacy, Protestant revisionism that downgraded celibacy and rehabilitated marriage, the ideology of companionate marriage, Tudor state-sponsored domestic ideology, medical discourse, legal discourse, the *querelle des femmes,* chivalric romance, ballads about love, ballads about domestic murder, popular jests, folk tales—all these had something to say about sex and desire, and they contradicted each other wildly. They were also internally contradictory, one gynecological treatise advising on treatment for women's pathological lust (see Callaghan 140–41), other gynecological treatises assuming that men are "more quickly aroused than women" (Laqueur 102). Some discourses were deeply suspicious of sex, the body, and the life of the senses; others were more tolerant. As Margaret Mikesell reminds us, although Catholic writers went on warning against excessive sexual passion even within marriage, "in the more progressive Protestant handbooks, not the danger but the pleasure of sex tends to be stressed. Gouge, for instance, cites 'due benevolence' . . . as one of the most 'proper and essential actions of marriage'—not only for preservation of chastity and propagation but to increase mutual affection. 'Benevolence' means 'it must be performed with good will and delight, willingly, readily and cheerfully'" (269). Both attitudes get into Webster's play; indeed, the play dramatizes their collision. Mikesell reminds us that Ferdinand's "They are most luxurious [i.e., lecherous] / Will wed twice" (1.1.306–7) was a residual Catholic attitude, while Protestants found remarriage quite acceptable, in line with their revaluing of marriage as equal or superior in worthiness to celibacy. But Mikesell is in the minority in taking care, when writing about Renaissance sexuality, to recognize the complexity of such competing and intersecting discourses: most writers fix shamelessly upon one narrow discourse that they pronounce the norm.[3] Montrose, for example, blandly equates "sexual passion" with "waste and idleness, a dangerous lack of bodily and spiritual self-definition" as if this were the only attitude in town during the sixteenth century. How would he account for the fact that sexual passion, and indeed orgasm by both sexual partners, was considered essential to conception and carefully cultivated by couples wishing for a child? As Laqueur notes,

> Ambroise Paré, the foremost surgeon of his day, opens his widely translated account of generation by emphasizing the importance of flirtation, caressing, and excitement. . . . When a husband comes into his wife's chamber, "he must

entertain her with all kind of dalliance, wanton behavior, and allurement to venery." If he finds her "to be slow, and more cold, he must cherish, embrace, and tickle her"; he should "creep" into the "field of nature," intermix "wanton kisses with wanton words and speeches," and caress her "secret parts and dugs until she is afire and enflamed in venery." (102)

Despite all the good recent scholarship on Renaissance sexuality, over-simplification about Renaissance sexual attitudes is endemic in criticism. *The Duchess of Malfi* clearly activates a number of attitudes common in its day: the Cardinal is tinged with late-medieval Catholic clerical misogyny (he is a Cardinal, after all); Bosola draws on hoary misogynistic tropes traceable back through what I have called "the formal controversy about women" to ancient Greek and Roman writers—the disgustingness of cosmetics, the corruption of the female body; in calling the Duchess a "lusty widow" Ferdinand enlists popular stereotypes about sexually insatiable widows visible in many Jacobean plays (Chapman's *The Widow's Tears,* Barry's *Ram-Alley,* Marston and Barkstead's *The Insatiate Countess*). The play also draws upon contradictory material in activating the ideal of companionate marriage, the valorization of the domestic, the ideal of love based on merit rather than rank, the contemporary debate (topic of many sermons) about arranged marriage versus free choice of spouse. We needn't see any one of these as dominant: any audience member might have reacted to any of these elements differently from the person in the next seat. Audiences are not entities holding uniform views, and this culture's ideas about sex were far from static or monolithic.

One Renaissance discourse about sexuality seems to me to have suffered particular neglect: Neoplatonically tinged humanism, whose footprints are clearly on *The Duchess of Malfi.* Humanists, of course, had a great deal to say about the body. At times they wrote about the body's health—about hygiene, about proper exercise through sport and dance. But especially in Neoplatonic humanism, which I think was much more influential and formative for English humanism than was, say, Aristotelian humanism[4]—ran a deep strain of suspicion of the body and the senses. Such suspicion was a logical outgrowth of the way Italian humanists were justifying their defense of human dignity, a central Renaissance project with crucial implications for early modern subjectivity. I think Neoplatonic humanism, along with certain strains of Christian doctrine already discussed by other critics, helps account for Ferdinand's extreme aversion to sexuality, and I want to complicate existing accounts of sexuality in *The Duchess of Malfi* by exploring the presence of this discourse in the play. Ferdinand, the play's major antisexual campaigner, is guilty of murdering of the Duchess, our hero of desire. He has been psychoanalyzed half to death; but I want to approach his strange aversion through examining the way humanists grounded human dignity in aversion to desire.

～～　～～　～～

Though Ferdinand regrets that sex, eating, and sleeping are necessary human activities, he ends up transformed into something very like an animal. More than a matter of individual neurosis, this pattern is visible in other characters in the drama too, who try to ascend above the merely physical. Tamburlaine wants to "be immortal like the gods," yet the imagery associated with him is increasingly that of blood and cannibalism. Dr. Faustus begins by regretting that he is no more than "Faustus, and a man"; yet he ends his life wishing he were a beast. Angelo in *Measure for Measure* tries to purify Vienna by executing people for extramarital sex, yet he eventually tries to extort sex from a novice nun. Such characters try, by denying humankind's animal nature, to rise above the merely human; but by trying to be more than human, they become less than human.

As Christianity taught that the soul was worthier than the body, Neoplatonic humanists founded human dignity upon intellectual and spiritual capacities that set man apart from animals. British Christian humanism united two traditions: the Christian, which (partly through the mediation of Thomist theory) based humanity's limited dignity on its ability to approach God through reason; and the Neoplatonic, which based humanity's almost unlimited dignity on its ability to transcend the bounds of its earthly position. But elements of this Christian humanist synthesis were uncongenial to the stage. Partly because its medium was the bodies of actors, the drama declined to turn away from the human body. Tragedy stages a collision between the potential of the spirit and the vulnerability of the flesh, and comedy celebrates human happiness in which fruition and wholesome sexuality loom large. But dramatists were alert to the claim that to be human one must transcend one's physical nature, and the dangers of such aspiration became the stuff of some plays.

Not only Pico della Mirandola and Marsilio Ficino, but thinkers like Pomponazzi and Telesio who in other respects contradicted them, share one article of faith: to be fully human, one must ascend above the life of the senses. This principle of ascent is the very essence of Neoplatonism. Pico, in effect, makes mobility the defining human characteristic. He envisions God informing man that "a limited nature in other creatures is confined within the laws written down by Us. In conformity with thy free judgment, in whose hands I have placed thee, thou art confined by no bounds; and thou wilt fix limits of nature for thyself." Man can degenerate to "the lower levels which are the brutes," or by the use of reason, recreate himself at the level of the divine (4–5). This apparent mobility within the Great Chain of Being is in fact mobility within that microcosmic Great Chain of Being, the tripartite soul: to degenerate to "the lower levels which are the brutes" really means to live a life of the senses, since the vegetable, animal, and rational souls reiterate the earthly levels of the Great Chain of Being. Oddly, though, to live a fully rational life is, for Pico, to be not a man, but an angel. A philosopher is a celestial creature, while one "delivered over to the senses" is "a brute, not a man" (6). Here, and at every point where he enumerates the levels of the Great Chain of Being, Pico elides the human level altogether. To be human, it would seem, is to enjoy the freedom to be anything but human.

Understanding this uncomfortable paradox is crucial to reading Webster's Ferdinand. Pico's freedom of movement is largely illusory. To be human, in Pico's scheme, one must transcend the human. Although the freedom that defines humanity demands that the option to become a "beast" be kept open, this "beast option" is clearly the wrong choice. One must maintain the freedom to live a sensual life, because not to be free is not to be human, but if one chooses to exercise this freedom, one's humanity is forfeited by the very act. When man's only "right" choice is to ascend, the defining human characteristic is no longer freedom or mobility; it is aspiration. And this in turn requires rejection of the senses: to aspire to the life of angels, one must eschew the life of the senses.

Ficino, who does not insist as strongly as Pico on maintaining the option to lead a beastlike existence, acknowledges man's composite nature grudgingly; he does not glory in it, as does Pico. Man's physical, animal component is for Ficino an unfortunate impediment, hindering the ascent into rational and spiritual realms. The main argument in support of Ficino's demonstration of the soul's immortality (the goal of his greatest work, *Theologia Platonica*) is that the human soul cannot find fulfillment while tied to a physical body and the life of the senses that it shares with animals. In one of the sections of his *Epistolae* Ficino sets out to demonstrate that "the immortal soul is always miserable in its mortal body"; and he declares in a later section that "we are all freighted with the burden of a most irksome body" and that "the more difficult it is for the celestial and immortal soul to pursue, persistently, its happiness while fallen into an earthly, intemperate body, the more easily it attains it when it is either free from the body, or in a temperate, immortal, celestial body" (680–82, my translation).

Where Ficino insists that thought can be divorced from sense and sense objects, Pomponazzi cannot conceive of thought separated from the concrete materiality of sense. The mind, for Pomponazzi, is an extension of the physical body, and as such must die with the physical body. As a corollary, Pomponazzi introduces the notion that the difference between man and the animals is merely quantitative, not qualitative, since man and animal alike are obliged to think, in varying degrees of efficiency, with physically based minds:

> Nature . . . proceeds by degrees. For vegetable things possess something of a soul, since they operate in themselves, though very materially. . . . Then come animals having only touch and taste and an indeterminate imagination. After them are animals which arrive at such perfection that they are thought to have intellect. For many operate like craftsmen, as by building houses; many like citizens, as bees; many have almost all the moral virtues. . . . Indeed, almost an infinite number of men seem to have less intellect than many beasts. (322–23)

But in spite of his blurring the distinction between man and beast by insisting on the physical nature of even the intellect, Pomponazzi still manages to assert that the life of reason (however mortal, however based on the data of sense) is to be preferred to the life of the senses. "Who would prefer," he asks, "to be a stone or a stag of long life, rather than a man of however low degree?" (359).

Pomponazzi, along with Telesio (who goes so far as to ascribe the faculty of reason to both man and beast, the difference being only one of degree), is skeptical of the mystique with which reason has been invested by Pico and Ficino. To these philosophers, reason is not the faculty that allows man to ascend to the immortal realms of the angels: it is merely a more refined version of a faculty man shares with the beasts. But interestingly enough, in practical terms the effect of Pomponazzi's and Telesio's philosophy is the same as that of Pico and Ficino. While Pico and Ficino believe that man should avoid descending to the brutal in order that he may more surely ascend to the angelic, Pomponazzi and Telesio believe that man should strive to ascend to the angelic for the sole purpose of avoiding descent to the brutal. The former doctrine values ascent for its own sake; the latter is based on an assumption not unlike Toynbee's questionable thesis that cultures that do not progress necessarily decline. The two formulations are really two sides of the same coin; both display an intense fear of backsliding in the direction of the animals. In the milieu of humanism, all arguments (even those that began by demonstrating the affinities between human and animal intelligence) conspired against the sensuous life man shares with beasts.

What is lacking in this Neoplatonic humanism is what is present in other brands of humanism not so influential as Neoplatonism in the formulation of justifications for human dignity: namely, acceptance of man's dual, physical-rational nature; the more Aristotelian advocacy of temperance, moderation, and the middle way. According to Neoplatonic doctrine, one must not seek to control one's sensual urges or contain them within reasonable limits: like Sir Guyon in the Bower of Bliss, one must seek to obliterate them. If a man is not totally spiritual and intellectual, he will be totally sensual. Not to ascend is to descend.

Ferdinand can be read as a man who has bought into—or perhaps absorbed unthinkingly along with his Italian humanist education—this body-denigrating philosophical system. His distaste for ordinary physicality surfaces early: on the topic of delegating military leadership he demands, "Why should [a leader] not as well sleep, or eat, by a deputy? This might take idle, offensive, and base office from him, whereas the other deprives him of honor" (1.1.99–101). Indeed, we never see Ferdinand eat, and although he at one point declares "I'll instantly to bed, for I am weary" (3.1.38–39), the nap is only a ruse: he goes off to spy on the Duchess instead. But it is lust to which Ferdinand has a most particular (and ultimately obsessive) aversion. He reports having "grown mad" with learning of the Duchess's giving birth (2.5.2). The fierce extremism of his response to sexuality can be measured against Angelo's response in *Measure for Measure:* even though Angelo is pretty serious about lust—he thinks it merits death, after all—when he catches himself in lustful feelings he remarks mildly, "Ever till now, / When men were fond [i.e., foolishly lustful], I smiled, and wondered how" (2.2.193–94). Ferdinand, well beyond smiling and wondering, sounds downright unbrotherly:

> I would have their bodies
> Burnt in a coal-pit, with the ventage stopp'd,
> That their curs'd smoke might not ascend to heaven;
> Or dip the sheets they lie in, in pitch or sulphur,
> Wrap them in 't, and then light them like a match;
> Or else to boil their bastard to a cullis,
> And give 't his lecherous father to renew
> The sin of his back. (2.5.66–73)

The Cardinal's response to Ferdinand's ravings, "Are you stark mad?" (2.5.66), is one of several instances of Webster's careful contrast between the Cardinal and Ferdinand. The Cardinal's opposition to the Duchess's remarriage is temporary—she may remarry eventually, as long as the marriage is one of honor (1.1.291–98); Ferdinand believes that "they are most luxurious / Will wed twice" (1.1.297–98). Ferdinand dwells on the "lustful pleasures" of that "rank pasture," the court, branding the Duchess a "lusty widow" (1.1.305, 326, 340). The presence of the Cardinal's mistress, Julia, reminds the audience that the Cardinal's antimarital advice does not arise from any distaste for lust in general.

In contrast to Ferdinand, the Duchess tells Antonio she is "flesh and blood" (1.1.453), and her actions bear this out. She gives birth to four children, suffers from morning sickness, "pukes," "waxes fat i' th' flank" (2.1.67–69), "vulturously" devours apricots (2.1.138, 2.2.2), screams during childbirth (2.3.1), sprawls all over the bed when she sleeps (3.2.13), worries about grey hairs (3.2.58), and enjoys sex ("Alas, what pleasure can two lovers find in sleep!" [3.2.10]). Her robust physicality is thoroughly wholesome: "In that look / There speaketh so divine a countenance / As cuts off all lascivious and vain hope" (1.1.198–200). Nothing could be healthier than the happy, mirthful bedroom scene where Antonio proposes to his wife, "we'll sleep together" (3.2). And the complete physical and spiritual humanity of the Duchess appears in the courage with which she faces torment and death.

Ferdinand's moral stand becomes merely hypocritical if we accept the common view that his dislike of the Duchess's sexuality grows out of his own incestuous desires for her. At first glance, such desire does seem suggested by the voyeuristic relish of passages such as this one:

> My imagination will carry me
> To see her in the shameful act of sin . . .
> Happily with some strong thigh'd bargeman,
> Or one o' th' woodyard that can quoit the sledge,
> Or toss the bar, or else some lovely squire
> That carries coals up to her privy lodgings. (2.5.40–45)

Or, "Damn her! that body of hers, / While that my blood ran pure in 't, was more worth / Than that which thou wouldst comfort, call'd a soul" (4.1.121–23). But since Ferdinand seems unconscious that his ascetic pronouncements mask incestuous desires, it is possible that "incestuous" is not an accurate description of his passions at all; given his strong identification with the Duchess (the fact that they are twins is stressed), Ferdinand's recoil from acknowledging her sexuality may be a recoil from his own. By denying a sexuality that is not to be denied, he attempts to deceive not others but himself. And although he has renounced the senses, he indulges in covert sensual feelings precisely because of the psychological warping caused by his deprivation of sense.

Ferdinand's feeling that sexual desire is unworthy of humanity is complicated by two further pressures. First, he certainly is, as Whigham argues, "obsessively preoccupied" with defense of his class position, and this runs parallel to the humanist-inspired anxiety insofar as the class system as a subdivision of the Great Chain of Being was subject to the same principles of climbing and aspiration that animated the whole system. Norbert Elias has argued that increasing refinement in manners among the aristocracy arose from an effort to maintain distinctiveness against hordes of social climbers pressing up from below, who were—as part of the project of maintaining distinction—increasingly denigrated as more bodily, more lustful, more gluttonous than their social betters. That the Duchess is openly sexual and also consorts with a member of the lower orders, Antonio, threatens Ferdinand as both a human being and an aristocrat. Second, a queer reading of Ferdinand seems to me to illuminate a number of things about his sexual hysteria.

Ferdinand has never married and shows no amorous interest in women. His identification with his female twin takes strange forms: for example, while we might expect a reference to the blood of one's family or parents running in the veins of both twins, Ferdinand imagines that *his own* blood runs in the Duchess's body: "that body of hers, / While that my blood ran pure in 't," suggesting a strong female-identified personality. (See Enterline's Lacanian reading, especially 282.) And look again at his famous fantasy about his sister's sex life: "My imagination will carry me / To see her in the shameful act of sin . . . / Happily with some strong thigh'd bargeman, / Or one o' th' woodyard that can quoit the sledge, / Or toss the bar, or else some lovely squire / That carries coals up to her privy lodgings" (2.5.40–45). It isn't *the Duchess's* thighs or loveliness he sees in his mind's eye. How much time each day does he spend hanging around canals or woodyards watching the strong thighs of bargemen or the biceps of sledge quoiters? How lovely are the squires who carry coals up to Ferdinand's privy lodgings? Like some demented Petrarchan lover, Ferdinand fetishizes body parts, but instead of emblazoning them in sonnets, he tends to cut them off bodies and carry them around—a dead man's hand, the leg of a man. His equivocating message in act 3, scene 5 suggests that he wants to cut off Antonio's head and cut out his heart. And there's that reference to "the part that hath no bone." And again, these are all *male* body parts he is fetishizing. Concerning the scene in which seven men are onstage making sports talk about a recent jousting match (1.1.87–91), Laura L. Behling finds sexual double entendre in Ferdinand's talk of taking the "ring" and winning a "joust," adding that this "game between men is set up as a sexual quiting to prove masculinity" (34). This is probable, though I would point out that if Ferdinand is alluding to body parts here, there's no reason to assume they are female body parts. Granted, the early modern homoerotic closet was very different from ours; but if for the reasons I have discussed, *all* sexuality troubles Ferdinand, and queer sexuality might seem to him even more threatening than straight sexuality—threatening enough to account for a denial that could prompt him to project his own desires onto his sister. (It isn't I who feel promiscuously attracted to a range of lower-class hunks—it's my twin sister.) To some extent, the Duchess functions like the naughty imaginary friend on whom a child can blame his own misdeeds.

Ferdinand does not succeed—either in his project (not unlike Angelo's in *Measure for Measure*) of forcing his sexual mores on other people or in his own attempt to rise above the world of sense. He has bought into the system, and not to ascend is to descend: Ferdinand becomes a beast. The animal song and the lust-obsessed conversations of the madmen in act 4, scene 2 prepare the way for the lust-connected animality of Ferdinand's madness. Animal images precede his lapse into lunacy—he speaks of a howling wolf, dogs, and monkeys (3.2.88, 104), calls the Duchess's children cubs (4.1.33) and young wolves (4.2.258), prophesies that "the wolf shall find her grave, and scrape it up" (4.2.308), and finally metamorphoses into an animal, beginning "I'll go hunt the badger by owl-light" (4.2.333) and ending in the throes of the richly symbolic disease "lycanthropia" (5.2.6):

> One met the duke 'bout midnight in a lane
> Behind St. Mark's church, with the leg of a man
> Upon his shoulder; and he howl'd fearfully;
> Said he was wolf. (5.2.13–16)

Ferdinand never fully recovers, but acts the part of an animal to the end: "Give me some wet hay; I am broken-winded. I do account this world but a dog-kennel" (5.5.66–67).

※   ※   ※

I have compared Ferdinand to Angelo, and to help widen our perspective from Ferdinand's individual psychology, I'd like briefly to show that these ideas are operative in other plays, by exploring the pattern of failed ascent followed by precipitous descent in *Measure for Measure* and in Marlowe's *Tamburlaine* plays.

Isabella's mournful comment on human pretension sets forth man's position between ape and angel:

> But man, proud man,
> Dressed in a little brief authority,
> Most ignorant of what he's most assured,
> His glassy essence, like an angry ape,
> Plays such fantastic tricks before high heaven
> As make the angels weep. (2.2.122–27)

Appropriately enough, given Pico's belief that man could rise to the level of angels, the failed Neoplatonist in this play is named Angelo. In the Duke's words, Angelo is "a man of stricture and firm abstinence"; "Lord Angelo is precise, / . . . scarce confesses / That his blood flows or that his appetite / Is more to bread than stone" (1.3.12, 50–53). In Lucio's words, Angelo is a man "not made by man and woman after this downright way of creation," a man whose "urine is congealed ice," an "ungenitured agent" who will "unpeople the province with continency" (3.2.102–68). Angelo has abjured the life of the senses to the point where it has become impossible for others to imagine him carrying on such normal biological functions as eating, copulating, or urinating. We are reminded of the way Ferdinand disgustedly dismisses eating and sleeping as "idle, offensive, and base." The change in Angelo's character, from his initial attempts to force sensual abstemiousness on the whole of Vienna, to his later declaration to Isabella ("I have begun, / And now I give my sensual race the rein. / Fit thy consent to my sharp appetite" [2.4.160–62]) is abrupt. Such an instantaneous character reversal could be put down to the conventions of Elizabethan/Jacobean comedy, but it is also explainable in terms of the philosophic all-or-nothingism of Neoplatonic doctrine. Not to ascend is to descend; if one cannot be an angel, one will be a beast.

The play, it would seem, ultimately denies the desirability of either extreme. The rehabilitation of Angelo is accomplished not by any move to set him back on his abstemious path of ascent above the world of the senses, but by an attempt to guide him into the middle path so neglected by Neoplatonists. The Duke, significantly called, in a phrase redolent of the *via media,* "a gentleman of all temperance" (3.2.232), maneuvers Angelo into channeling his physical impulses in a lawful direction; first in the bed-trick and finally in marriage. The principle of ascent is repudiated: Angelo is forced to accept human physicality. But rather than providing, as a counter to its desire-repressing male figure, a freely desiring woman as does *The Duchess of Malfi,* this play provides a desire-repressing female figure, Isabella, whose renunciation of all things sensual is foregrounded, as she contemplates taking the strictest possible monastic vows. Her ascetic ideals are undercut by the callous self-righteousness of her moral stand: "Then, Isabel, live chaste, and Brother, die. / More than our brother is our chastity" (2.4.185–86). True, she has spoken of honor (2.4.180); but honor in the abstract, divorced from other human considerations, is almost always suspect in Shakespeare, and allies her more with Ferdinand and his abstract honor than with the Duchess. (Also suspicious is Isabella's sudden use, in this passage, of what seems to be the royal "we.") Isabella's attempted ascent has been at the expense of her humanity, and her "cure" is similar to Angelo's: she must forgive two counts of lechery (Claudio's and Angelo's) and then be married. Sex must be accepted; asceticism is denied. The proliferation of marriages and engagements in the denouement is more than comic convention: two characters with a penchant for asceticism have been forced by the playwright to live in the real sensual world—not the world of beastly, subhuman desire, but the world of healthy human sexuality.

The ordinary world of sense exerts its power over other sky-aspiring dramatic characters, too. Take Tamburlaine who, one feels pretty sure, wouldn't be regarded by Ferdinand as much of a marriage prospect for his sister, and who certainly doesn't appear, at first glance, to be a typical Neoplatonic humanist. He is neither aristocratic nor scholarly, nor even well bred. True, he takes pains over his sons' education, but their schooling is hardly what Elyot and Ascham had in mind. Yet there are unmistakable calling cards of Neoplatonism in the play. The most obvious is Zenocrate, who represents the elevating power of beauty. Few who have read Spenser's thoroughly Neoplatonic "Hymne in Honour of Beautie" and "Hymne of Divine Beautie" could mistake the mold into which Zenocrate has been cast. The appreciation of earthly beauty, according to Neoplatonists, was to lead up the Neoplatonic ladder toward appreciation of divine beauty, away from things physical and toward things spiritual. At the close of part 1 of *Tamburlaine,* Beauty in the person of Zenocrate seems to have succeeded in spiritually elevating Tamburlaine. Earlier, when Tamburlaine had shown less respect than "Tartarian steeds" for the beauty of the virgins of Damascus, Zenocrate herself had despaired of the power of beauty to mitigate Tamburlaine's bloodthirstiness (5.2.266–73). But the soliloquy beginning "Oh fair Zenocrate, divine Zenocrate" (5.2.72–128), evidencing rare internal conflict as Tamburlaine debates whether to accede to Zenocrate's wishes by sparing her father, prepares for the resolution in which it is clear that Zenocrate's beauty *has* elevated Tamburlaine spiritually: the father is spared, and even Bajazeth is included (posthumously) in Tamburlaine's "truce with all the world" (5.2.466). In *Tamburlaine 2,* however, we witness the failure of beauty's power. Tamburlaine has broken his truce with the world, and in answer to Zenocrate's first words in the play, "Sweet Tamburlaine, when wilt thou leave these arms?", he asserts categorically, "When heaven shall cease to move on both the poles" (1.4.9–10). Cardinal Bembo's Neoplatonic lesson in Castiglione's *The Courtier,* that appreciation of a woman's physical attractions should elevate a man's spirit so that the physical finally becomes unimportant, is lost on Tamburlaine, who, inconsolable upon the death of Zenocrate, vows to carry her physical body with him wherever he goes.

This pattern in Tamburlaine's response to beauty—an attempt at spiritual elevation followed by a relapse into the world of the physical—is part of a larger pattern of attempted ascent and relapse. Like the Neoplatonists, Tamburlaine is obsessed with the desire to ascend above the level of the merely human. At times, he sees himself as the instrument of the gods, or as a god on earth. At times he wants to be greater than a god, clearly agreeing with Theridamas that "a god is not so glorious as a king" (*Part 1,* 2.5.57). And he often gives notice of intention to do battle with the gods (*Part 1,* 2.3.19, 21; 5.2.389–90; *Part 2,* 4.2.39–42; 5.2.48–50). But the question of how, in practical terms, one goes about doing battle with gods is not entirely a frivolous one. One can only assume that Tamburlaine wishes he knew. For Tamburlaine's presumptuous aspirations remain frustratingly limited to the physical world. His best-known comment on his own aspirations is ironic indeed:

> Nature, that framed us of four elements
> Warring within our breasts for regiment,
> Doth teach us all to have aspiring minds.
> Our souls, whose faculties can comprehend
> The wondrous architecture of the world
> And measure every wandering planet's course,
> Still climbing after knowledge infinite,
> And always moving as the restless spheres,
> Wills us to wear ourselves and never rest,
> Until we reach the ripest fruit of all,
> That perfect bliss and sole felicity,
> The sweet fruition of an earthly crown. (*Part 1*, 2.7.18–29)

If Tamburlaine does not often sound like a humanist, he sounds like one here. Humankind is defined (as Pico finally defines humanity) by its aspirations; a human being is a restless seeker after knowledge whose questing spirit and aspiring mind are associated with the spiritual state of "bliss"— and then, suddenly, anticlimactically, "an earthly crown." If Marlowe did not intend the incongruous conclusion to jar, he might easily enough have avoided the use of the charged word "earthly."

Part of Tamburlaine's project too, in aspiring beyond a mundane physical life, is an asceticism not unlike Ferdinand's. He twice disdains offers of gold (*Part 1*, 1.2.83–85; 3.3.261–62). He carefully preserves Zenocrate from "all blot of foul unchastity" (*Part 1*, 5.2.423–24). He disapproves of the dishonorable lives of Turkish concubines (*Part 2*, 4.4). As for food, Tamburlaine banquets only to celebrate military victories (*Part 1*, 3.3.272–73; *Part 2*, 1.6.91–98)—one of his banquets features an unappetizing "course of crowns" (*Part 1*, 4.4.104 s.d.). His failure to rise above the mundane physical world is not the result of an undue absorption with the life of the senses, but (as Pomponazzi would have believed) of the inevitable limitation of thought to the objects of sense. Tamburlaine's diction is revealing: his vaguely defined aspirations toward something beyond this world are often couched in appetitive terms—hunger, thirst, gluttony, satiety. When Cosroe describes Tamburlaine as "that fiery thirster after sovereignty" and then as "bloody and insatiate Tamburlaine," Tamburlaine responds, "The thirst of reign . . . / Moved me to manage arms against thy state" (*Part 1*, 2.6.32, 2.8.11, 2.7.12); he describes his joy in the multitude of his crowned followers as a surfeit (*Part 2*, 2.6.25).

Tamburlaine's attempt to deny his ordinary human physicality is buttressed by his insistence on the physical nature of others. His characteristic mode of punishing enemies is to debase them to the animal level, by calling them animals (the Turkish kings are likened to "sheep," "curs," "dogs," and "bellowing bulls" [*Part 2*, 4.2]), by treating them like animals (Bajazeth is kept in a cage and fed scraps in *Part 1;* the Turkish kings become "jades" to draw Tamburlaine's chariot in *Part 2*), and by making them aware of their mere physicality by depriving them of physical necessities—food, drink, rest (cf. Bajazeth, the Turkish kings, the land punished with famine because Zenocrate has died there). But although Tamburlaine seems to be trying to reassure himself that he is ascending by forcing his enemies to descend, his ascent by means of this trick remains something of an optical illusion. *Part 1* affords a stage emblem of this habit of Tamburlaine's: in 4.2.36–37 he compares himself to the rising sun; the occasion for this hyperbole is his ascending to his chair by stepping upon Bajazeth's back. It is not unlike the way Ferdinand reassures himself of his own superhuman purity by interpreting his sister's ordinary human sexuality as bestial desire.

Tamburlaine does not ascend, either spiritually or in terms of confronting the gods directly, and (as in Neoplatonic philosophy) not to ascend is to descend. Preying on his own kind, he is debased to the animal level. He who had thirsted after sovereignty now thirsts after blood. In *Part 1*, when Tamburlaine indicates that his mind is at present "satiate with spoil" and "refuseth blood" (4.1.52–54), the implication is that blood-satiety will eventually follow. In *Part 2*, Calyphas repudiates his father's blood-quaffing habits: "I know, sir, what it is to kill a man; / It works remorse of conscience in me. / I take no pleasure to be murderous, / Nor care for blood when wine will quench my thirst" (4.1.27–30). Tamburlaine describes to another son the way in which one's valor should *feed* on one's enemies: "Cherish thy valor still with fresh supplies, / And glut it not with stale and daunted foes" (*Part 2*, 4.2.12–13). And toward the end, Tamburlaine is described as "the monster that hath drunk a sea of blood / And yet gapes still for more to quench his thirst" (*Part 2*, 5.2.13–14). Tamburlaine's obsession with *shedding* blood is part of an attempt to establish his own immunity to physical laws by demonstrating the contrasting physicality of his foes, and the imagery of *feeding* on enemies and *drinking* blood shows that his own triumph is based on the life of the senses. He does not seem to see the irony of his proud declaration that "his honor . . . consists in shedding blood" (*Part 1*, 5.2.414). His ascetic denial of any ordinary appetite for ordinary human food results not in ascension above the world of sense, but in a decline to subhuman predation.

Tamburlaine's boast, "Sickness or death can never conquer me" (*Part 2*, 5.1.221), is more than simply hubristic. It indicates that Tamburlaine actually believes that he has, by slaughtering other human beings, ascended above the merely mortal. It is a belief he will have to revise. He never wonders whether his cannibalistic imperialism has made him less than a man, but he does finally ask, "Shall sickness prove me now to be a man?" (*Part 2,* 5.3.44). To entertain even this possibility is crushing enough to one who had aspired to more. For Neoplatonic humanism was really super-humanism: the daily business of living—a partly spiritual and partly physical affair— was never felt to be enough. Only once in either play does Tamburlaine wish that he and Zenocrate were simply human, could simply live together. Significantly, this would involve a reversal of Zenocrate's ascension out of the physical world, for she is dead, and Tamburlaine must ask, like that humbler Marlovian shepherd who echoes him, "Come down from heaven, and live with me again" (2.4.118). This plain Anglo-Saxon line marks the only moment when Tamburlaine accepts the value of ordinary life on earth.

In an age of Tamburlainian and Faustian overreaching, the great triumph of *The Duchess of Malfi* is its daring affirmation of ordinary life on earth. I have called the Duchess a hero of desire; what is remarkable is that she is a hero of *ordinary* desire. Ferdinand fantasizes a duchess whose insatiable lusts are epic: the strong-thighed bargeman, the sledge-hefting woodcutter, the lovely squire seem to his aspiring mind only a random sample of her legion of lovers, whom he thinks she must pursue with the monomania of a Tamburlaine pursuing new kingdoms to conquer. Early Jacobean drama abounds in representations by men of world-conquering lust in women, for example this exclamation from Dekker's *The Honest Whore, Part 2:* "Oh, who would trust your cork-heeled sex? I think / To sate your lust, you would love a horse, a bear, / A croaking toad, so your hot itching veins / Might have their bound" (3.3.175–78). During the first decade or so of the seventeenth century, the voracious sexual appetites of women in plays by men approached what the 1950s would have called nymphomania: as a character in Middleton's *The Phoenix* marvels, "A man so resolute in valor as a woman in desire, were an absolute leader" (1.5.37–38). But the Duchess of Malfi disclaims such sexual leadership, declaring "I have not gone about, in this, to create / Any new world, or custom" (3.2.9–11)—she wants no fantasyland of exotic desires but an ordinary everyday marriage, in which a loving parent can give a little boy "some syrup for his cold" (4.2.202–3). As Mikesell observes, "the scenes between husband and wife bespeak quite ordinary domestic intimacies rather than grand passion. The sexuality of the bedchamber scene is an integral part of the casual, affectionate badinage shared by husband, wife and maid" (272). Companionate marriage was a third term that deconstructed the binary of supramundane asceticism and rampant animal lust; and ordinary earthly sexual desire, as affirmed by the Duchess, obviated the choice between angel and beast by reestablishing the neglected median between them, elided by Pico and other theorists: the just plain human. In arguing that the paradox "that human beings may aspire to heaven or sink to the level of the beasts is among the main implications of the play's pattern of contrasts" ("Emblem and Antithesis" 126), Catherine Belsey reproduces the binary that the Duchess's median, earthly, human sexuality has heroically deconstructed. Hers is a heroism not of grandeur but of dailyness, and what's heroic is her daring to defend the tiny fortress of her ordinary desire against massed armies of hyperbolic superhumanism. In a world of humanists, the Duchess of Malfi is a human. A hero of the people.

In *Measure for Measure,* which takes up similar issues, the exoneration of sexual desire is more grudging; that play represents the extreme of a life separated from sense as simply impossible, however desirable it might be: people will be people, and will indulge their sexual desires. Lucio's and Pompey's criticisms of Angelo's enforcement of antilechery laws are suspect because (as libertine and bawd respectively) they have a vested interest in lust's continuance; the Provost's is a disinterested criticism. But all three argue that legislation aimed at forcing human beings to rise above the sensual is not so much illaudable as impracticable. Lucio believes it is "impossible to extirp" lechery (3.2.100); Pompey inquires of Escalus, "Does your Worship mean to geld and splay all the youth of the city?" and volunteers, after Escalus's negative response, "Truly sir, in my poor opinion, they will to't, then" (2.1.229–33); and concerning Claudius's case, the Provost marvels, "All sects, all ages smack of this vice, and he / To die for't!" (2.2.5–6). In its realistic view of the irrepressibility of human sensuality, the play's attitude toward Neoplatonic ascent is not so much critical as pessimistic: the suppression of human physical urges is not unhealthy but merely impossible. Indulgence in the life of the senses is a necessary vice, but a vice nonetheless. But Webster goes much farther than that: *The Duchess of Malfi* represents aspiration toward a life separated from sense as unhealthy and ultimately inhuman. The Duchess's wooing and marriage present us with a healthy and positive alternative to the common Renaissance pattern of aborted ascent followed by precipitous descent.

Since *The Duchess* is not a play that deprecates human physicality, why does it so often compare humans to animals?[5] The two ways in which *The Duchess* uses animal analogy correspond to the two main ways Shakespeare's *King Lear* uses it: evil or criminally insane characters are compared with predatory animals—tigers (3.5.86), wolves (5.2), "cruel biters" (5.2.340)—while the uniformly helpless good characters are compared with prey—birds lured to nets, pheasants and quail fattened to be eaten (3.5.103–13), tied mastiffs (4.1.13), salmon ready to be cooked (3.5.125–39), "beasts for sacrifice" (5.2.80). (Tellingly, all these "prey" have been victimized by humans rather than by other animals.) Webster was willing to concede that man is part beast. But the horrors dramatized in the play do not result from man's animal nature. They result from the mental warping that is a consequence of trying to deny that animal nature.

The physicality that humanity shares with beasts finds acceptance in Webster's play, whose action seems to imply that in the worst times, human vulnerability to physical pain gives occasion for the indomitability of the human spirit to shine forth, while in the best times, a healthy life of the senses is one of life's legitimate joys. The ending of *The Duchess of Malfi* is as affirmative as the ending of a tragedy can be: "Integrity of life is fame's best friend, / Which nobly, beyond death, shall crown the end" (5.5.120–21)—for the primary meaning of "integrity" in Webster's day was "wholeness." Both the Duchess and Antonio have integrated body and spirit, and although they have died, they have died as complete human beings.

The many contemporary critics of the "love is not love" school, who write sexuality out of the Renaissance literary picture, declaring it only a displacement of political or careerist desire, might perhaps be regarded as Neo-Neoplatonists, striving to ascend out of this mundane world of sexuality. They replicate a move made in the Renaissance by Pico, Ficino, Pomponazzi, Telesio, Ferdinand, Angelo, Isabella, Tamburlaine, and many others. It never worked.

The Duchess of Malfi dates to a period when a number of plays (such as Nathan Field's *Amends for Ladies* or Middleton's *More Dissemblers Besides Women*) were overturning the conventional plot device of the wealthy, lustful widow victimized by marrying a lower-class fortune hunter. (I attribute this turnabout largely to the market pressure exerted by female playgoers—see my *Women and the English Renaissance,* chapter 10.) But other playwrights exonerated widows mainly by showing that they were *not* lustful and did *not* make scandalous marriages with men below their station. Webster, in contrast, flirts perilously with the old widow stereotype. As I have written elsewhere, "Any defender of women could show a widow remaining chaste. But to turn a widow who does not remain chaste into a tragic hero was revolutionary. Ferdinand sneeringly calls the duchess a 'lusty widow.' A lesser dramatist would have absolved her of this charge; Webster makes clear that she really is a lusty widow and implies that there is nothing in the world the matter with that" (*Women* 260).

Surprisingly, given that we live on the other side of the sexual revolution, modern critics have a lot of problems with the Duchess's sexuality, and with other aspects of her life of the senses: for example, from the amount of ink spilled over the apricot episode you'd think apricot-eating was right up there with murder in the hierarchy of crimes. Examining links in the play between "the gastronomic and the sexual," Lori Haslem writes that the apricot's reputation as a female aphrodisiac "cannot but aggravate a Ferdinand-like suspicion of the Duchess's appetite, namely, that it is somehow connected with her appetite for sex. . . . Her labor pains immediately follow her eating of the fruit, a sequence which strongly implies that the processes of female reproduction and digestion are directly related" (452–55). James T. Henke writes that "Bosola's comments on the greed with which she eats [the apricots] . . . can hardly fail to call up the association between gastronomic appetite and sexual appetite" (635; see also Randall).[6] Well, so what? The many critics who have written about apricots in this play seem to regard eating as wicked, and to conclude by extension that if sex is linked with eating, both must be wicked and the play must therefore be tapping into misogynistic discourses suggesting that women are creatures of sense. But that is my point: the play agrees that women are creatures of sense, and that furthermore, men are creatures of sense, and that this is an important part of being human. At least in the world of this play, and in others such as *Measure for Measure* and *Tamburlaine,* it is those who try to *deny* the senses, to do without sex, eating, drinking, and sleeping and to curtail these sense activities in others, who become destructive to themselves and to other people.

Writers in other genres, too, became disenchanted with Neoplatonic denigration of the bodily: in his poem "No Platonique Love," William Cartwright voices the inevitabilities of the body and sex and recounts an instance of that tumble into the physical (both sexual and gastronomic) that—as we have seen—often follows an attempt at ascetic ascent:

> I was that silly thing that once was wrought
>   To practice this thin love;
> I climb'd from sex to soul, from soul to thought;
>   But thinking there to move,
> Headlong I rowl'd from thought to soul, and then
> From soul I lighted at the sex again.
>
> As some strict down-look'd men pretend to fast,
>   Who yet in closets eat;
> So lovers who profess they spirits taste,
>   Feed yet on grosser meat;
> I know they boast they souls to souls convey,
> Howe'er they meet, the body is the way. (246–57)

John Donne, too, rejects a disembodied, angelic, Platonic sort of love: "Since my soul, whose child love is, / Takes limbs of flesh, and else could nothing do, / More subtle than the parent is / Love must not be, but take a body too" ("Air and Angels"). But it was preeminently the dramatists who were struggling to come to terms, in their anthropocentric plays, with an inherited brand of philosophic humanism that remained, for the drama, unacceptably inhuman. The great neurotics of English Renaissance drama are those who turn beast because they cannot turn angel. It was mainly Christian humanism that was responsible for suggesting that such a choice was necessary in the first place. Philosophers taught that human dignity resided in the freedom to be either beast or angel. The best drama of the English Renaissance is built on the insight that the human condition consists of the necessity, and the opportunity, to be both.

In this struggle to assert a humanity in which ordinary human desires have a place, our Duchess plays an honorable part. Women have long been demonized as creatures of the senses, and it was risky for Webster to enlist a woman as a hero of desire. Just how risky it was appears in the number of readers who can't get beyond demonizing her for her desire, or at least claiming that Webster and his audiences did. But just as the view of *Othello* as a racist play founders on the stubborn fact that in an age when black characters were villains or served as comic relief, Shakespeare cast a black man as tragic hero, so the view of *The Duchess of Malfi* as a cautionary tale about widows, gluttony, and lust founders upon a similar stubborn fact: Webster cast this sexy, desiring widow as a tragic hero.

And so, echoing Sir Philip Sidney, I conjure you all no more to scorn the human appetites; but if (fie of such a but) you have so earth-scorning a mind that it must needs lift itself up to the Neoplatonic skies, then, though I will not wish upon you that an Angelo be placed in charge of law enforcement in your city, or your brother metamorphose into a Ferdinand, or a Sir Guyon be let loose in your garden, yet thus much curse will I send you: that while you live, you live in love, and never get favor because you regard sonnets as only political; and, when you die, you die from starvation for want of a bowl of apricots.

Notes

1. Lynn Enterline complains, rightly I think, that "such readings, though sensitive to historical context, tend to evacuate sexuality itself of any particular meaning" (253).

2. Joyce E. Peterson is unusually forthright in recognizing the problems inherent in taking (as she does) the views of Ferdinand, the Cardinal, and Bosola to represent some Jacobean World Picture: "Here, we have the villains of the piece presenting what is apparently authorial comment on the action, and it seems to me that this paradoxical technique has been partly responsible for leading many critics astray from the paths of Websterian virtue. Webster took a great risk in giving them the play's voice. . . . The audience may be so put off by the quality of the speakers that it will miss the validity of their judgment on the Duchess's actions." Peterson finds Bosola's "Sometimes the devil doth preach" (1.1.291) "a fair description of what we get in the brothers' counsel. The devil may quote Scripture for his own ends, but that

speaker and those ends do not invalidate Scripture. . . . Although right for the wrong reasons, in light of the results of the Duchess's actions, they truly express the play's perspective" (55–56). Peterson is like many in regarding "the play's perspective" as single-minded, monoglossic, didactic, and reflective of monolithic, uncontested values in society. (Later she claims that the play can "yield up its rhetorical perspective to a close analysis" [79]—there's one single point of view in there, and once a determined critic ferrets it out, we'll know what the play means.) She does not entertain the possibility that Webster placed such a "perspective" in the mouths of villains in order to discredit or at least challenge it, nor does she explain what her didactic Webster had to gain by taking such a "great risk," that would compensate for the risk of being misunderstood. To be fair, my own argument encounters a somewhat similar difficulty when I maintain that Webster took a great risk in making a sensual woman into a tragic hero; but at least I don't have such a seedy character as Ferdinand, the Cardinal, or Bosola to contend with: I would argue that Webster's defending wholesome sexuality and companionate marriage was, all things considered, less risky than his placing his own views in the mouths of murderers, torturers, spies, voyeurs, grave-robbers, and body-snatchers.

3. Another critic sensitive to such complexities, Sara Jayne Steen, writes that critics "have overgeneralized the Renaissance reaction to a marriage like the Duchess's. The marriage of Arbella Stuart to William Seymour long has been recognized as a close contemporary parallel to the Duchess of Malfi's case, and responses to Stuart suggest a more complex historical interpretation is in order" (62). Finding that "some people indeed criticized Stuart's actions, but others were sympathetic to and even supportive of what they perceived as a romantic match" (61), Steen concludes that "if many Jacobeans were capable of sympathizing with and even supporting Stuart, . . . they were capable of sympathizing with the Duchess" (76).

4. There is a historical reason for the strong influence of Neoplatonism on developing English humanism: the founding generation of Christian humanists in England was intimately associated with Italy and especially with the Florence of Pico and Ficino. (If one wishes to look earlier, John Tiptoft, teacher of Free, Grey, Gunthorpe, and others, was in Italy at about the time of the founding of Cosimo de Medici's Platonic Academy, of which Ficino would be the leading light.) Between 1487 and 1490, Thomas Linacre lived in Florence and was permitted by Lorenzo de Medici to share the Greek instruction given by Chalkondylas to Lorenzo's sons. During the same period (1488–94), Pico was residing in Fiesole, three miles from Florence, in a villa provided for him by Lorenzo de Medici. In 1504, Linacre, back in England, was Sir Thomas More's teacher at the time More translated the biography of Pico. William Grocyn studied at Florence from 1488 to 1490, also under Chalkondylas; in addition, Linacre and Grocyn both studied under Poliziano, with whom Pico had been well acquainted since his visit to Florence in 1470. John Colet traveled in France and Italy from 1493 to 1496

and on his return corresponded with Ficino: his writings are studded with references to Pico and Ficino as well as Plato and Plotinus. William Latimer was in Italy at about the same time as Linacre. These founding English humanists were closely connected with each other, in teacher/pupil relationships, as colleagues, or as friends; and as reforming educators they bestowed the influence of Florentine humanism on later generations of English humanists. In 1516 Erasmus was able to write with enthusiasm that "in this age England *contains* Italy."

5. The presence of animal analogy in the play has often been used to discredit the Duchess's sexuality. Peterson, for example, enlists *all* the play's references to animals as evidence of the disastrous subhumanity the Duchess has visited upon her duchy by engaging in the life of the senses humankind shares with animals (chapter 5).

6. Exceptions to this gastrophobia include Christina Luckyj's wholesome statement, "the 'apricocks' scene (2.1) becomes, in performance, not an indictment of the Duchess, but a further confirmation of the directness and sensual delight she exhibited in the wooing scene" (85). Luckyj is also one of the only critics to defend rather than excoriate the sexuality of Julia in the play's subplot.

The "Morris Witch" in
The Witch of Edmonton ◄═══▶

Laura Denker and Laurie Maguire[1]

Old Carter concludes *The Witch of Edmonton* on a note of emotional compromise: "So, let's every man home to Edmonton with heavy hearts, yet as merry as we can, though not as we would" (5.3.166–67).[2] Given that he has just lost a daughter, Susan (murdered impulsively by her bigamous husband), Carter's mixed response is understandable, as is that of his remaining child, Katherine, who anticipates her forthcoming marriage with trepidation: "And but my faith is passed, / I should fear to be married. . . . Excuse me that / I am thus troubled" (5.3.151–54).

The play, of course, is itself generically mixed—a tragicomedy—and such duality characterizes its plot, its characters, and its ambiance from the beginning. Frank, the selfish, bigamous protagonist, is first introduced as victim rather than villain (he marries a fellow servant, Winnifred, whom he believes he has made pregnant, although it is the couple's employer, Sir Arthur, who has, in all probability, fathered Winnifred's child); as the plot develops, however, Frank's narcissism, mendacity, and immorality render him increasingly a villainous subject rather than victimized object, no matter how much he sees himself as the latter (see 3.2.22–23, 25–26; 4.2.102).

Mother Sawyer, the eponymous witch, is characterized with similar moral duality. She becomes a villain only because she is a victim, as several critics have pointed out. "Mother Sawyer is a victim, yes, though she is not exactly innocent," writes Anthony B. Dawson (83), and Larry Champion invokes the same binary, albeit with a reversal of Dawson's emphasis: Mother Sawyer "exercises free will in choosing evil," but she is "victimized by external pressures that render her ability to withstand temptation all the more difficult" (119). The most sustained analysis of Mother Sawyer's dual position comes in Frances Dolan's discussion of the paradoxes of witchcraft. Accusations of witchcraft "often began when a poor, elderly, unmarried woman demanded charitable assistance and was denied; those who denied her, fearing her bitterness and vengefulness, ameliorated their panic and guilt by turning the tables: they accused her of be-witching them. Thus the accuser and the accused each perceived him or her self as the injured party" (172). Dolan goes on to examine the ways in which Mother Sawyer is powerless yet "chooses to seize whatever power she can through the outlaw status by which she is constituted." Neither simply villain nor victim, Mother Sawyer "positions herself as both" (219). Symbiotic rather than opposite, dual rather than dialectic, victim/villain, powerless/powerful, object/subject jostle uncomfortably throughout *The Witch of Edmonton* in all three plots.

Binaries, inversions, parallels, reversals, symbioses, dualities are a unify-ing feature of this collaborative play. Such a generalized statement could, of course, apply to any early modern play, where the double-plot convention encourages thematic counterpoint and parallel (see Levin, and Maguire), but it seems more than usually pertinent to *The Witch of Edmonton,* as the fol-lowing summary indicates.

The comic subplot of Cuddy Banks, dismissed by Robert Cushman as "some appalling yokel business" (534) presents the main plot's witchcraft theme in its benigner Petrarchan form, romance ("Kate Carter . . . hath be-witch'd me. . . . I saw a little devil fly out of her eye"; 2.1.215–20). As Kate McLuskie notes, the "context . . . gives the commonplace metaphor of love as witchery a striking resonance" (*Renaissance Dramatists* 71). More domi-nantly, Cuddy's May Morris activity, which occupies four scenes in the sub-plot, illustrates the socially sanctioned male side of pagan tradition—dancers heralding spring by "waking up the earth" with their heels—and contrasts with the socially suspicious female side of paganism, witchcraft. Thus, the social ritual in the subplot and the social threat in the main plot are "linked in a kind of chiastic parallelism" (Dawson 91).

The Thorney plot presents duality in its most conspicuous form: bigamy. Frank resorts to this drastic expedient because of dual imperatives—filial duty (which requires he save his family's fortune by marrying Susan Carter) and paternal duty (which calls him to legitimize his unborn child by marry-ing Winnifred). From the beginning Frank's problem is one of binaries: he takes two wives because he serves two masters. As a servant in Sir Arthur Clarington's household, he is directed by his employer; as a son he is guided by his father. Frank's later crisis of identity is prefigured here: he is not al-lowed to be an individual but is simply a function (in fact, two functions). Elsewhere in this strand of the action, the aristocratic Sir Arthur, who goes back on his word and stalls Frank's payment (he has offered Frank financial incentive to marry Winnifred), contrasts with the "honest Hertfordshire yeom[a]n," Old Carter, whose "word and . . . deed shall be proved one" in providing Susan's dowry: "My security shall be present payment" (1.2.5–7; 16–17). In the witchcraft plot, the "black cur," Banks, does to Mother

Sawyer metaphorically what her dog does literally—"barks and bites, and sucks the very blood / Of me and of my credit" (2.1.116–18; Comensoli, "Witchcraft" 51). In both witchcraft and bigamy plots, repetition and duplication link the old witch, Mother Sawyer, with the young bride, Susan. Both talk too much and are chastised for unrestrained speech. Both are presented as one-eyed (Mother Sawyer's single eye is part of her physical deformity, and Susan's coffined corpse "stares / With one broad open eye"; 4.2.149–50). Both are associated with the devil (Mother Sawyer's canine familiar is known only as Dog; Susan's assertiveness prompts Frank to accuse her of having "dogged [her] own death"; 3.3.39). Binaries, both localized and pervasive, continue. Winnifred is an honest whore. Susan is a "rose" whom Frank discovers has thorns (3.2.118). The witchcraft plot explains the natural (agricultural failure, adultery) in terms of the supernatural. In an ironic paradox, Frank's downfall is prompted by his first act of selflessness: his concern for Winnifred, disguised as his page, reveals her identity and subsequently his crime (Brodwin 321).

In this essay we want to consider another binary in the play: gender. Gender is the ne plus ultra of binary constructs, from Galen to Montaigne, from Platonic theory to deconstruction. Femininity has long been simply a position within patriarchy; behaviors forbidden to men (emotional expression, tears, sympathy to other men, economic failure) are defined pejoratively as feminine, and behaviors forbidden to women (anger, aggression, intelligence, independence, strong appetites) are defined as masculine (Tyson 86–87). This symbiotic ideology is physiological in origin. Galen believed that all foetuses began as female, and that superior strength enabled a foetus to expel its internal genital organs outwards to become a male. Thus the male position was considered the evolved one, the female sex being simply an imperfect, underdeveloped version of the male (Orgel, *Impersonations* 20).

As Stephen Orgel reminds us, early modern childhood had only one gender: female. Both boys and girls wore skirts until about the age of seven (Orgel 15), and it is notoriously difficult to distinguish children's gender in early modern portraits. In one extreme example, Randall McLeod examines the different states of a portrait engraving of James I's children, which show boys' and girls' heads palimpsestically substituted without any alteration to the bodies that support them. Montaigne chronicles two case histories of women who became men by the power of thought, a natural if belated Galenic *renversement* (see P. Parker passim).

Such gender reversals are common metaphorically, where love has the power to turn men into women. Romeo's love for Juliet makes him "effeminate" (3.1.114); the lovesick Troilus loses his appetite for fighting, becoming "weaker than a woman's tear" (1.1.10); Robert Burton states bluntly that "love . . . turns a man into a woman" (3.2.4.1, cited by Orgel 26). The same situation obtains in reverse, where assertive behavior turns women into men. In Elizabeth Cary's *The Tragedy of Mariam,* Salome presents Constabarus with divorce papers, and he reacts as one would expect: "Are Hebrew women now transformed to men? / Why do you not as well our battles fight, / And wear our armor?" (ll. 421–23). The witches in *Macbeth,* powerful and controlling, are gender-anomalous: female but bearded. Stephen Orgel corrects a powerful misconception about early modern women when he reminds us that women were not precluded from "operating in a public world: it was just that, when they did, they were thought of as masculine" (Orgel 127).

The complex nature of binary association in *The Witch of Edmonton* is revealed in the prefatory distych, not all of whose couplings are logical: "Forc'd marriage, murder; murder, blood requires. / Reproach, revenge; revenge hell's help desires."

As Dawson points out, the "parallelism, balance, anadiplosis" offer "a sense of indissoluble connection" that is "belied by semantic asymmetries. For one thing, forced marriage does not require murder; beyond that, there is no forced marriage in the play" (78). Here Dawson introduces a topic that we wish to pursue: the artificial nature of binary constructs in this play. The binaries we are interested in are victim/villain, male/female, and witchcraft/Morris dancing. The first dyad has been much noticed by critics, if only *en passant,* as the quotations cited earlier from Dawson, Comensoli, and Dolan indicate. The second is neglected, Comensoli's essay being a notable exception, and the third is mentioned only by Dawson and then but briefly. If the positions of victim/villain are fluid in *The Witch of Edmonton,* so are the positions of male and female, and the two are, as we argue, connected to the cultural histories of witchcraft and Morris dancing. The common denominator of all three dyads is gender. Frank occupies the structural position conventionally marked as female, while his wife, Susan, is given masculine license, masculine vocal freedom, and is coded as male. This gender reversal complicates the concepts of villain and victim in the play (concepts already, and presumably purposefully, complicated by the dramatists), and adds to the generic and thematic clashes and compromises that are the hallmark of this accomplished play.

Haec vir, hic mulier

Frank Thorney is one of the most criticized of Jacobean protagonists, and justly so: a coward, a bigamist, a murderer, his only aim in the play is the localized and improvisatory one of extricating himself from the current crisis. He opens the play with the glib self-congratulation, "why here's a business soon dispatched" (1.1.1), referring to the far-from-minor transaction of marriage. He tells his bride Winnifred that they need to keep their marriage secret until "th'inheritance, / To which I am born heir, shall be assured" (1.1.28–29), although this hope is self-delusory as the play makes it clear that the inheritance has dwindled. Frank has no qualms about involving others in his schemes for survival (he asks Sir Arthur to lie to his father, in writing, about his marriage to Winnifred), and he himself is blatantly mendacious (1.2.149ff.). When challenged by his father, who has heard news of his son's marriage, Frank's reaction is one of unimaginative denial—"I must outface it" (1.2.163).

Frank has an unhealthy need for approval, and it is this that leads him into immoral and illegal territory. Sir Arthur's "honest Frank" and "witty Frank" (1.1.116, 151), his father's praise of him as dutiful (1.2.105 and cf. 1.2.158–59) are paramount, and in act 4 he explains his bigamy simply as follows: "To please a father I have heaven displeased" (4.2.102). His decision to murder his wife is made as easily as his decision to take a second wife, and the notable absence of anguish may perhaps be explained by the two references in which Frank sees himself, Giovanni-like, as being led by fate (1.2.193, 227).[3] Certainly, Frank does not see himself as culpable. He blames his bigamous dilemma on his father who "forced me to take the bribe" (3.2.22–23, and cf. 4.2.102), and he blames the murder of his second wife, Susan, on Susan herself, whose devoted attendance has "dogged" him to this desperate course. Thereafter he has no qualms about accusing two innocent men of the deed, and it is only thanks to the intervention of Dog that Warbeck and Somerton are saved from the gallows. Frank's first moment of selflessness comes in act 4 when he reveals Winnifred's female identity beneath her male disguise. He does this to protect her from Old Carter's "tyranny" (4.2.173), but by this stage in the play one can hardly admire Frank for chivalry in protecting one woman when he has just murdered another. Even among prodigal son protagonists Frank emerges badly, but he goes to the gallows forgiven by all, whereas Mother Sawyer, whose crimes are far less, is haled to execution in the same scene with taunts and jibes.

Few critics have dared defend Frank Thorney; indeed, it is the witchcraft plot that has received the lion's share of critical attention. Several critics, however, have commented sympathetically on Frank's predicament. Leonora Leet Brodwin deems Frank "not a malicious miscreant but, on the contrary, one who, trying to be good to everybody sins against all" (314), and David Atkinson discerns in him a "troubled conscience," crediting him with moral growth by act 4 ("Moral Knowledge" 427). Anthony Dawson analyzes Frank's bigamy and the "contradictions inherent in the mixing of sexual and economic interests," arguing that, like the witchcraft in the play, "Frank's transgression imitates the structure of the socially acceptable, and in so doing renders unstable the very oppositions it seeks to uphold" (88). Dawson's comment returns us to the binaries and dualities with which we began, and introduces us to the crucial opposition in the play: man and woman, husband and wife, Frank and Susan.

Susan is granted unaccustomed freedom and autonomy by her father, treated in many ways as a son rather than a daughter. We first meet Susan and her sister Katherine in 1.2 where the women are out walking with their suitors Warbeck and Somerton. The women are to all intents and purposes unchaperoned, for the quartet has split into pairs. "Every day play-day with you? Valentine's day too, all by couples?" teases Old Carter (1.2.34–35). He tells the suitors that his daughters shall make their own marital choice, a privilege that Warbeck admiringly calls a "liberty": "Sue, thou hearest / The liberty that's granted thee. What sayest thou? / Wilt thou be mine?" (1.2.40–42).

Susan responds with confident badinage—"Your what, sir? I dare swear, / Never your wife"—and as the scene progresses Warbeck complains about his treatment: "Do you scorn me, Mistress Susan? / Am I a subject to be jeered at?" (1.2.95–96). Susan's reply is illuminating. She rejects the role of "property for you [Warbeck] to use," and her father, for the second time in the scene, comments approvingly on his daughter's rhetorical ability: "She'll firk him, on my life" (1.2.97, 100).

The Revels editors do not provide a gloss for "firk," but the verb is so strong that it requires commentary. The *OED* overlooks the word's sexual valences, offering only "press hard" (vb.2a), "drub, beat" (vb.4), "play a fiddle" (vb.4b), all of which give the play's phrase the meaning "She'll get the better of him in conversation," a meaning the phrase undoubtedly carries. But even the briefest survey of Renaissance drama illustrates the bawdy associations of the verb, associations "aided by the word's similarity to *fuck*," as Gordon Williams points out (I, 490). "When I was young and had an able backe, . . . I . . . could have ferd, and ferkt . . . as eare a man a liue" boasts an old man in Barry's *Ram-Alley;* one woman "had rather be firkt on the bare floor then a Feather bed" in *Wandring Whore* VI; "To make it rise betwixt her thighs / And firk her is a pleasure" confesses one character in *Merry Drollery* (all cited by Williams, I, 490–91). Further examples from Jonson, Dekker, Middleton, Beaumont and Fletcher (Williams, I, 490–91), and from Shakespeare's *Henry V* ("I do not know the French for fer, and ferret, and firk"; 4.4.30–31) make it clear that Carter grants Susan not just male verbal license: he gives her sexual license.

Clearly, Susan has been encouraged to exercise verbal freedom, and it is her frank and persistent speech that prompts Frank to murder her in act 3, in a sequence to which we shall return. The first stab wound does not silence her, however, and Frank is forced to stab her again before her death is assured. It is this unusual silence on the part of his daughter that offends Old Carter when he sees the corpse, and he, comically, tries to exchange offspring with Old Thorney:

> Sir, take that carcass there, and give me this.
> I'll not own her now, she's none of mine.
> Bob me off with a dumb-show? No, I'll have life.
> This is my son too, and while there's life in him,
> 'Tis half mine. Take you half that silence for't.
> When I speak I look to be spoken to.
> Forgetful slut! (3.3.99–105)

The sentiment is extreme, and may be an expression of extreme grief. Lear too, when faced with the death of Cordelia, listens desperately for speech, willing his daughter to talk and hence furnish proof of life. But Carter's half-line, "Forgetful slut," contains a strong and highly specific condemnatory noun, usually applied to promiscuous women and women who speak, the early modern logic being that if a woman opened one orifice (her mouth) she could not be trusted to keep another (her vagina) closed. The opposite of all Renaissance fathers, Old Carter wants his daughter to be the opposite of all Renaissance women: independent, articulate. For him, silence is insurgence.

Susan shows her independence and vocal assertiveness most in the scenes that lead to her death (2.2 and 3.2). Although Susan (conventionally) blames herself for the discontent she detects in Frank, she "thwarts convention by passionately voicing her sexual desire" (Comensoli "*Household*," 128):

> You, sweet, have the power
> To make me passionate as an April day;
> Now smile, then weep; now pale, then crimson red.
> You are the powerful moon of my blood's sea,
> To make it ebb or flow into my face
> As your looks change. (2.2.91–96)

This is not healthily physical but aggressively masculine. Orgel reminds us that early modern culture "construed as 'masculine' . . . aggressive sexual display, the flaunting of desire" (Orgel 119), and Lois Tyson points out that patriarchy deems "healthy appetite (*for anything*)" unfeminine (87; emphasis added).

Frank is uncomfortable, and tries to put Susan back in her modest "feminine" category: "Change thy conceit, I prithee. / Thou art all perfection" (2.2.96–97). He replaces her passionate images with those of chaste "Diana herself," invoking Susan's "chaste breast" and "modesties," extinguishing Susan's "unchaste desires," and characterizing her as "a perfect emblem of . . . modesty" (2.2.97, 101, 102, 104, 106). He concludes by telling her to be quiet: "maintain no more dispute" (2.2.107). Susan, however, refuses to be silenced: "Come, come, those golden strings of flattery / Shall not tie up my speech" (2.2.109–10). For as long as Frank sees Susan as a "paragon of modesty, Susan is exempt from mutability" (Comensoli *"Household,"* 129); he tells her, " Thou art so rare a goodness / As death would rather put itself to death / Than murder thee" (2.2.140–41). But in ignoring the injunction to be silent, Susan prompts her own death. The fault is not hers but her father's; and Old Carter's obsession with filial sound is now transferred to his son-in-law, Frank: "'tis well you can speak yet. / There's no music but in sound, sound it must be" (3.3.109–10).

If Susan expresses her independence by voicing her own opinions, Frank speaks only what others want to hear. Like Annabella in Ford's *'Tis Pity She's a Whore,* he is malleable and impressionable, overeager to please. Whereas Susan's father grants her liberty of conjugal choice, Frank's father places his son in a more typically female position on the marriage market, dictating his son's choice of spouse. This is what Stephen Orgel means when he describes everyone as in some way feminized by early modern society: "Everyone in this culture was in some respects a woman, feminized in relation to someone" (124). The hierarchical structure of patriarchy feminizes everybody inasmuch as it places people in relations of power and subjection. "Patriarchy was not single nor uninflected: the patriarchy of fathers impinged on that of husbands, both were at odds with the patriarchy of the crown, and even the crown could be charged with usurping the prerogatives of God the Father" (Orgel 124).[4] Whether patriarchy worked horizontally ("through the class system") or vertically ("through primogeniture") it worked to stratify, to institutionalize, to discipline (Orgel 124–25). And men could be controlled and disciplined just as much as women. In submitting to an arranged marriage, Frank, like other prodigal son heroes (Bertram in *All's Well* for instance), is controlled, objectified, feminized.

Old Thorney offers as incentive paternal approval and financial remuneration:

> If you marry
> With wealthy Carter's daughter there's a portion
> Will free my land, all of which I will instate
> Upon the marriage to you. (1.2.130–32)

Whereas Susan explicitly disassociates herself from the notion of woman as conjugal property, Frank accepts that position: "When I was sold, I sold myself again—/ Some knaves have don't in lands, and I in body" (3.2.27–28).

Earlier in this speech he complains that his father "would not bless, nor look a father on me, / Until I satisfied his angry will" (3.2.25–26). This is not supported by the earlier events of the play, but it is clear that Frank's relationship with his father is emotionally fragile. In 1.2 son and father meet, and the exchange is revealing:

> Frank: Sir, my duty.
> Old Thorney: Now
>   You come as I could wish. (1.2.104–6)

The subtext is clear: only dutiful sons are welcome. And so Frank acts dutifully, even if it means a split identity and a split life.

As the scene progresses, we see a mild and obedient Frank who "humbly yield[s] to be directed by [his father] / In all commands" (1.2.145–46). When Old Thorney challenges him with marriage to Winnifred, calling him a "graceless, godless son," Frank feels the accusation deeply ("To me, sir, this? O my cleft heart!"; 1.2.158–59), and he reveals in act 4 that his aim throughout has been "but to please a father." It is, in fact, not just his father he wishes to please, but everyone with whom he comes into contact: Sir Arthur, Winnifred, Old Carter. For instance, he tells Sir Arthur that he will marry Winnifred "to right / A wronged maid *and to preserve your favour*" (1.1.106–7; my emphasis). The opposite of Susan, who voices her own preferences, Frank is silent: "Alas, sir, / Am I a talker?" (1.1.148–49). Feminized through passivity, through his position on the marriage market, through his acceptance of his status as object, Frank is further feminized through silence.

Edmonton society, like early modern society, does not approve of women who talk. Mother Sawyer's transgression is, predictably, speech. She has a "bad tongue" (2.1.11), and in 4.1 the Justice three times admonishes her for her lack of verbal restraint: "Be not so furious"; "You are too saucy and too bitter"; "Know whom you speak to?" (4.1.75, 82, 86). In her madness Anne Ratcliffe lets loose with her tongue. Susan Carter pays with her life for her verbal freedom. Yet, even at the end, Old Carter still seeks female vociferousness, imaginatively reinvesting his dead daughter with the power of speech: "O, now I see her; 'tis a young wench, my daughter, . . . she looks out at a casement and cries, 'Help, help! Stay that man!'" (4.2.144–47).

The nature of Susan's transgression is made apparent by her position at the casement. As Lena Orlin suggests in her survey of women at doors and windows, these two areas were "coded differently in social convention" ("Women on the Threshold" 53). Women on doorsteps were still technically "at home" (53) even though the threshold sometimes led to accusations of whoredom because of its literally liminal position. The casement was less ambivalent. Women above—at upper windows, as in *Women Beware Women, Volpone, The Broken Heart*—invited public attention. Following Proverbs 7:12, Henry Smith equated women at windows with whores: "therefore Solomon, depainting the Whore, setteth her at the door, now walking in the streets, *now looking out of the windows,* like curled Jezebel, as if she held forth the glass of temptation for vanity to gaze upon" (cited by Orlin 52).

That Susan appears at the window only to call for help is beside the point. She is crossing a spatial boundary, from the domestic, feminine, private "within" to the masculine, public "without." The gender bifurcation in *Witch of Edmonton* breaks down around Mother Sawyer. If Susan is coded as male and Frank as female, the witch is uncategorizable. Susan's masculine power is an anomaly, and the contradictions in her character so great that she has to be killed off, her power categorized and then punished as a species of masculinity. Frank is similarly controlled by gender: subjected and disciplined, he becomes the good woman of the play. This, presumably, is why he can be forgiven by Edmonton in act 5. Mother Sawyer, on the other hand, is so far outside the hierarchical order—which is to say, so gender-anomalous—that she has to be demonized, exiled, and banished from the play's partially eirenic conclusion of reconciliation and forgiveness. Mother Sawyer frustrates ontological categorization (let alone binary definition). Despite the appellation "Mother," she is single, the dramatists having eliminated the husband and daughter of the play's source, Henry Goodcole's pamphlet, *The Wonderful Discovery of Elizabeth Sawyer* (1621); she suckles not a child but a dog; and though she traffics with the devil, her relationship with her familiar is one of domestic affection rather than diabolism ("Let's tickle"; 4.1.160). At no point does Mother Sawyer ever identify herself as a witch. "I am called witch," she laments, "Yet am myself bewitched from doing harm" (5.1.2–3). She is the name not the thing, the label not the entity. Her frustration of the play's, and of early modern society's, taxonomic binary is made apparent in 4.1 when Old Banks details the putative sexual evidence of witchcraft: "having a dun cow tied up in my backside, . . . I cannot choose, though it be ten times in an hour, but run to the cow and taking up her tail kiss, saving your worship's reverence, my cow behind" (4.1.53–57). The town laughs at him, and Sir Arthur and the Justice dismiss this witchcraft as harmless "sports" (4.1.64), but Old Banks insists. In the play's context he is right to be alarmed. Bestiality and the anus are conspicuously ungendered (Smith, "L[o]cating the Sexual Subject" 111), and in a culture structured on gender hierarchies, such perceived effects of bewitchment are insidious indeed.

The Morris Witch

The play's binary of victim/villain cannot be separated from its binary of masculine/feminine. Wherever there is repression there will be resistance, *tout court.* Comedy's way of dealing with this is to represent the social victim as a villain; thus Mother Sawyer keeps dramatic company with Shylock.

But, unlike *The Merchant of Venice, The Witch of Edmonton* is not a comedy. Although described on the 1658 quarto title-page as a "tragicomedy," the play is a subgenre of tragedy, that generic hinterland marked by a qualifying adjective: *domestic* tragedy.

Domestic tragedy depicts nonaristocratic characters—the Frankfords (in *A Woman Killed with Kindness*), the Ardens (in *Arden of Faversham*), the Thorneys—at a moment of crisis when domestic violence (Anne Frankford's adultery and banishment, Alice Arden's petty treason, Frank Thorney's uxoricide) spills over into public life. Like tragedy generally, domestic tragedy "problematizes communal relations by responding to the breaking, not the sustaining, of rules and order" (Liebler 9). Unlike other domestic tragedies, however, *The Witch of Edmonton,* in an unexpectedly literal way, fits Naomi Liebler's definition of "festive tragedy." For Liebler, festive tragedy, like its counterpart festive comedy, celebrates social survival, ritual, ceremony, civic values and constructs, but, unlike comedy, festive tragedy "interrogates not only the capability of representative human communities to act for their own continuing good, but also what *constitutes* 'the good,' the 'common weal' in each dramatized case" (Liebler 8). "'Festive,'" Liebler explains, "means something more socially complex than 'merry.' The Latin root, *festum* ('feast') incorporates the sacramental, patterned, and entirely serious functions and meaning of ritual and communal activity. In this sense, the meaning of the word 'festive' expands to include 'ceremonial,' 'solemn,' 'celebratory,' and 'consecrative'" (Liebler 12). Nowhere is this more evident than in *The Witch of Edmonton,* where the Cuddy Banks plot focuses on a "sacramental," "patterned," "entirely serious," "consecrative" ritual: Morris dancing.

Morris dancing is a ritual folk ceremony that is part play, part dance. The dance element requires colorful costumes, with long handkerchiefs, ribbons, streamers, or scarves (waved in stylized fashion in the air), and metal bells (attached to the costumes, particularly at the legs and the feet). The play element involves improvisation on a traditional plot that is passed down orally from fathers to sons (it sometimes has dialogue but more usually is dumbshow); performance requires only five or six players; and anonymity (often to the extent of performers blacking their faces) is key to the ceremonial nature of the performance (Brody; and Helm). The word "mummer" comes from the Dutch *mommen* or Middle Low German *mummen,* meaning "to keep silent," but is also related to the Old and Middle French *momer,* meaning "to disguise oneself with a mask" (see Brody 4 on the complicated etymology). "Morris" derives from the Middle English *Moreys* = Moorish.

Closely tied to annual festival rhythms and to the agricultural calendar (the arrival of spring or fall, the harvest gathering, the "death" of foliage in winter, and so on), Morris dancing/mumming punctuated the year at appropriate times: plays about St. George on St. George's Day, Pace-Egg or Pasch-Egg plays at Easter, the Souling Play or Soul-Cakers play on All Souls' Day, the Sword Dances (with symbolic slaying) in winter. Pagan in origin, these ritual markings of the agricultural cycle originally facilitated communication with the spirit of the earth Goddess who was believed to reside in nature (Brody 117–27), and Morris dancing/mummers' plays functioned as fertility rites: the ringing of bells and the tapping of the feet awoke the earth; high leaps were mimetic magic to make crops grow tall; and the plays' action represented the seasonal structure of combat, death, and renewal. By the sixteenth and seventeenth centuries, Morris dancing had become a folk custom rather than a religious ritual, and its pagan origins were comfortably and almost invisibly assimilated.[5]

This was not the case with witchcraft, which has, in most other respects, much in common with Morris dancing. It is pagan in origin; it is as exclusively female as Morris dancing is male; it is associated with seasonal rhythms (e.g., celebration of the summer solstice), with nature (witches were often herbalists, community healers), and with fertility (the "wise woman" provided contraception, aided childbirth delivery, practiced abortion). Simply and summarily put, witchcraft is the female side of Morris dancing. The parallel is made clear in one of the many synonyms for Morris dancer— "Morris witch." In *The Witch of Edmonton* Cuddy Banks, as Morris dancer, is literally a black (Moorish) witch, whereas Mother Sawyer, who is given the diabolic label, is simply an old destitute woman in search of firewood.

The May Day Morris dance both celebrates the arrival of spring, and cues the very arrival that it celebrates, for (as mentioned above) the noise of the dancers' bells as they tap their feet is intended to waken the dormant earth spirit. In a Christian society, dancing to celebrate spring remains a logical response, particularly in an agricultural community like Edmonton;[6] dancing in order to *create* spring is not logical. Such topocosmic superstition is essentially no different from the cause-and-effect relations of which the Edmonton men accuse Mother Sawyer: Mother Sawyer's sow licked Anne Ratcliffe's soap, and now Old Ratcliffe blames Mother Sawyer for his wife's madness; Old Banks catches his wife in adultery and attributes his misfortune to Mother Sawyer; a countryman's horse catches a contagious disease and Mother Sawyer is deemed responsible (4.1.1–9). One survival of pagan tradition—the Morris dance—is accepted, another—witchcraft—is shunned; one is dignified, another is criminalized. We might proffer logical reasons for this bifurcated development—Morris dancing is socially cohesive, witchcraft is not (except inasmuch as it bonds the community that persecutes the witch)—but at root there is no obvious good reason. The cultural binary of witchcraft/Morris dancing is shown to be as arbitrary and artificial a construct as the other binaries under interrogation in *The Witch of Edmonton:* moral status (victim/villain) and gender ontology (male/female). The play's refusal to distinguish main plot from subplot, and to nominate a tragic hero/heroine, seems relevant here, the authors illustrating their point about distinction. Is Mother Sawyer the heroine of the play that takes her name? Frances Dolan points out that Mother Sawyer has only four of the play's 13 scenes whereas Frank has seven (219). Does this make Mother Sawyer's plot technically a subplot? (Critics variously refer to her storyline as main plot and subplot.) Is Mother Sawyer or Frank the tragic protagonist? If the latter, does the play's gendering of his structural position make him a tragic hero or heroine?

"Witch" was not always a condemnatory term, and in the phrase "Morris witch" we have a fossilized pagan meaning, connoting the celebratory ritual magic of the Morris dancer. "Morris" functions in its Middle English adjectival sense, "witch" describes the spiritual element, and the compound epithet is a neutral term invoking the performer, the artiste. When the terms are used disjunctively in the medieval and early modern periods, the sense shifts. "Morris" becomes male and positive, "witch" female and pejorative. That Morris dancing is a masculine tradition, witchcraft a female tradition, is presumably relevant. Throughout *The Witch of Edmonton* Dekker, Ford, and Rowley ask us to reassess the taxonomic opposites of gender that structure (and ruin) lives.

Gender, however, is a means rather than an end in this play. *The Witch of Edmonton* is not about women's historical resistance or oppression, whether as wives or witches, nor is it about gender as biological or social facticity. Dekker, Ford, and Rowley use gender, and the polarity inevitably associated with it, to expose the artificial constructs of early modern culture in status (victim/villain), behavior (male/female), and tradition (witchcraft/Morris dancing). In examining the structure and epistemology of gender, the play and its authors lament the ideological double bind that traps people's lives, as sons and daughters, as youthful marriage partners, and as single, handicapped seniors.

Notes

1. As ever, Dympna Callaghan provided crucial help and advice during the development of this essay.
2. Citations of *The Witch of Edmonton* in this essay follow the edition by Peter Corbin and Douglas Sedge (Manchester: Manchester UP, 1986).
3. John Ford, one of the play's three named authors, is generally held responsible for the creation of Frank Thorney. Thus, the parallels between Frank and Giovanni in Ford's *'Tis Pity She's A Whore* are of particular interest.
4. We see this in act 1 of *Witch of Edmonton,* where the plot is instigated by patriarchy coming in conflict with itself. Sir Arthur's claim on Frank as patron/employer conflicts with Old Thorney's claim on Frank as father, but instead of one overriding the other, Frank chooses to obey both. Similarly,

Frank's role as father-to-be conflicts with his role as son, the two linked by society's emphasis on family labels. In 1.1 Frank earns the name of father by marrying the pregnant Winnifred ("Thy child shall know / Who to call dad now"; 1.1.4–5); in 1.2 he earns the name of "son Frank" (1.2.204) by marrying Carter's daughter, Susan. But, as the dramatists ruefully show, in this plot he cannot be both dutiful father and dutiful son.

5. In Shakespeare's *Richard II,* for instance, Richard wishes himself a "mockery king of snow, / Standing before the sun of Bolingbroke / To melt [him] self away in water-drops!" (4.1.250–52). The pagan invocation of the seasons contributes to the balanced political struggle of *Richard II* in which deposee and deposer battle for supremacy, like autumn and summer, the old year and the new, in a ritual and repetitive cycle of natural and political history (Cornford). Richard II is replaced by Henry IV, who in turn will be replaced by a younger, newer king.

6. Barry Kyle's RSC production of *The Witch of Edmonton* in 1981–82 was filled with agricultural detail, activity, and sound effects, and the characters spoke with rural accents, reminding us that Edmonton was not always a North London suburb.

Sex and the Female Tragic Hero 🖾

Jeanne Addison Roberts

T ragedy has often been defined as a representation of the struggle between the individual and the community. Opinions have varied
about whether audiences tend to side with the individual or the
community. The question is of particular interest in the Renaissance because
of what seems to be growing recognition of the individual and a growing
imagination of identity apart from the community.[1] As this sense of separate
identity grows, there also develops in the drama at least the illusion of a subjectivity defined by the perception of an individuality of character. This illusion of subjectivity is particularly powerful, of course, with the male
characters who are the focus of the tragedies.

In Shakespearean tragedy male tragic heroes—Titus, Hamlet, Macbeth,
Lear, Coriolanus, Timon, Romeo, and even Othello and Antony—seem to
move from central spots in their communities to the fringes and beyond to
become geographical or psychic outsiders, individuals distanced from their
communities with a growing sense of separateness and individual subjectivity. One might argue that tragic heroes develop as personifications of the
fears of a community that finds in drama ways of dealing with those fears.
Thus the poison/remedy theory of tragedy discussed by Naomi Liebler and
other theorists seems appropriate.[2] In every case these "heroic" individuals
are, in the end, subordinated to or overcome by their societies, although also
in every case their communities seem modified to varying extents by their
deaths. In this process the "poison" finds a "remedy."

The question of possible subjectivity in the male characters of Renaissance drama has been variously argued, with some critics denying it, some
finding it in nascent form particularly in characters like Prince Hal and
Hamlet, and some insisting on it as a recurring feature. In any case, discussion of the possibility is muddied by the fact that in searching for subjectivity we are inevitably confused by our own (possible) subjectivity, our sense

of the author's, the actor's, the audience's subjectivities (then and now), and the cumulative opinions of readers and critics.

If the case for male characters is difficult, the case for the possible subjectivity of female characters is exponentially more so. In the overwhelming majority of cases they are seen from a male, and therefore inevitably limited, point of view. Their situation is notably different from that of the males, especially in their relation to the community. I have argued elsewhere that for Renaissance England the community, the cultural center of the imagined world was hierarchical, patriarchal, male-centered, and relatively static and exclusive (*The Shakespearean Wild* 1–22). Women, aliens, and animals existed on the fringes—often useful and indeed necessary but foreign and therefore potentially frightening. The few women who might be nominated for heroic status—Tamora, Juliet, Desdemona, Lady Macbeth, Lear's daughters, Gertrude, Cleopatra, and Volumnia—already exist on the margins of the community and cannot serve as typical representatives of it. Because they are marginal, one might suppose that they would communicate a sense of individualism and subjectivity. But this is rarely the case. Instead they often seem rather representations of male fantasies or male fears, as simple or modified stereotypes, or as mere devices of plot. Understandably, because they are already marginal, they only rarely leave their communities changed in major ways, but they do threaten them. With very rare exceptions their threats are sexual. All of the women listed above, with the possible exception of Volumnia, can be thought of as sex objects; and all, with the possible exception of Gertrude, Cleopatra, and Volumnia, can be perceived as fertile. It is, of course, the potential for fertility that makes women inescapably vital to a male-centered community unable to reproduce itself without at least minimal contact with women. Thomas Campion has put it neatly: "How can man Perpetual be, / But in his owne Posteritie?" (1614, sig. B3v). Because this contact with women is necessary, but risky, it is a chief concern of the community to maintain the status quo by keeping it under control. Judging from English Renaissance drama, some male writers imagine women rather monochromatically in terms of their sexuality. In Shakespeare sexuality, with its potential for fertility, is the primary concern in the depiction of all the female hero candidates except Lady Macbeth and Volumnia; and even Lady Macbeth makes a point of having given suck (1.7.54)[3] and is urged to bring forth men children only, advice that certainly suggests that her fertility is in the mind of her husband (1.7.72).

Historically this fearful obsession with sexuality does not always seem central to drama, and perhaps it is foregrounded in the English Renaissance precisely because of the changing landscape. A continually intriguing puzzle in the study of Greek drama is why an Athenian society, which according to all accounts suppressed and ghettoized women, should have produced plays with such strong central female characters as Clytemnestra, Electra, Jocasta, Phaedra, Helen, Iphigenia, Agave, Alcestis, Medea, and Antigone. Perhaps sex was so thoroughly under control that male playwrights were more worried about regicide, matricide, suicide, kidnapping, infanticide, filicide, defiance of authority, deception, and self-sacrifice. All of these women violate established community values. Clytemnestra, Electra, Medea, and Agave are murderous; Jocasta is suicidal; Antigone and Iphigenia defy their rulers. It is true that Jocasta is incestuous and Helen is adulterous, but neither intentionally. Only Phaedra is sexually obsessed, but she has been set up by Aphrodite; and the real sin in her case is the deception of her husband. Each of these women is compelling and to a degree sympathetic. They threaten community values in much more varied ways than the women of Shakespeare's plays. Each of the Greek women leaves her society profoundly changed with her departure. And because they have long speeches and are subjects of choruses, they achieve some real sense of individuality.

But in spite of the far narrower possibilities of heroic women in Shakespeare, both male and female audiences have felt subjective presence in Shakespeare's women. To demonstrate self-evident female subjectivity in Shakespeare's tragedies is an enterprise almost certainly doomed to failure; but since some sense of subjectivity seems essential to a tragic hero, I will focus on a few factors that help to create at least such an illusion. Pertinent questions to ask about a female character are:

1. How many lines does she have?
2. Does she have soliloquies?
3. Does she speak in a distinctive voice?
4. Does she change and develop?
5. Does she represent stereotypes of Renaissance male views of women? Sex? Death?
6. Does she reveal internal conflicts?
7. Does she act in ways that shape her destiny rather than simply suffering as victim?
8. Are there unexplained mysteries in her behavior?
9. Is the world changed by her death?

The matter of the number of lines is relatively straightforward. According to the Pelican Shakespeare count (Harbage, ed. 31), only five female characters out of the whole canon speak more than 500 lines (no one in the histories, Portia and Rosalind in the comedies, Juliet [509] and Cleopatra [622] in the tragedies, and Imogen in the romance). We need no ghost come from the grave to tell us that the tragedies are about men. It is surprising that Juliet and Cleopatra speak as much as they do.

On the basis of soliloquies Juliet seems to qualify as Shakespeare's most fully revealed tragic woman. Unlike other women of the tragedies, she has two major soliloquies ("Gallop apace," 3.2.1–31, and her extended imagining of herself waking up in the tomb, 4.3.14–58). Particularly in the last half of the play she is perhaps the major figure. Her voice is distinctive—passionate, sensitive, and imaginative. In the early scenes the men banter extensively in couplets that come across as the easy "boy talk" of male bonding. Only after Romeo meets Juliet does he learn to master the complexities of the sonnet. And even then his language pales in comparison with the richness of Juliet's fertile imagination (sometimes almost grotesque as in her imagining of Romeo cut out in little stars, 3.2.22). Juliet also grows significantly as she moves from virgin to lover to wife, rejects her parents and nurse, and faces death. The deaths of the two lovers also promise to have major consequences for their society, healing the ancient rift between Montagues and Capulets; but it is not likely to change broader social customs or the system of controlling sexuality.

It is tempting to imagine that Shakespeare's interest in Juliet was enhanced by his being at the time of composition himself the father of a 13-year-old daughter. But this fantasy is dampened by the thought that, although Juliet is certainly not a mere plot device, she is tied by language and action to the two major stereotypical associations with women—sex and death. She has few internal conflicts and no real mysteries. But I am quite prepared to grant her the illusion of subjectivity and to award her the status of tragic hero on the grounds that she knows what she wants, works to achieve it, develops in the process, and acts bravely and deliberately in extremely difficult circumstances. She even fits the pattern developed by Liebler of tragic hero as poison and remedy. Her rebellious actions are thought to be poisonous to her community, but her death provides at least a temporary remedy, parochial if not society-wide, in the reconciliation of the two families. I am certainly saddened by her unnecessary death, and I do regret her limitation of experience and her early passing; but at the same time I feel a certain elation that her love remains untarnished—forever will she love and he be fair.

Cleopatra is, of course, a considerably more complicated case. She speaks 113 lines more than Juliet, and she obviously is deeply involved in major world affairs. But she does not speak alone to the audience. Her voice is distinctive, but I am never quite sure how much is self-revelation and how much is theater. Paradoxically, her very mystery contributes to the illusion of subjectivity. She certainly seems to grow and change, but I continually sense the presence of subtexts that I cannot fully fathom (e.g., does she or does she not mean to betray Antony as she toys with Thidias [3.13.47–85]?). Even more than Juliet she emanates an aura of sex and death—standard female associations. But she also has wealth, worldly power, friends, emotional depth, and wide experience of the political arena. She dies deliberately and gloriously, and her death ensures her own enduring fame. However, Egypt is altered, probably for the worse, and the communal values of Rome seem solidly triumphant. Unlike most of the women of Shakespeare's tragedies, who, interesting though they may be, conform to the stereotypical patterns of virgin, villain, and victim, Juliet and Cleopatra escape the bounds of typecasting.

Other candidates for heroism qualify less clearly. Gertrude functions primarily as a plot device, but Hamlet imagines her "In the rank sweat of an enseamed bed / Stewed in corruption" (3.4.93–94). Desdemona, already on the fringe because of her gender, moves farther away by marrying an alien without her father's consent. Like Juliet's and Cleopatra's sexual independence, Desdemona's is a threat to the community's values, but her sacrifice as victim does nothing to cleanse or alter her society. She has nearly 400 lines but no soliloquies, and her subjectivity is increasingly shadowy after her splendid first speech. Her voice becomes muffled, and she does not seem to grow or change. She has threatened her father by her independence, but it is the misreading of her sexuality by her husband that threatens society, leading him finally to reject marriage itself:

> O curse of marriage!
> That we can call these delicate creatures ours,
> And not their appetites! I had rather be a toad
> And live upon the vapor of a dungeon
> Than keep a corner in the thing I love
> For others' uses. (3.3.267–72)

Desdemona does have a distinctive voice, but her one independent action precedes the action and she personifies a male stereotype in which sex leads to death. She is certainly sympathetic, but hardly heroic.

Being bad is no bar to being a tragic hero. Indeed the modern playwright Paula Vogel has spoken of the importance of "negative empathy" in certain plays where "audience members resist identifying with the protagonist, because they're doing things we don't want to admit we have in common" [*sic*].[4] This may explain why we're willing to award the title of hero to Macbeth (although my students usually say that all the bad things he does are his wife's fault). Goneril and Regan might have qualified more easily if they hadn't been guilty of the cardinal sin of disrespect to Daddy and later of the urge to sexual promiscuity. They also needed a few more lines and a bit more subtlety of development. They change little and have no apparent inner conflicts; and they are inextricably joined to sex and death. Their actions have been poisonous, but their death offers no remedy. Cordelia, who might have qualified more clearly as poison and remedy, has too few lines. Although her very silence is eloquent, and her actions show independence, there is not enough evidence to establish subjectiveness, and the world does not seem changed by her death.

Lady Macbeth and Tamora might also be nominated for heroism. They have the same number of lines (257), and both are to me initially sympathetic. Although Lady Macbeth is frequently portrayed as sexy on the modern stage, the text does not require that she be so. It shows no one lusting after her, and she does not express sexual lust. However, making her sexy on the stage adds an intriguing dimension to her portrait—is her sexuality seductively "feminine" or frighteningly "masculine"? Or perhaps both? If her sexuality is not emphasized, she may become even more interesting. She is a strong-minded woman acting on principle rather than emotion—the principle of achieving her ends. Lady Macbeth assumes the conventional community role for women of aiding and supporting her husband. Her voice is distinctive, and she speaks memorably whether alone or in company. Shakespeare editors Charlotte Porter and Helen Clarke note that she is "so vital and influential a personage that she tempts the reader or hearer of the play to conceive of her outside the play" (21). But although they credit her with a conscience sensitive enough to force her to acknowledge her own evil, they finally concede that she exists only in relation to Macbeth (21). Her lines about being willing to dash out the brains of her baby (1.7.54–58) are among the most shocking in Shakespeare, but they are certainly memorable. She has, in effect, weighed a child against her spouse and chosen him. From a community point of view this might even be defensible. And, of course, the choice is only theoretical. She definitely develops inner conflicts; she changes; and she acts to shape her destiny, perhaps even by suicide. She qualifies on most counts as heroic. But the world seems unchanged by her death, and even her husband cannot take time to mourn her. She simply disappears from the crucial last half of the play. Although she is remembered in passing as a "fiend-like queen" (5.9.35), it is the death of Macbeth that opens up a future leading ultimately to King James.

Tamora, on the other hand, is there from start to bitter end. Both female and alien, she is an outsider on two counts. Defeated in battle and condemned to witness the senseless slaughter of her son, she has valid grounds for revenge. She is a sexual threat both in her marriage to Saturninus and her dalliance with the black Aaron—a sexual alliance that is doubly alarming because it seems to be both extramarital and miscegenistic. Her revenge on Titus is actually no more violent or extreme than his on her or those of other revengers. Both she and Titus lose multiple sons. Titus's daughter is violated and maimed through Tamora's machinations, but his cannibalistic banquet and universal slaughter finally outdo her in violence. Both seem to me about equally "heroic." Both act as poison and remedy—he by erasing a perverted generation and she, astonishingly, by bequeathing a future. The extraordinary thing about the ending is that her people (the Goths) enter to "save" Rome, though she is not there to participate, and that her son by Aaron, whom she has ordered killed at birth, survives like Titus's grandson, with a chance, however tenuous, to populate the future. Her heritage does indeed change the course of Roman history. I feel inclined to honor her as a tragic hero. In my mind she certainly has a better claim than Titus Andronicus.

The only two possible female heroes in Shakespearean tragedy whose threat to society is not linked to their potential for sexual activity are Lady Macbeth and Volumnia. In each case their apparent rejection of sexuality and traditional "feminine" virtues poses even more frightening prospects. One might argue that the threat is still sexual but that it has taken on a negative charge; the very denial of gender stereotypes is "unnatural." Janet Adelman has argued forcefully and persuasively that the threat projected by these two characters is that they arouse the male fear of feminization in the husband and the son respectively (*Suffocating Mothers* 130–64). But this is to see them only from a masculine point of view. Each woman embodies some aspect of accepted social "values." Lady Macbeth is the childless woman who wants to help her husband get ahead and Volumnia is a Roman matron, apparently a single parent who has inculcated in her son the values of a Roman soldier. Like Lady Macbeth she has truly shocking lines: "The breasts of Hecuba, / When she did suckle Hector, look'd not lovelier / Than Hector's forehead when it spit forth blood . . ." (1.3.40–42). But shocking as they are we recognize them as an inherited Spartan ideal.

Both these women seem to me especially poignant. In their own right they have distinctive voices, and both certainly change and develop. They escape the most common male stereotypes of sex object and victim, and they certainly reveal inner conflicts. They try to shape their destinies; but, since their success is dependent on uncontrollable males, they fail. But their defeats are hardly simply pathetic. More central to their communities than any of the other female candidates for heroism, both are intent on upholding community principles—the one in her loyalty to her husband, the other in her internalization of the Roman patriotic ethic. They may be faulty in their failure to humanize their principles when they conflict with other social values, but they are powerful figures respected, at least at the start, by their communities. Lady Macbeth is rapidly revealed as excessive; and her ambition, like her husband's, may emerge as a precipitator of tragedy. But we do respond to her voice, perhaps even admire her determination and resourcefulness. We may even feel cheated by her abrupt disappearance and want to know more about her last days. And we may give her credit finally for a conscience too sensitive to accept her own crimes. However, her heroism, if it exists, is short lived.

By contrast, even though Volumnia has more lines than Lady Macbeth (310 to 257), we never hear her speak in soliloquy. Some of her speeches may be as shocking as Lady Macbeth's, but she is essentially a public person ruled by society but isolated by her singular role as a public Roman matron. She clearly changes as Rome is threatened. Her conflicts are profoundly moving. She acts finally to shape the destiny of Rome but only at the expense of her son and her hopes. Volumnia does in fact change Rome, but it is for her a crushing victory. Her son expresses his anguish at her action:

> O mother, mother!
> What have you done? Behold the heavens do ope
> The gods look down, and this unnatural scene
> They laugh at. O my mother, mother! O!
> You have won a happy Victory to Rome;
> But for your son, believe it—O, believe it—
> Most dangerously you have with him prevailed. . . . (5.3.182–88)

But after Volumnia's long and eloquent plea for her son to spare Rome, once she has won she does not speak again. There are few more heartbreakingly ironic moments in all of Shakespeare than her return to her city and the empty acclamation of her people:

> Behold our patroness, the life of Rome!
> Call all your tribes together, praise the gods,
> And make triumphant fires! Strew flowers before them!
> [Unshout] the noise that banish'd Martius!
> Repeal him with the welcome of his mother.
> Cry, "Welcome, ladies, welcome!" (5.5.1–6)

She is acclaimed for precisely the victory that she already knows enough to mourn. Volumnia is for me truly a tragic hero. Her effort to support the martial standards of her culture becomes for her poisonous, and the "remedy" she provides is almost unbearable for her. She has no words to express her grief, and perhaps her true tragedy is that she does not die. Her life rather than her death has altered the destiny of her community.

Shakespeare's women fit surprisingly well into the format described by Liebler. They incorporate both poison and remedy. The most notable difference between the genders is the obsessive male concern with female sexuality, a concern that seems to reflect society's fixation on the "purity" and sanctity of the family tree. Women's obsessions are broader. Sex certainly figures, but a broader sense of family dominates. Husbands, parents, and children are what move women to action.

These concerns no doubt relate to actual events of the period, and I should like to end with a discussion of three plays that I think show a connection with the events of 1613 and the years preceding. I have described these events and public reactions in great detail elsewhere ("Marriage and Divorce," 161–78), but briefly I suggest that the publication of John Marston's *The Insatiate Countess,* John Webster's *White Devil,* and Elizabeth Cary's *Mariam*[5] may be linked to Frances Howard's career as wife of Robert Devereux, Earl of Essex, her instigation of successful annulment proceedings against him in 1613, her rapid remarriage to Robert Carr in the same year, and her trial in 1616 for the 1613 murder of Sir Thomas Overbury.

Howard was married to Essex when she was 13, but during his protracted absence abroad she early excited gossip and sustained prurient interest.[6] As early as 1606 she is said to have prostituted herself to Prince Henry and soon after was thought to have taken up with Robert Carr, a favorite of King James who later created Carr Earl of Somerset. However, as late as the annulment trial Howard claimed to be *virgo intacta* because her husband was impotent with her. She actually submitted to a virginity test possibly similar to the rigged test in *The Changeling,* and was (with the intervention of James) granted the annulment. At a later trial in 1616 she admitted to complicity in the 1613 murder of Sir Thomas Overbury who had opposed the annulment. Whatever the truth, gossip, scurrilous poetry, and jokes were rampant; and the assumption of her lasciviousness was widespread. An obscene contemporary verse refers to Howard in the virginity test as

> She that could reek within the sheets of lust,
> And there be searched, yet pass without mistrust;
> She that could surfle up the ways of sin
> And make strait posterns where wide gates had been. (LeComte 211)

And similar cynicism is expressed by another:

> There was a court lady of late
> That none could enter she was so strait
> But now with use she is grown so wide
> There is a passage for a Carr to ride. (LeComte 133)

Barely disguised by humor, the revulsion and fear reflected in these verses is echoed in the three tragedies.

The idea of a woman in effect divorcing her husband was almost unheard of, although Penelope Rich had persuaded her husband to divorce her in 1605 after she had left him to live with another man. The threat of Howard's actions to the patriarchal fabric was sensational and widely discussed. She herself may have demonstrated the qualities of a tragic hero. Her actions clearly seemed poisonous to many, but she did, in fact, find a remedy to a bad marriage and demonstrate a certain exhilarating courage and self-confidence. If she did not change her society, she did offer a prophetic glimpse of future developments.

All three of the plays in question, probably written earlier, were published in 1612–13. Two were sold by the same publisher. All three deal with wives who have disposed of their husbands and moved on to one, two, or three lovers. In the two plays by males the central female character has essentially one characterizing trait—lechery. The play by a woman features a major character, Salome, who speaks eloquently in favor of divorce, who has choreographed the death of her first husband, and who manages in the end to have her current husband executed so that she can take up with husband number three. She, however, is balanced against the chaste and virtuous Mariam.

Marston and Webster may have been inspired by Howard's affairs. Although Marston's play cannot have originated later than 1608 when he retired from the stage, it seems to have been revised by hired hacks and published in 1613. Interestingly it was reprinted in 1616, the year of Howard's second trial. Webster's play was performed in 1612 with little success and printed the same year. The two plays seem to have some relation to each other, but the relation is unclear.[7] Neither play seems to have been a great success with audiences. Georgio Melchiori (1984) has suggested that Thomas Archer, the publisher, collected derelict playscripts for publication. The Howard trial may have provided a reading audience for these two works. Cary's play was probably written between 1602 and 1606 but not printed until 1613. My suggestion is that the publication of all three plays was motivated by hope of profit from the scandal of the Howard divorce. It is worth noting that Shakespeare's *Henry VIII,* a reminder of a famous husband-initiated divorce, was probably written and definitely performed in 1613.

Of all the plays that center on the sexuality of female characters, none is more extreme or more single-minded than *The Insatiate Countess.* It focuses on questions of sexual fidelity on two levels, a main plot about the lustful Countess and a subplot about the failed sexual adventures of middle-class men in their pursuit of cleverly faithful women. The Countess Isabella, in the title role, has really only one distinguishing trait. Her lust is demonstrated at considerable length as she moves from a dead husband to a second marriage and to a succession of three lovers. She has twice as many lines (550) as any other character in the play, and she is awesomely active. We first see her in black supposedly in mourning for her late husband. But she quickly corrects that view:

> I wail his loss! Sink him ten cubits deeper,
> I may not fear his resurrection:
> I will be sworn upon the Holy Writ
> I mourn thus fervent, 'cause he died no sooner:
> He buried me alive,
> And mewed me up like Cretan Dedalus,
> And with wall-eyed Jealousy kept me from hope
> Of any waxen wings to fly to pleasure.
> But now his soul her Argos eyes hath closed,
> And I am free as air. (1.1.43–52)

She rushes into matrimony again with Roberto, but at her wedding feast Guido catches her eye. She instantly transfers her affection, declaring,

> My heart's on fire, and unto mine eyes
> The raging flames ascend, like to two Beacons,
> Summoning my strongest powers, but all too late:
> The conqueror already opes the gate. (2.1.113–17)

She goes to her nuptial bed imagining that " . . . when my loathed mate / Shall struggle in due pleasure for his right, / I'll think't my love, and die in that delight" (2.2.256–58). Isabella moves on from Guido to Gniaca, to Sago, persuading Sago to kill Guido, who has tarnished her reputation. Significantly, the murderer is pardoned, but his inciter is condemned to death—apparently not for murder but for lust. The Duke pronounces an irreversible sentence, spelling out her offenses:

> O Heavens!
> Is she not weary yet of lust and life?
> . . . . her lust
> Would make a slaughter house of Italy.
> Ere she attained to four and twenty years,
> Three earls, one viscount, and this valiant Spaniard
> Are known to ha' been the fuel to her lust:
> Besides her secret lovers, which charitably
> I judge to have been but few, but some they were. (5.1.50–66)

On the scaffold the Countess blithely asks for a reprieve:

> You're all for this world, then why not I?
> Were you in health and youth, like me, my Lord,
> Although you merited the crown of life
> And stood in state of grace, assured of it,
> Yet in this fearful separation,

> Old as you are, e'en to your latest gasp,
> You'd crave the help of the physician,
> And wish your days lengthened one summer longer,
> Though all be grief, labour and misery,
> Yet none will part with it, that I can see. (5.1.115–24)

Failing a reprieve, she prays for a pardon, asking the Duke to show [his] creator's image and be like Him the Father of mercy (5.1.139–40). She also asks pardon of her abandoned husband who has retired to a monastery, conceding,

> Had I with you enjoyed the lawful pleasure,
> To which belongs, nor fear, nor public shame,
> I might have lived in honour, died in fame.
> Your pardon on my falt'ring knees I beg,
> Which shall confirm more peace unto my death,
> Than all the grave instructions of the Church. (5.1.185–90)

And she dies certain of salvation:

> Murder and Lust, down with my ashes sink,
> But like ingrateful seed perish in earth,
> That you may never spring against my soul,
> Like weeds to choke it in the heavenly harvest;
> I fall to rise, mount to thy Maker, spirit,
> Leave here thy body, death has her demerit. (5.1.220–25)

The female portraits in the play are not all one-sided. The three women of the subplot are clever, virtuous, and faithful, although they too are presented primarily as objects of sexual desire. But the men in both plots are so stupid, besotted, foolishly rash, and inanely macho that Isabella shines in comparison. It may be a bit hard to identify lust, honesty, and self-esteem as heroism, but Isabella's sheer exuberance in her zest for the pleasures of life and the proliferation of her speeches, often spoken alone, have their appeal as does her nearly guiltless enjoyment of her hobby. Her death promises to cut down significantly on unbridled lust, but it also seems to promise her own absolution. She is certainly one-dimensional, but I am willing to think of her as a hero, however sadly undeveloped. She may even fit the poison/remedy pattern since it seems possible that her death may temporarily exorcise the pervasive lust and suspicion that characterize the males of the community. In truth, though she may be more of a male fantasy than a character, she could have been lifelike enough to remind readers and audiences of the reputation of Frances Howard.

By comparison with Isabella, Vittoria Corombona of Webster's *The White Devil* (1996) seems relatively tame. Although presumably the title character, she has only 270 lines, whereas her brother Flamineo has more than 900. And her character is curiously blank. She never speaks alone to the audience, and we are never quite sure how much she has had to do with the murder of her first husband or indeed exactly how she feels about the second. Like Isabella in Marston, she is tried for lust rather than murder, and her lover apparently escapes trial altogether. The trial is her great scene. She shows independence and anger, rejects the charges of her accusers, and, as the English ambassador concludes, "She hath a brave spirit" (3.2.140). Refusing guilt, she challenges her judge,

> Terrify babes, my lord, with painted devils,
> I am past such needless palsy; for your names
> Of whore and murd'ress, they proceed from you,
> As if a man should spit against the wind,
> The filth returns in's face. (3.2.147–50)

And after being condemned anyway to a house of convertites (reformed whores), she boasts,

> It shall not be a house of convertites.
> My mind shall make it honester to me
> Than the Pope's palace, and more peaceable
> Than thy soul, though thou art a cardinal,
> Know this, and let it somewhat raise your spite,
> Through darkness diamonds spread their richest light. (3.2.28–34)

This trial has something of the tone of Frances Howard's, arousing a similar shadow of doubt over the protestations. Of course, Howard was not on trial for her life, and Vittoria did not have a powerful king on her side. But the two women, one real and one fictional, are similarly objects of male suspicion of female lust and the effort to control it.

Soon after the trial, like a haunting reprise, Vittoria's lover/husband falsely accuses her of infidelity. She lashes out at him angrily, and in a line eerily reminiscent of Iago declares, "I'll speak not one word more" (4.2.187). And indeed her speech is dramatically reduced for the rest of the play. She rallies briefly before her death to insist "I will not in my death shed one base tear, / Or if look pale, for want of blood not fear" (5.6.223–24). Unlike Marston's Isabella, she never speaks of her lust—in fact one wonders if she has moved rather passively from husband to lover at his initiative more than hers. We hear much more loudly the misogynistic voices of the men—all apparently

terrified by their fear of female sexuality. Flamineo is probably the most eloquent on this subject. He sums up his position in one of his last speeches:

> O men
> That lie upon your death-beds, and are haunted
> With howling wives, ne'r trust them; they'll remarry
> Ere the worm pierce your winding sheet; ere the spider
> Make a thin curtain for your epitaphs.
> . . . Trust a woman? Never, never;
> . . . we lay our souls to pawn to the devil for a little
> pleasure, and a woman makes the bill of sale. (5.6.152–61)

If Vittoria is a tragic hero, and I think she does barely qualify, she seems
as much victim as villain. She acquiesces more than acts in the acceptance of
a lover and the murder of her first husband. Her voice becomes muted. And
if her acts are poisonous to her society, her death provides no remedy. She
can only conclude "My soul, like to a ship in a black storm, / Is driven I
know not whither" (5.5.246–47).

Portraits of possible female tragic heroes are not necessarily ambiguous.
In late 1613 Webster depicted the career of another Italian noblewoman in
his greatest play, *The Duchess of Malfi* (1965). The Duchess is brave, strong-
minded, and heroic, but she too is tainted in the eyes of surrounding men,
in this case her brothers, by their discovery of a sexuality that has driven her
to marry in secret a man of inferior degree. In the same year Shakespeare and
Fletcher's *Two Noble Kinsmen* features Emilia, another innocent woman who
exists in the play to inspire sexual infatuation and rivalry in the two kinsmen. Neither of these plays, however, seems relevant to the Howard divorce.

Elizabeth Cary's *Mariam* (1994) is unique in its female authorship. It is also
probably the product of a somewhat earlier period than the other two. In
many ways it is an extraordinary exception to the pattern we have been tracing. In the beginning, Herod the patriarch is absent and the climate is relatively peaceful. We are presented at first with a world of women. All is not
sweetness and light, but people are thinking radical thoughts. Mariam and her
mother are more worried about dynastic history, family, and status than lust.
Mariam debates whether she is happy or sad that her husband is supposed
dead. She rejects the idea that she might envy the power and career of Cleopatra. Even when Salome appears, the conversation is mainly about ancestry.
Outside the family, young love between Pheroras and Graphina, specified as
virginal but previously forbidden by Herod, seems poised to prosper. It is soon
clear, however, that Salome is driven by lust, and that having disposed of Jose-
phus, her first husband, she is musing about divorcing the second. Her famous
lines on divorce suggest why this play might have been printed for the enter-
tainment of those following Howard's annulment proceedings,

> Why should the privilege to men be given?
> Or given to them, why barr'd from women then?
> Are men than we in greater grace with Heaven?
> Or cannot women hate as well as men?
> I'll be the custom-breaker: and begin
> To show my sex the way to freedom's door,
> And with an off'ring will I purge my sin;
> The law was made for none but who are poor. (1.4.305–12)

Salome, unlike Marston's Isabella, seems less really lustful, however, than practical. But she is, like Isabella, strong-minded. When her husband expresses society's view, she affirms her confidence in her own powers:

> Constabarus. You are the first, and will, I hope, be last,
> That ever sought her husband to divorce.
> Salome. I mean not to be led by precedent,
> My will shall be to me instead of Law. (1.6.451–54)

The fixation on lustful women really enters the play only with the men—with Salome's husband Constabarus and with the return of Herod. Constabarus, who has some cause, utters the standard line that women are made "to be the human curse" (4.6.315) and accuses them of much more than just lechery: "You are the wreck of order, breach of laws. / [Your] best are foolish, froward, wanton, vain, / Your worst adulterous, murderous, cunning, proud . . ." (4.6.332–34). But even Herod, who allows Salome to command Mariam's death because he believes in her infidelity, never voices his fear of her lust with the violence of an Othello or a Flamineo. He waffles endlessly, crediting her virtues at greater length than her imagined vice. His strongest condemnation is: "She is deceitful, light as vanity: / Oh, she was made for nothing but a bait, / To train some hapless man to misery" (4.7.490–92).

In fact, Mariam's "sin" is foreswearing her husband's bed; but, in spite of her very ambivalent feelings toward him, she concludes that she has been wrong, and has brought about her own fate:

> Had I but with humility been grac'd,
> As well as fair I might have prov'd me wise:
> But I did think because I knew me chaste,
> One virtue for a woman might suffice. (4.8.559–62)

Mariam is certainly a tragic hero. She has long soliloquies that reveal both her feelings and especially her conflicts. She acts on an impressively brave conviction that she is a free agent, and her very vacillation makes her seem believable. She escapes briefly from conformity to the law of female sub-servience to even a tyrannous male, but she is drawn back inexorably. Her rejection of her husband's marital rights may be as transiently "poisonous" to her society as it is to Herod. He does agonize interminably, but no rem-edy is provided unless his celebration of her in death may show some dawn of real recognition.

Elizabeth Cary's great achievement is to imagine a multifaceted female hero who displays resentment, female rivalry, concern for her children, pride, guilt, and a gift for asexual friendship with males. Her sexuality is of major significance only to Herod, and even he focuses on other qualities as well. Mariam is ultimately a victim, but Cary has balanced her with the vil-lainous Salome (they have almost exactly the same number of lines—245 to 240), who might herself be a tragic hero if she were tragic. But she seems to end happily, poised for a third marriage, blamed by Herod for envy of Mariam, but apparently a survivor. One can only wonder how a Renaissance audience might have compared her to Frances Howard who won her di-vorce, married her lover, and only later was confined to the Tower for her complicity in murder.

Ironically and perhaps prophetically, Herod, who doesn't even enter the play until act 4, has twice as many lines as Mariam and Salome combined. Patriarchy is firmly reestablished. It is a little disappointing to discover or re-discover the limitations of female tragic heroes. Although there are genuine flashes of heroism in both Salome and Mariam, we are also confronted forcibly with the reality of the special dilemmas posed by the limits of female choice. If Salome is poisonous, her remedies are presumably unacceptable to her audience; and if Mariam is poisonous in rejecting her husband, this "remedy" was probably also unacceptable to the original audience. The com-munity remains unchanged.

I end with a new appreciation of tragic women who do not fit neatly into stereotypes: Tamora, Juliet, Lady Macbeth, Cleopatra, Volumnia, Isabella, the Duchess of Malfi, and in particular Salome and Mariam. These women can be judged by some of the same criteria as male tragic heroes. Each of them moves out of her presumed place in the community—a place already on the fringes—and in so doing threatens to be poisonous. But the over-whelming majority are stopped short of providing remedy. For most of them their sexuality is crucial and in fact probably still adds to their interest to both genders. Judging by my experience with students, it is hard to generate sympathy for the asexual Lady Macbeth and Volumnia. But in these plays sexuality breeds death, and ambivalence toward sexuality is at the root of most female tragedy—the poison that rarely promises remedy. Elizabeth Cary stands alone, not only as a female playwright, but as one who, while exposing us to one of the dullest male "heroes" in drama, leaves us with an intriguing double vision of the complexity of the female. She reveals with shocking clarity the two unsatisfactory solutions to the female problem: neither the unwilling sex object nor the free-thinking manipulator of men can provide a remedy for the irresolvable double bind generated by the male need of female sexuality and his paralyzing fear of it.

Notes

1. The question of the development of self-consciousness in the Renaissance has been much debated, going back at least to Jacob Burckhardt's essay in 1860. See 1944 reprint. A brief selection of other contributors important to drama would include Stephen J. Greenblatt, Catherine Belsey, Naomi J. Miller, Roy Porter, and Elizabeth Hanson. It is hard to imagine deliberate depiction of subjectivity without some conception of self-consciousness.

2. See especially Liebler's note on *Romeo and Juliet* in *Shakespeare's Festive Tragedy,* 148–55.

3. All quotations from Shakespeare refer to *The Riverside Shakespeare.*

4. Quoted from a phone interview, *The Washington Post,* May 18, 1999, C5.

5. *Mariam* was the first book published by new publisher Richard Hawkins; *The White Devil* was published by its author and sold by Thomas Archer, who also published and sold *The Insatiate Countess.*

6. Frances Howard's reputation has suffered from an almost universal bad press: see for example Edward LeComte. For a more sympathetic portrait see David Lindley.

7. Giorgio Melchiori discusses this in some detail in his edition of *The Insatiate Countess,* 1984, 30–39. It is interesting that Marston changed the rank of his central character from the lady of his source to Countess, the appropriate title for the wife of an Earl.

Contributors

LAURA DENKER is an editor and writer who lives in Ottawa, Ontario.

MIMI STILL DIXON is Professor of English at Wittenberg University. She has published articles on medieval drama and Shakespeare. The present essay is part of a longer study of verbal and visual constructions of female subjectivity in medieval and Renaissance drama.

NAOMI CONN LIEBLER is Professor of English and University Distinguished Scholar at Montclair State University. She is the author of *Shakespeare's Festive Tragedy: the Ritual Foundations of Genre* (1995) and of articles on Shakespeare and other early modern authors, and coeditor, with John Drakakis, of *Tragedy* (1998). She is currently working on a critical edition of Richard Johnson's *Seven Champions of Christendom.*

LAURIE MAGUIRE is Tutorial Fellow in English at Magdalen College, Oxford. She is the author of *Shakespearean Suspect Texts* (1996) and the coeditor, with Thomas L. Berger, of *Textual Formations and Reformations* (1998).

ROBERT S. MIOLA is the Gerard Manley Hopkins Professor of English at Loyola College in Maryland. He has published books and articles on classical backgrounds to Renaissance literature, especially Shakespeare. He is currently editing *The Case is Altered* for the Cambridge Ben Jonson and compiling an anthology of male and female writers called *The Catholic Renaissance.*

MARTIN ORKIN is the author of *Shakespeare Against Apartheid: Drama and the South African State* and coeditor of *Post-Colonial Shakepeare.* Currently he is head of the Department of Theatre at the University of Haifa.

JEANNE ADDISON ROBERTS, Emerita Professor of Literature at American University, is the author of *The Shakespearean Wild: Geography, Genus, and Gender,* and most recently of forthcoming articles on the Crone in English Renaissance drama and on Elizabeth Cary's *Mariam* as a Revenge Tragedy.

KAY STANTON, a professor of English at California State University at Fullerton, has spoken on Shakespeare in six countries, and has presented over 60 professional conference papers. She has published on Shakespeare, Marlowe, Milton, and Arthur Miller and is completing her book *Shakespeare's "Whores": Spirited Erotics, Politics, and Poetics.*

THERESIA DE VROOM is Marymount Chair for Faith, Culture, and the Arts at Loyola Marymount University. She has written articles on medieval and Renaissance drama and she is currently completing a book called *"The Lady Vanishes": Fantasies of Female Heroism in Shakespeare's Last Plays.*

JUDITH WEIL is Professor of English at the University of Manitoba. She is the author of *Christopher Marlowe: Merlin's Prophet* (1977) and coeditor, with Herbert Weil, of the New Cambridge *King Henry IV, Part One* (1997). She is currently working on a study of service and dependency in Shakespeare's plays.

LINDA WOODBRIDGE is Professor of English at Pennsylvania State University. Her publications include *Women and the English Renaissance: Literature and the Nature of Womankind, 1540–1620* (1984); *True Rites and Maimed Rites: Ritual and Anti-Ritual in the Age of Shakespeare* (coedited, 1992); *The Scythe of Saturn: Shakespeare and Magical Thinking* (1994); *Vagrancy, Homelessness, and Renaissance Literature* (2001). She is a former president of the Shakespeare Association of America.

Works Cited

Adams, H. *English Domestic and Homiletic Tragedy 1575–1652.* New York: Columbia UP, 1943.

Adelman, Janet. *The Common Liar: An Essay on* Antony and Cleopatra. New Haven: Yale UP, 1973.

———. *Suffocating Mothers: Fantasies of Maternal Origin in Shakespeare's Plays "Hamlet" to "The Tempest."* New York and London: Routledge, 1992.

Aeschylus. *The Eumenides.* Trans. Richmond Lattimore. Greek Tragedies Volume 3. Ed. David Grene and Richmond Lattimore. Chicago: U of Chicago P, 1960. 1–41.

Amussen, S. D. "Gender: Family and the Social Order, 1560–1725." In *Order and Disorder in Tudor and Stuart England.* Cambridge: Cambridge UP, 1985.

Anderson, Bonnie S. and Judith P. Zinsser. *A History of Their Own: Women in Europe from Prehistory to the Present.* Vol. 1. New York and London: Penguin, 1988.

Aristotle. *Poetics.* Trans. Kenneth A. Telford. Chicago: Henry Regnery, 1968.

Arrowsmith, William. Introduction to *Hecuba.* By Euripides. *Euripides III.* Ed. David Grene and Richmond Lattimore. Chicago: U of Chicago P, 1960. 2–7.

Arrowsmith, William and Herbert Golder. Foreword. *Hecuba.* By Euripides. Trans. Janet Lembke and Kenneth J. Reckford. New York: Oxford UP, 1991. v-ix.

Arthur, Marilyn B. "The Curse of Civilization: The Choral Odes of the *Phoenissae.*" *Harvard Studies in Classical Philology* 81 (1977): 163–93.

Ashcroft-Nowicki, Dolores. *The Tree of Ecstasy: An Advanced Manual of Sexual Magic.* York Beach, Maine: Weiser, 1999.

Aston, Trevor, ed. *"Crisis in Europe 1560–1660": Essays from Past and Present.* London: Routledge and Kegan Paul, 1965.

Atkinson, David. "An Approach to the Main Plot of Thomas Heywood's *A Woman Killed With Kindness.*" *English Studies* 70 (1989): 15–27.

———. "Moral Knowledge and the Double Action in *The Witch of Edmonton.*" *SEL* 25 (1985): 419–37.

Aughterson, Kate, ed. *Renaissance Woman: A Sourcebook.* London and New York: Routledge, 1995.

Austin, William. *Haec Homo Wherein the Excellency of the creation of Woman is described by way of an Essaie.* London. Printed for R[alph] M[abbe], 1639. (STC 976)

Bakhtin, M. M. "Author and Hero in Aesthetic Activity" (ca. 1920–23). *Art and Answerability.* Ed. Michael Holquist and Vadim Liapunov. Trans. Vadim Liapunov. Austin: U of Texas P, 1990. 4–256.

Bamber, Linda. *Comic Women, Tragic Men: A Study of Gender and Genre in Shakespeare.* Stanford: Stanford UP, 1982.

Baring, Anne and Jules Lashford. *The Myth of the Goddess: Evolution of an Image.* New York: Penguin, 1993.

Barton, Anne. "'Nature's Piece 'Gainst Fancy': The Divided Catastrophe in *Antony and Cleopatra.*" *An Inaugural Lecture* (to the Hildred Carlile Chair of English Literature in the University of London, Bedford College, October 1972). Rpt. *William Shakespeare's Antony and Cleopatra.* Ed. and intro. Harold Bloom. New York: Chelsea, 1988. 35–55.

Baym, Nina. "The Madwoman and her Languages: Why I Don't Do Feminist Literary Theory" (1984). In *Feminisms: An Anthology of Feminist Literary Criticism.* Ed. Robyn R. Warhol and Diane Price Herndl. New Brunswick: Rutgers UP, 1991.

Beanland, J. "The Sex War in Language." *The Vote* (18 Feb. 1911): 207–8. Rpt. in *Language, Gender, and Professional Writing: Theoretical Approaches and Guidelines for Nonsexist Usage.* Ed. Francine Wattman Frank and Paula A. Treichler. MLA Commission on the Status of Women in the Profession. New York: MLA, 1989. 208.

Behling, Laura L. "'S/He Scandals Our Proceedings': The Anxiety of Alternative Sexualities in *The White Devil and The Duchess of Malfi.*" *English Language Notes* 33 (1996): 24–43.

Belfiore, Elizabeth S. *Tragic Pleasures: Aristotle on Plot and Emotion.* Princeton: Princeton UP, 1992.

Belsey, Catherine. "Alice Arden's Crime." *Renaissance Drama* 13 (1982): 83–102.

———. "Emblem and Antithesis in 'The Duchess of Malfi.'" *Renaissance Drama* 11 (1980): 115–34.

———. *The Subject of Tragedy: Identity and Difference in Renaissance Drama.* London and New York: Methuen, 1985.

Berger, John. *Ways of Seeing.* London: BBC and Penguin Books, 1972.

Berry, Philippa. *Of Chastity and Power: Elizabethan Literature and the Unmarried Queen.* London and New York: Routledge, 1989.

———. *Shakespeare's Feminine Endings: Disfiguring Death in the Tragedies.* London: Routledge, 1999.

Black, Maria and Rosalind Coward. "Linguistic, Social, and Sexual Relations: A Review of Dale Spender's *Man Made Language.*" In *The Feminist Critique of Language.* Ed. Deborah Cameron. London and New York: Routledge, 1990. 111–33.

Blundell, Sue. *Women in Ancient Greece.* London: British Museum Press, 1995.

Bolgar, R. R. *The Classical Heritage and Its Beneficiaries.* Cambridge: Cambridge UP, 1954.

Bono, Barbara J. *Literary Transvaluation: From Vergilian Epic to Shakespearean Tragicomedy.* Berkeley: U of California P, 1984.

Bourdieu, Pierre. *The Logic of Practice.* Trans. Richard Nice. Stanford: Stanford UP, 1990.

Braden, Gordon. *Renaissance Tragedy and the Senecan Tradition: Anger's Privilege.* New Haven: Yale UP, 1985.

Brockbank, Philip. Introduction. *Coriolanus.* By William Shakespeare. London: Methuen, 1976.

Brodwin, Leonora Leet. "The Domestic Tragedy of Frank Thorney in *The Witch of Edmonton.*" *SEL* 7 (1967): 311–28.

Brody, Alan. *The English Mummers and their Plays: Traces of Ancient Mystery.* Philadelphia: U of Pennsylvania P, 1970.

Bromley, Laura G. "Domestic Conduct in *A Woman Killed with Kindness.*" *Studies in English Literature* 26 (1986): 259–76.

Bronfen, Elizabeth. *Over Her Dead Body: Death, Femininity and the Aesthetic.* Manchester: Manchester UP, 1992.

Brooks, Peter. *The Melodramatic Imagination: Balzac, Henry James, Melodrama, and the Mode of Excess.* New Haven: Yale UP, 1976.

Brown, Arthur. "Thomas Heywood's Dramatic Art." In *Essays on Shakespeare and the Elizabethan Drama in Honor of Hardin Craig.* Ed. Richard Hosley. London: Routledge and Kegan Paul, 1963. 327–40.

Bryan, M. B. "Food Symbolism in *A Woman Killed with Kindness.*" *Renaissance Papers.* Durham: Duke UP, 1974. 9–17.

Burckhardt, Jacob. *The Civilization of the Renaissance in Italy,* 1860. Repr. London: Phaidon, 1944.

Burke, Peter. *Popular Culture in Early Modern Europe.* London: Temple Smith, 1978.

Burton, Robert E. *The Anatomy of Melancholy.* Ed. Thomas C. Faulkner, Nicholas K. Kiessling, and Rhonda L. Blair. Oxford: Clarendon, 1989.

Bushman, Mary Ann. "Representing Cleopatra." *In Another Country: Feminist Perspectives on Renaissance Drama.* Ed. Dorothea Kehler and Susan Baker. Metuchen, New Jersey, and London: Scarecrow, 1991.

Bynum, Carolyn Walker. *Fragmentation and Redemption: Essays on Gender and the Human Body in Medieval Religion.* New York: Zone Books, 1992.

Bynum, Edward Bruce. *The African Unconscious: Roots of Ancient Mysticism and Modern Psychology.* New York and London: Teachers College P, 1999.

Cairncross, A., ed. *The Third Part of King Henry VI.* The Arden Shakespeare. London: Methuen, 1964.

Callaghan, Dympna. *Shakespeare Without Women: Representing Gender and Race on the Renaissance Stage.* London and New York: Routledge, 2000.

———. "The Terms of Gender: 'Gay' and 'Feminist' *Edward II.*" *Feminist Readings of Early Modern Culture: Emerging Subjects.* Ed. Valerie Traub, M. Lindsay Kaplan, and Dympna Callaghan. Cambridge: Cambridge UP, 1996. 275–301.

———. *Woman and Gender in Renaissance Tragedy: A Study of "King Lear," "Othello," "The Duchess of Malfi" and "The White Devil."* Atlantic Highlands, New Jersey: Humanities Press, 1989.

Camera Obscura: The Spectatrix (1989) 20–21.

Cameron, Deborah. *Feminism and Linguistic Theory.* New York: St. Martin's P, 1985.

Cameron, Deborah, ed. *The Feminist Critique of Language.* London and New York: Routledge, 1990.

Campion, Thomas. *The Description of a Maske* (A poem celebrating the marriage of Frances Howard and Robert Carr). London: 1614

Canuteson, John. "The Theme of Forgiveness in the Plot and Subplot of *A Woman Killed With Kindness.*" *Renaissance Drama* n.s. 2 (1969): 123–41.

Carey, Cecile Williamson. "'Go Break This Lute': Music in Heywood's *A Woman Killed With Kindness.*" *Huntington Library Quarterly* 37 (1974): 111–22.

Cartwright, William. *Comedies, Tragi-comedies, with other Poems.* London: Humphrey Moseley, 1651.

Cary, Elizabeth. *The Tragedy of Mariam.* In Cerasano and Wynne-Davies.

———. *The Tragedy of Mariam, The Fair Queen of Jewry.* Ed. Barry Weller and Margaret W. Ferguson. Berkeley and Los Angeles: U of California P, 1994.

Cavell, Stanley. *Disowning Knowledge in Six Plays of Shakespeare.* Cambridge: Cambridge UP, 1987.

Cavendish, Margaret, Duchess of Newcastle. *Bel In Campo.* In *Playes.* London. J. Martin, J. Allestrye, and T. Dicas. 1662.

Cerasano, Susan P. "Alleyn's Fortune: The Biography of a Playhouse." Diss., U of Michigan, 1981.

Cerasano, S. P., and Marion Wynne-Davies, eds. *Renaissance Drama by Women: Texts and Documents.* London and New York: Routledge, 1996.

Champion, Larry S. *Thomas Dekker and the Traditions of English Drama.* New York: Peter Lang, 1985.

Chaney, Earlyne, and William L. Messick. *Kundalini and the Third Eye: The Eye of the Soul in Antiquity and in the Aquarian Age.* Part 1 by Chaney, Part 2 by Messick. Commerce, Calif.: Stockton, 1980.

Comensoli, Viviana. *"Household Business": Domestic Plays of Early Modern England.* Toronto: U of Toronto P, 1996.

———. "Witchcraft and Domestic Tragedy in *The Witch of Edmonton.*" *The Politics of Gender in Early Modern Europe. Sixteenth-Century Essays and Studies* 12 (1989): 43–60.

Conacher, D. J. *Euripidean Drama: Myth, Theme, and Structure.* Toronto: U of Toronto P, 1967.

Cook, David. "*A Woman Killed with Kindness:* An Unshakespearian Tragedy." *English Studies* 45 (1964): 353–72.

Cornford, Francis M. *The Origin of Attic Comedy.* London: Arnold, 1914.

Cox, John D. and David Scott Kastan, eds. *A New History of Early English Drama.* New York: Columbia UP, 1997.

Cunliffe, John W., ed. *Supposes and Jocasta.* Boston: D.C. Heath, 1906. [Contains Dolce's *Giocasta* and Gascoigne and Kinwelmersh's *Jocasta]*

Cushman, Robert. "The Witch of Edmonton." Directed by Barry Kyle, Royal Shakespeare Company. *Observer* review, reprinted in *London Theatre Record,* 23 September–6 October 1982: 534.

Cutner, Herbert. *A Short History of Sex-Worship.* London: Watts, 1940.

Dawson, Anthony B. "Witchcraft/Bigamy: Cultural Conflict in *The Witch of Edmonton.*" *Renaissance Drama* n.s. 20 (1989): 77–98.

de Certeau, Michel. "The Arts of Dying: Celibatory Machines." In *Heterologies: Discourse on the Other.* Trans. Brian Massumi. Minneapolis: U of Minnesota P, 1986.

de Lauretis, Theresa. *Alice Doesn't: Feminism, Semiotics, Cinema.* Bloomington: Indiana UP, 1984.

de Vroom, Theresia. "Beatrice of Nazareth and the Seven Ways of Loving." *Women Writing in Dutch.* Ed. Kristiane Aercke. New York: Garland, 1994. 61–91.

———. "In the Context of 'Rough Music': The Representation of Unequal Couples in Some Medieval Plays." *European Medieval Drama* 2 (1998): 237–60.

Dekker, Thomas. *The Honest Whore, Part 2*. In *The Dramatic Works of Thomas Dekker*. Ed. Fredson Bowers. Cambridge: Cambridge UP, 1953-.

Dekker, Thomas, with John Ford and William Rowley. *The Witch of Edmonton*. Ed. Peter Corbin and Douglas Sedge. Manchester: Manchester UP, 1986.

Dening, Sarah. *The Mythology of Sex: An Illustrated Exploration of Sexual Customs and Practices from Ancient Times to the Present*. New York: Macmillan, 1996.

DiGangi, Mario. *The Homoerotics of Early Modern Drama*. Cambridge and New York: Cambridge UP, 1997.

Diodorus Siculus. *Diodorus of Sicily in Twelve Volumes with an English Translation*. Ed. and trans. C. H. Oldfather et al. New York and London: The Loeb Classical Library, 1933–67.

Doane, Mary Ann. *The Desire to Desire: The Woman's Film of the 1940s*. Bloomington: Indiana UP, 1987.

———. *Femmes Fatales: Feminism, Film Theory, Psychoanalysis*. New York: Routledge, 1991.

Dolan, Frances E. *Dangerous Familiars. Representations of Domestic Crime in England 1550–1700*. Ithaca: Cornell UP, 1994.

Dolce, Lodovico. *Giocasta*. Venice, 1549.

———. *Giocasta*. In Cunliffe, ed.

———. *Tragedie*. Venice, 1560.

Donaldson, Ian. *The World Upside Down: Comedy from Jonson to Fielding*. Oxford: Oxford UP, 1970.

Donne, John. *John Donne's Poetry*. Ed. Arthur L. Clements. 2nd ed. New York: Norton, 1992.

Doran, Madeleine. *Endeavors of Art*. Madison: U of Wisconsin P, 1954.

Douglas, Mary. *Purity and Danger: An Analysis of the Concepts of Pollution and Taboo*. London: Routledge and Kegan Paul, 1966.

Dusinberre, Juliet. *Shakespeare and the Nature of Women*. 2nd ed. New York and London: St. Martin's P, 1996.

Eisler, Riane. *Sacred Pleasure: Sex, Myth, and the Politics of the Body*. San Francisco: HarperSanFrancisco, 1996.

Elias, Norbert. *The Civilizing Process*. Trans. Edmund Jephcott. New York: Urizen, 1978. First published in German, 1939.

Eliot, T. S. *Essays on Elizabethan Drama*. 1932. Rpt. New York: Harcourt, Brace and World, 1960.

Enterline, Lynn. *The Tears of Narcissus: Melancholia and Masculinity in Early Modern Writing*. Stanford: Stanford UP, 1995.

Erasmus, Desiderio. *Erasmi Epistolae*. Ed. P. S. Allen et al. No. 457, trans. D. F. S. Thomson. Oxford: Oxford UP, 1906–58.

Euripides. *Euripides Poeta*. Basel, 1562.

———. *Euripides with an English Translation*, The Loeb Classical Library. Ed. and trans. Arthur S. Way. Vol. 3. 1912, rpt. 1979.

———. *Hecuba*. Trans. William Arrowsmith. *Euripides III*. Ed. David Grene and Richmond Lattimore. Chicago: U of Chicago P, 1960. 1–68.

———. *Hecuba.* Trans. Janet Lembke and Kenneth J. Reckford. New York: Oxford UP, 1991.

———. *Hecuba & Iphigenia in Aulide.* Trans. Desiderius Erasmus. Venice, 1507.

———. *Iphigenia in Aulide.* Trans. Jane Lumley (1555). Ed. H. H. Child, Malone Society Reprints, 1909; ed. Gustav Becker, *Shakespeare Jahrbuch* 44 (1910): 28–59.

———. *Phoenissae.* Ed. Donald J. Mastronarde. Cambridge: Cambridge UP, 1994.

Ficino, Marsilio. *Opera Omnia.* Basel: Adam Henripetri, 1576.

Findlay, Alison. *A Feminist Perspective on Renaissance Drama.* Oxford: Blackwell, 1999.

Fitz, L. T. (Linda Woodbridge). "Egyptian Queens and Male Reviewers: Sexist Attitudes in *Antony and Cleopatra* Criticism," *Shakespeare Quarterly* 28 (1977): 297–316.

Foley, Helene P. *Ritual Irony: Poetry and Sacrifice in Euripides.* Ithaca: Cornell UP, 1985.

Foucault, Michel. *Discipline and Punish: The Birth of the Prison.* Trans. Alan Sheridan. 2nd ed. London: Penguin, 1991.

———. "What Is an Author?" In *Language, Countermemory, Practice.* Trans. D. F. Bouchard and S. Simon, ed. D. F. Bouchard. Oxford: Basil Blackwell, 1977.

Freedberg, David. *The Power of Images: Studies in the History and Theory of Response.* Chicago and London: U of Chicago P, 1991.

Freud, Sigmund. "The Question of Lay Analysis." *Standard Edition of the Complete Psychological Works of Sigmund Freud.* Ed. James Strachey. London: Hogarth P, 1959. 20:212.

Friedrich, Paul. *The Meaning of Aphrodite.* Chicago and London: U of Chicago P, 1978.

Frye, Susan. *Elizabeth I: The Competition for Representation.* Oxford and New York: Oxford UP, 1993.

Gajowski, Evelyn. *The Art of Loving: Female Subjectivity and Male Discursive Traditions in Shakespeare's Tragedies.* Newark: U of Delaware P, 1992.

Garber, Marjorie. *Vested Interests: Cross Dressing and Cultural Anxiety.* London and New York: Routledge, 1992; repr. Harper Perennial, 1993.

Garner, Shirley Nelson and Madelon Sprengnether, eds. *Shakespearean Tragedy and Gender.* Bloomington: Indiana UP, 1996.

Garrard, Mary. *Artemisia Gentileschi: The Image of the Female Hero In Italian Baroque Art.* Princeton: Princeton UP, 1989.

Gascoigne, George. *A Hundreth Sundrie Flowres.* 1573.

Gascoigne, George. *Jocasta.* In Cunliffe, ed.

Gohlke, Madelon. "'I wooed thee with my sword': Shakespeare's Tragic Paradigm." In *The Woman's Part: Feminist Criticism of Shakespeare.* Ed. Carolyn Ruth Swift Lenz, Gayle Greene, Carol Thomas Neely. Urbana and Chicago: U of Illinois P, 1983.

Goldhill, Simon. *Reading Greek Tragedy.* Cambridge: Cambridge UP, 1986.

Gowing, Laura. *Domestic Dangers: Women, Words, and Sex in Early Modern England.* Oxford: Clarendon, 1996.

Grande, Troni Y. *Marlovian Tragedy: The Play of Dilation*. Lewisburg, Penn. and Cranbury, New Jersey: Bucknell UP, 1999.

Green, Lyn. "Isis, the Egyptian Goddess Who Endured in the Græco-Roman World." *KMT: A Modern Journal of Ancient Egypt* 5.4 (1994): 60–70.

Greenblatt, Stephen. "Invisible Bullets: Renaissance Authority and its Subversion," *Glyph* 8 (1981): 40–61.

Greenblatt, Stephen J. *Renaissance Self-Fashioning: From More to Shakespeare*. Chicago: U of Chicago P, 1980.

Grigson, Geoffrey. *The Goddess of Love: The Birth, Triumph, Death and Return of Aphrodite*. London: Constable, 1976.

Guillaume, Jean. "Cleopatra Nova Pandora," *Gazette Des Beaux-Arts*, October 1972, 185–94.

Gutierrez, Nancy C. "Exorcism by Fasting in *A Woman Killed with Kindness:* A Paradigm of Puritan Resistance?" *Research Opportunities in Renaissance Drama* 23 (1994): 43–62.

———. "The Irresolution of Melodrama: The Meaning of Adultery in *A Woman Killed with Kindness*," *Exemplaria* 1 (Fall 1989): 265–91.

———. "Philomela Strikes Back: Adultery and Mutilation as Female Self-Assertion." *Women's Studies* 16 (1989): 429–43.

Hall, Kim F. *Things of Darkness: Economies of Race and Gender in Early Modern England*. Ithaca and London: Cornell UP, 1995.

Hanson, Elizabeth. *Discovering the Subject in Renaissance England*. Cambridge: Cambridge UP, 1998.

Harbage, Alfred. *Shakespeare and the Rival Traditions*. New York: Macmillan, 1952.

Harbage, Alfred and Samuel Schoenbaum, eds. *Annals of English Drama 975–1700*. London: Methuen, 1964.

Hart, Lynda. "Introduction: Performing Feminism." In *Making a Spectacle: Feminist Essays on Contemporary Women's Theatre*. Ed. Lynda Hart. Ann Arbor: U of Michigan P, 1992.

Haslem, Lori Schroeder. "'Troubled with the Mother': Longings, Purgings, and the Maternal Body in *Bartholomew Fair* and *The Duchess of Malfi.*" *Modern Philology* 92 (1995): 438–59.

Hattaway, Michael. "Drama and Society." *The Cambridge Companion to English Renaissance Drama*. Ed. A. R. Braunmuller and Michael Hattaway. Cambridge: Cambridge UP, 1990. 91–126.

Hawkins, Harriett. *Poetic Freedom and Poetic Truth: Chaucer, Shakespeare, Marlowe, Milton*. Oxford: Clarendon, 1976.

Hazlitt, W. *Lectures on the Dramatic Literature in the Age of Elizabeth* (1818). New York: Derby and Jackson, 1859.

Heal, Felicity. *Hospitality in Early Modern England*. Oxford: Clarendon, 1990.

Heilman, Robert Bechtold. *The Iceman, the Arsonist, and the Troubled Agent: Tragedy and Melodrama on the Modern Stage*. Seattle: U of Washington P, 1973.

———. *Tragedy and Melodrama: Versions of Experience*. Seattle and London: U of Washington P, 1968.

Helm, Alex. *The English Mummers' Play*. Woodbridge, Suffolk: D. S. Brewer, 1981.

Helms, Lorraine. *Seneca by Candlelight and Other Stories of Renaissance Drama.* Philadelphia: U of Pennsylvania P, 1997.

Hendricks, Margo and Patricia Parker, eds. *Women, "Race," and Writing in the Early Modern Period.* London and New York: Routledge, 1994.

Henke, James T. "John Webster's Motif of 'Consuming.'" *Neuphilologische Mitteilungen* 76 (1975): 625–41.

Herndl, George C. *The High Design: English Renaissance Tragedy and the Natural Law.* Lexington: U of Kentucky P, 1970.

Heywood, Thomas. *Apology for Actors.* London: 1612.

———. *The Fair Maid of the West, Part 1* (ca.1600). Ed. Robert K. Turner, Jr. Regents Renaissance Drama Series. Lincoln: U of Nebraska P, 1968.

———. *A Woman Killed with Kindness.* Ed. Brian Scobie. New Mermaid Ed. London: A. & C. Black, 1985.

Hillman, David and Carla Mazzio. *The Body in Parts: Fantasies of Corporeality in Early Modern Europe.* London and New York: Routledge, 1997.

Hodgdon, Barbara. *The End Crowns All: Closure and Contradiction in Shakespeare's History.* Princeton: Princeton UP, 1991.

Horne, David H., ed. *The Life and Minor Works of George Peele.* New Haven: Yale UP, 1952.

Hornstein, Lillian Herlands, et al. *The Reader's Companion to World Literature.* New York: Mentor, 1956.

Howard, Jean E. *The Stage and Social Struggle in Early Modern England.* New York and London: Routledge, 1994.

Howard, Jean E. and Phyllis Rackin. *Engendering a Nation: A Feminist Account of Shakespeare's English Histories.* New York and London: Routledge, 1997.

Hughes-Hallett, Lucy. *Cleopatra: Histories, Dreams and Distortions.* New York: Harper, 1990.

Hunter, G. K. and S. K. Hunter. *John Webster.* Harmondsworth: Penguin, 1969.

Ions, Veronica. *Egyptian Mythology.* London: Hamlyn, 1968.

Jankowski, Theodora A. "Defining/Confining the Duchess: Negotiating the Female Body in John Webster's *The Duchess of Malfi.*" *Studies in Philology* 87 (1990): 221–45.

Jardine, Lisa. *Still Harping on Daughters, Women and Drama in the Age of Shakespeare.* Sussex: Harvester, 1983. Rpt. New York: Columbia UP, 1989.

———. "Cultural Confusion and Shakespeare's Learned Heroines: 'These are old paradoxes.'" *Shakespeare Quarterly* 38 (1987): 1–18.

Jay, Martin. *Downcast Eyes: The Denigration of Vision in Twentieth-Century French Thought.* Berkeley: U of California P, 1993.

Jespersen, Otto. *The Philosophy of Grammar.* 1924. New York: Norton, 1965.

Jones, Ann Rosalind. "Italians and Others." *Staging the Renaissance: Reinterpretations of Elizabethan and Jacobean Drama.* Ed. David Scott Kastan and Peter Stallybrass. London and New York: Routledge, 1991.

Jones, Emrys. *The Origins of Shakespeare.* Oxford: Clarendon, 1977.

Jones, Robert C. *These Valiant Dead: Renewing the Past in Shakespeare's Histories.* Iowa City: U of Iowa P, 1991.

Kahn, Coppélia. *Roman Shakespeare: Warriors, Wounds, and Women.* London and New York: Routledge, 1997.

Kaplan, E. Ann. *Women and Film: Both Sides of the Camera.* New York, Methuen, 1983.

Kastan, David Scott. "Shakespeare and 'The Way of Womenkind.'" *Daedalus* 111, no. 3 (1982): 115–30.

Kerrigan, John. *Revenge Tragedy: Aeschylus to Armageddon.* Oxford: Clarendon, 1996.

Kimbrough, Robert. *Shakespeare and the Art of Humankindness: The Essay toward Androgyny.* Atlantic Highlands, New Jersey: Humanities, 1990.

Kintz, Linda. *The Subject's Tragedy: Political Poetics, Feminist Theory, and Drama.* Ann Arbor: U of Michigan P, 1992.

Kitto, H. D. F. *Greek Tragedy: A Literary Study.* Garden City: Doubleday, 1954.

Knights, L. C. *Drama and Society in the Age of Jonson.* New York: W. W. Norton, 1937.

Kristeller, Paul Oskar, ed. *Catalogus Translationum et Commentariorum.* 7 vols. Washington, D.C.: Catholic UP, 1960 -.

Lanyer, Aemilia. *The Poems of Aemilia Lanyer.* Ed. Susanne Woods. New York and Oxford: Oxford UP, 1993.

Laqueur, Thomas. *Making Sex: Body and Gender from the Greeks to Freud.* Cambridge, Mass.: Harvard UP, 1990.

LeComte, Edward. *The Notorious Lady Essex.* New York: Dial, 1969.

Le Moyne, Pierre, S. J. *La Gallerie des Femmes Fortes.* 1647. Translated into English as *The Gallery of Heroick Women* by the Marquesse of Winchester. Printed by R. Norton for Henry Seile. London, 1652. Wing L1045.

Lenz, Carolyn Ruth Swift, Gayle Greene, and Carol Thomas Neely, eds. *The Women's Part: Feminist Criticism of Shakespeare.* Urbana: U of Illinois P, 1983.

Lerner, Gerda. *The Creation of Patriarchy.* New York and Oxford: Oxford UP, 1986.

Levin, Richard. *The Multiple Plot in English Renaissance Drama.* Chicago: U of Chicago P, 1971.

Lévi-Strauss, Claude. *The Savage Mind.* 2nd ed. Chicago: U of Chicago P, 1960.

Liebler, Naomi Conn. *Shakespeare's Festive Tragedy: The Ritual Foundations of Genre.* London and New York: Routledge, 1995.

Liebler, Naomi Conn and Lisa Scancella Shea. "Shakespeare's Queen Margaret: Unruly or Unruled?" In *Henry VI: Critical Essays.* Ed. Thomas Pendleton. New York and London: Routledge, 2001. 79–96.

Lindley, David. *The Trials of Frances Howard.* London and New York: Routledge, 1993.

Lloyd, Michael. *The Agon in Euripides.* Oxford: Clarendon, 1992.

Lloyd-Jones, Hugh. *The Justice of Zeus.* Berkeley: U of California P, 1971.

Loomba, Ania. "The Color of Patriarchy" in Hendricks and Parker, eds.

Loraux, Nicole. *The Experiences of Tiresias: The Feminine and the Greek Man.* Trans. Paula Wissing. Princeton: Princeton UP, 1995.

———. *Façons Tragiques de Tuer une Femme.* Paris: Hachette, 1985.

———. *Mothers in Mourning. With the essay "Of Amnesty and Its Opposite."* Trans. Corinne Pache. Ithaca: Cornell UP, 1998.

———. *Tragic Ways of Killing a Woman.* Trans. Anthony Forster. Cambridge and London: Harvard UP, 1987, 1991.

Lucas, F. L. *Euripides and His Influence.* New York: Longmans, Green, and Co., 1928.

Luckyj, Christina. *A Winter's Snake: Dramatic Form in the Tragedies of John Webster.* Athens: U of Georgia P, 1989.

Macfarlane, A. *Witchcraft in Tudor and Stuart England.* London and New York: Routledge, 1970.

Maguire, Laurie. "The Girls from Ephesus." In *Comedy of Errors. Critical Essays.* Ed. Robert S. Miola. New York: Garland, 1997. 355–92.

Manniche, Lise. "Divine Reflections of Female Behavior." *KMT: A Modern Journal of Ancient Egypt* 5.4 (1994): 52–59.

Marlowe, Christopher. *Edward the Second.* Ed. W. Moelwyn Merchant. London: Benn, 1967.

———. *The Works and Life of Christopher Marlowe.* Ed. R. H. Case. London: Methuen, 1930–33.

Marotti, Arthur F. "'Love is Not Love': Elizabethan Sonnet Sequences and the Social Order." *ELH* 49 (1982): 396–428.

Marshall, Cynthia. "Wound-Man: Coriolanus, Gender, and the Theatrical Construction of Interiority." In *Feminist Readings of Early Modern Culture: Emerging Subjects.* Ed. Valerie Traub, M. Lindsay Kaplan, and Dympna Callaghan. Cambridge: Cambridge UP, 1996.

Marston, John, et al. *The Insatiate Countess.* Ed. Georgio Melchiori. Manchester: Manchester UP, 1984.

Maus, Katharine Eisaman. *Inwardness and Theater in the English Renaissance.* Chicago and London: U of Chicago P, 1995.

Mayne, Judith. *Cinema and Spectatorship.* London: Routledge. 1993.

Mazzio, Carla. "Sins of the Tongue." In Hillman and Mazzio.

McConnell-Ginet, Sally. "The Sexual (Re)Production of Meaning: A Discourse-Based Theory." In *Language, Gender, and Professional Writing: Theoretical Approaches and Guidelines for Nonsexist Usage.* Ed. Francine Wattman Frank and Paula A. Treichler. The Commission on the Status of Women in the Profession. New York: MLA, 1989. 35–50.

McEachern, Claire. "Fathering Herself: A Source Study of Shakespeare's Feminism." *Shakespeare Quarterly* 39 (1988): 269–90.

McLeod, Randall (Ana Mary Armygram). "The Triumph of King James and his August Descendants." *Shakespeare Quarterly* 52 (2001): (forthcoming).

McLuskie, Kathleen, E. *Dekker and Heywood: Professional Dramatists.* New York: St. Martin's P, 1994.

———. *Renaissance Dramatists.* Atlantic Highlands, New Jersey: Humanities Press, 1989.

———. "'When the Bad Bleed': Renaissance Tragedy and Dramatic Form." In William Zunder and Zuzanne Trill, eds. London: Longman, 1996.

McLuskie, Kathleen E. and Felicity Dunsworth. "Patronage and the Economics of Theatre." In Cox and Kastan, eds. 423–40.

Middleton, Thomas. *The Phoenix. The Works of Thomas Middleton.* Ed. A. H. Bullen. New York: AMS, 1964 (first published 1885).

Mikesell, Margaret. "Catholic and Protestant Widows in *The Duchess of Malfi*." *Renaissance and Reformation/Renaissance et Reforme* 7 (1983): 265–79.

Miller, Casey and Kate Swift. *Words and Women*. Garden City, New York: Anchor/Doubleday, 1976.

Miller, Naomi J. *Changing the Subject: Mary Wroth and Figurations of Gender in Early Modern England*. Lexington: U of Kentucky P, 1996.

Minturno, Antonio Sebastiano. *De Poeta* (1559). Facs. rpt. Munich: W. Fink, 1970.

Mirandola, Giovanni Pico della. *Oration on the Dignity of Man*. 1487. Trans. Charles Glenn Wallis. Indianapolis: Bobbs-Merrill, 1965.

Modleski, Tania. *The Women Who Knew Too Much. Hitchcock and Feminist Theory*. London: Methuen, 1988.

Moi, Toril. *Sexual/Textual Politics: Feminist Literary Theory*. London and New York: Routledge, 1985.

Montrose, Louis Adrian. "Of Gentlemen and Shepherds: The Politics of Elizabethan Pastoral Form." *ELH* 50 (1983): 415–59

———. "'The Perfecte Paterne of a Poete': The Poetics of Courtship in *The Shepheardes Calender*." *Texas Studies in Literature and Language* 21 (1979): 34–67.

Mossman, Judith. *Wild Justice: A Study of Euripides' Hecuba*. Oxford: Clarendon, 1995.

Muir, Kenneth, ed. *Macbeth*. London and New York: Methuen, 1962.

Mulvey, Laura. "Visual Pleasure and Narrative Cinema." *Screen* 16:3 (Autumn 1975): 6–18.

Mussmann, Linda. *M.A.C.B.E.T.H.* Performed by Time & Space Limited at the Cunningham Dance Studio, New York, November 1–18, 1990.

Neill, Michael, ed. and intro. *The Oxford Shakespeare: The Tragedy of Anthony and Cleopatra*. Oxford: Clarendon, 1994.

Newton, Judith, and Deborah Rosenfelt. Introduction. *Feminist Criticism and Social Change: Sex, Class and Race in Literature and Culture*. Ed. Judith Newton and Deborah Rosenfelt. New York: Methuen, 1985. xv–xxxix.

Norbrook, David and H. R. Woudhuysen, eds. *The Penguin Book of Renaissance Verse*. Harmondsworth: Penguin, 1993.

Norland, Howard B. "Formalizing English Farce: *Johan, Johan* and Its French Connection," *Comparative Drama* 17 (Summer 1983): 141–52.

Nussbaum, Martha C. *The Fragility of Goodness: Luck and Ethics in Greek Tragedy and Philosophy*. Cambridge: Cambridge UP, 1986.

———. *Poetic Justice: The Literary Imagination and Public Life*. Boston: Beacon, 1995.

———. *Sex & Social Justice*. New York: Oxford UP, 1999.

Orgel, Stephen. *Impersonations: The Performance of Gender in Shakespeare's England*. Cambridge: Cambridge UP, 1996.

———. "Nobody's Perfect: or Why Did the English Stage Take Boys for Women?" *South Atlantic Quarterly* 88:1 (Winter 1989): 7–29.

Orlin, Lena Cowen. *Private Matters and Public Culture in Post-Reformation England*. Ithaca: Cornell UP, 1994.

———. "Women on the Threshold." *Shakespeare Studies* 25 (1997): 50–58.

Ovid. *The Metamorphoses*. Trans. Frank Justus Miller. 2 vols. London: Heinemann, 1984.

Ozmet, Steven. *When Fathers Ruled: Family Life in Reformation Europe.* Cambridge, Mass.: Harvard UP, 1983.

Padel, Ruth. *In and Out of Mind: Greek Images of the Tragic Self.* Princeton: Princeton UP, 1992.

———. *Whom Gods Destroy.* Princeton: Princeton UP, 1995.

Parker, Patricia. "Gender Ideology, Gender Change: The Case of Marie Germain." *Critical Inquiry* 19 (1993): 337–64.

Parker, R. B. Introduction. *Coriolanus.* By William Shakespeare.

Parker, Robert B. *Miasma: Pollution and Purification in Greek Religion.* Oxford: Clarendon, 1983.

Pechter, Edward. *What Was Shakespeare? Renaissance Plays and Changing Critical Practice.* Ithaca: Cornell UP, 1995.

Penelope, Julia (Stanley). *Speaking Freely: Unlearning the Lies of the Fathers' Tongues.* New York: Pergamon, 1990.

Peterson, Joyce. *Curs'd Example: "The Duchess of Malfi" and Commonweal Tragedy.* Columbia: U of Missouri P, 1978.

Petroff, Elizabeth. *Medieval Women's Visionary Literature.* Oxford: Oxford UP, 1986.

Piper, Watty. *The Little Engine That Could.* New York: Platt and Munk, 1930; rpt. 2000.

Plotnick, Roy E. "In Search of Watty Piper: A Brief History of the 'Little Engine' Story." http://www.uic.edu/orgs/paleo/littleng.htm.

Plutarch. *Plutarch's "De Iside et Osiride."* Ed. and trans. J. Gwyn Griffiths. Cambridge: U of Wales P, 1970.

Pomeroy, Sarah B. *Goddesses, Whores, Wives, and Slaves: Women in Classical Antiquity.* New York: Schocken, 1975.

———. *Women in Hellenistic Egypt: From Alexander to Cleopatra.* Detroit: Wayne State UP, 1990.

Pompanazzi, Pietro. *On the Immortality of the Soul.* Trans. William Henry Hay II, revised by John Herman Randall, Jr. In *The Renaissance Philosophy of Man.* Ed. Ernst Cassirer et al. Chicago: U of Chicago P, 1948. 282–381.

Poole, Adrian. *Tragedy: Shakespeare and the Greek Example.* Oxford: Blackwell, 1987.

Porter, Charlotte E. and Helen A. Clarke. *Shakespeare Studies: Macbeth.* New York: American Book Co., 1901.

Porter, Roy, ed. *Rewriting the Self: Histories from the Renaissance to the Present.* London and New York: Routledge, 1997.

Prouty, C. T. *George Gascoigne: Elizabethan Courtier, Soldier, and Poet.* New York: Columbia UP, 1942.

Rabinowitz, Nancy Sorkin and Amy Richlin, eds. *Feminist Theory and the Classics.* New York and London: Routledge, 1993.

Randall, Dale B. J. "The Rank and Earthy Background of Certain Physical Symbols in *The Duchess of Malfi.*" *Renaissance Drama* 18 (1987): 171–203.

Rawson, Philip. *The Art of Tantra.* London: Thames and Hudson, 1973.

Reeder, Greg. "Musings on the Sexual Nature of the Human-headed Ba Bird." *KMT: A Modern Journal of Ancient Egypt* 9.3 (1998): 72–78.

Roberts, Jeanne Addison. "Marriage and Divorce in 1613: Elizabeth Cary, Frances Howard, and Others." In *Textual Formations and Reformations*. Ed. Laurie E. Maguire and Thomas L. Berger. Newark: U of Delaware P, 1998.

———. *The Shakespearean Wild: Geography, Genus, and Gender*. Lincoln: U of Nebraska P, 1991, rpt. 1994.

Rose, Mary Beth. *The Expense of Spirit: Love and Sexuality in English Renaissance Drama*. Ithaca: Cornell UP, 1988.

Rubinstein, Frankie. *A Dictionary of Shakespeare's Sexual Puns and their Significance*. 2nd ed. New York: St. Martin's P, 1989.

Schleiner, Louise. "Latinized Greek Drama in Shakespeare's Writing of *Hamlet*." *Shakespeare Quarterly* 41 (1990): 29–48.

Scholes, Robert. "The Orgastic Pattern of Fiction." *Fabulation and Metafiction*. Urbana: U of Illinois P, 1979.

Sedgwick, Eve Kosofsky. *Between Men: English Literature and Male Homosocial Desire*. New York: Columbia UP, 1985.

Shakespeare, William. *Antony and Cleopatra*. Ed. John Wilders. The Arden Shakespeare. London and New York: Routledge, 1995.

———. *The Complete Works*. Ed. Alfred Harbage. Baltimore: Penguin Books, 1969.

———. *The Complete Works*. Ed. David Bevington. 4th ed. New York: Longman, 1997.

———. *Coriolanus*. Ed. Philip Brockbank. London: Methuen, 1976.

———. *Coriolanus*. Ed. R. B. Parker. Oxford: Oxford UP, 1994.

———. *The Riverside Shakespeare*. Ed. G. Blakemore Evans. 2nd ed. Boston: Houghton Mifflin, 1997.

———. *The Winter's Tale*. Ed. Stephen Orgel. Oxford: Oxford UP, 1996.

Sharratt, P. and P. G. Walsh, eds. *George Buchanan: Tragedies*. Edinburgh: Scottish Academic P, 1983.

Shepherd, Simon. *Amazons and Warrior Women: Varieties of Feminism in Seventeenth-Century Drama*. Brighton: Harvester, 1981.

Sidney, Mary. *The Tragedie of Antony*. In Geoffrey Bullough, ed. *Narrative and Dramatic Sources of Shakespeare*. 8 vols. London: Routledge and Kegan Paul; New York: Columbia University Press, 1964. Vol. 5.

Smith, Bruce R. *Ancient Scripts & Modern Experience on the English Stage 1500–1700*. Princeton: Princeton UP, 1988.

———. "L[o]cating the Sexual Subject." In *Alternative Shakespeares 2*. Ed. Terence Hawkes. London: Routledge, 1996. 95–121.

———. *Shakespeare and Masculinity*. Oxford Shakespeare Topics. Oxford and New York: Oxford UP, 2000.

Smith, Hallet. "*A Woman Killed with Kindness*." *PMLA* 53 (1938): 138–47.

Spacks, Patricia M. "Honor and Perception in *A Woman Killed with Kindness*." *MLQ* 20 (1959): 321–32.

Spender, Dale. *Man Made Language*. London: Routledge and Kegan Paul, 1980.

Spenser, Edmund. *The Faerie Queene*. Ed. A. C. Hamilton. London and New York: Longman, 1977.

Spevack, Marvin, Michael Steppat, and Marga Munkelt, eds. *A New Variorum Edition of Shakespeare: Antony and Cleopatra.* New York: MLA, 1990.

Stafford, Barbara Maria. *Visual Analogy: Consciousness as the Art of Connecting.* Cambridge, Mass.: MIT, 1999.

Stanton, Kay. "'Made to write "whore" upon?': Male and Female Use of the Word 'Whore' in Shakespeare's Canon." In *A Feminist Companion to Shakespeare.* Ed. Dympna Callaghan. Oxford: Blackwell, 2000. 80–102.

Steen, Sara Jayne. "The Crime of Marriage: Arbella Stuart and *The Duchess of Malfi.*" *The Sixteenth Century Journal* 22 (1991): 61–76.

Steiner, George. *Antigones.* Oxford and New York: Oxford UP, 1984.

Stone, Merlin. *When God Was a Woman.* San Diego: Harcourt, 1976.

Storm, William. *After Dionysus: A Theory of the Tragic.* Ithaca and London: Cornell UP, 1998.

Surridge, Marie E. "Aspects of the Evolution of Feminine Titles in French: From Miresse and Ministresse to the Generic Masculine." In *On the Feminine.* Ed. Mireille Calle. Trans. Catherine McGann. Atlantic Highlands, New Jersey: Humanities Press, 1996. 157–71.

Swinburne, A. C. *The Age of Shakespeare.* London and New York: Harper, 1908.

Telesio, Bernardino. *De Rerum Natura.* Naples: Horatio Salviano, 1587.

Terpening, Ronnie H. *Lodovico Dolce, Renaissance Man of Letters.* Toronto: U of Toronto P, 1997.

Thomas, Keith. *Religion and the Decline of Magic: Studies in Popular Beliefs in Sixteenth and Seventeenth Century England.* London: Weidenfeld & Nicolson, 1971.

Thomas, Sandra P. Introduction. *Women and Anger.* Ed. Sandra P. Thomas. New York: Springer, 1993.

Thompson, E. P. "'Rough Music' et Charivari: Quelques Réflections Complémentaires." *Le Charivari.* Ed. J. le Goff and J. C. Schmitt. Paris, 1981. 251–64.

———. "'Rough Music': Le Charivari Anglais." *Annales* 37 (1972): 285–312.

Townsend, Freda L. "The Artistry of Thomas Heywood's Double Plots." *Philological Quarterly* 25 (1946): 97–119.

Traci, Philip J. *The Love Play of "Antony and Cleopatra": A Critical Study of Shakespeare's Play.* The Hague and Paris: Mouton, 1970.

Treichler, Paula A. "From Discourse to Dictionary: How Sexist Meanings Are Authorized." In *Language, Gender, and Professional Writing: Theoretical Approaches and Guidelines for Nonsexist Usage.* Ed. Francine Wattman Frank and Paula A. Treichler. The Commission on the Status of Women in the Profession. New York: MLA, 1989. 51–79.

Tyson, Lois. *Critical Theory Today.* New York: Garland, 1999.

Underdown, D. E. "The Taming of the Scold: the Enforcement of Patriarchal Authority in Early Modern England." *Order and Disorder in Early Modern England.* Ed. Anthony Fletcher and John Stevenson. Cambridge: Cambridge UP, 1985.

Ure, Peter. "Marriage and the Domestic Drama in Heywood and Ford." *English Studies* 32 (1951): 200–216.

Verrall, A. W. *Euripides the Rationalist.* 1895; rpt. New York: Russell & Russell, 1967.

Virgil. *Aeneid VII-XII, The Minor Poems.* Trans. H. Rushton Fairclough. London: Heinemann, 1934.

Vogel, Paula. Interview in *The Washington Post,* May 18, 1999, C5.

Walker, Julia M., ed. *Dissing Elizabeth: Negative Representations of Gloriana.* Durham and London: Duke UP, 1998.

Warhol, Robyn R. and Diane Price Herndl, eds. *Feminisms: An Anthology of Literary Theory and Criticism.* New Brunswick: Rutgers UP, 1991.

Wayne, Valerie, ed. *The Flower of Friendship: A Renaissance Dialogue Contesting Marriage.* By Edmund Tilney. Ithaca: Cornell UP, 1992.

————, ed. *The Matter of Difference: Materialist Feminist Criticism of Shakespeare.* Hemel Hempstead: Harvester Wheatsheaf, 1991.

Webster, John. *The Duchess of Malfi.* Ed. Elizabeth M. Brennan. New York: Hill and Wang, 1965.

————. *The Duchess of Malfi.* Revels edition. Ed. John Russell Brown. London: Methuen, 1964, 1969.

————. *The White Devil.* Ed. John Russell Brown. Manchester: Manchester UP, 1985, 1996

————. *The White Devil.* Ed. Christina Luckyj. London: A & C Black, 1996.

————. *The White Devil,* with commentary by Simon Trussler and notes by Jacqui Russell. London: Methuen, 1986.

Weil, Judith. "*The White Devil* and Old Wives' Tales." *Modern Language Review* 94 (1999): 328–40.

Weinberg, Bernard. *A History of Literary Criticism in the Italian Renaissance.* 2 Vols. Chicago: U of Chicago P, 1961.

Wells, Robin Headlam. *Elizabethan Mythologies: Studies in Poetry, Drama and Music.* Cambridge: Cambridge UP, 1994.

Whigham, Frank. *Seizures of the Will in Early Modern English Drama.* Cambridge: Cambridge UP, 1996.

————. "Sexual and Social Mobility in *The Duchess of Malfi.*" *PMLA* 100 (1985): 167–86.

Wiesner, Merry E. *Women and Gender in Early Modern Europe.* Cambridge: Cambridge UP, 1993.

Wiles, David. *Tragedy in Athens: Performance Space and Theatrical Meaning.* Cambridge: Cambridge UP, 1997.

Willbern, David. "Shakespeare's Nothing." *Representing Shakespeare: New Psychoanalytic Essays.* Ed. Murray M. Schwartz and Coppélia Kahn. Baltimore: Johns Hopkins UP, 1980. 244–63.

Williams, Bernard. *Shame and Necessity.* Berkeley: U of California P, 1993.

Williams, Gordon. *A Dictionary of Sexual Language and Imagery in Shakespearean and Stuart Literature.* 3 vols. London: Athlone, 1994.

Williams, Linda. *Viewing Positions: Ways of Seeing Film.* New Brunswick: Rutgers UP, 1994.

Wilson, Luke. "*Hamlet,* Hales v. Petit, and the Hysteresis of Action." *ELH* 60 (1993): 17–55.

Winnett, Susan. "Coming Unstrung: Women, Men, Narrative, and Principles of Pleasure." *PMLA* 105 (1990): 505–18.

Woodbridge, Linda. *The Scythe of Saturn: Shakespeare and Magical Thinking.* Urbana: U of Illinois P, 1994.

————. *Women and the English Renaissance: Literature and the Nature of Womankind 1540–1620.* Urbana: U of Illinois P, 1984.

Woolf, Virginia. *A Room of One's Own.* New York and Burlingame: Harcourt, Brace, and World, 1957.

Wright, Louis B. *Middle-Class Culture in Elizabethan England.* 1935. Rpt. Ithaca: Cornell UP, 1958.

Wymer, Roland. *Webster and Ford.* London: Macmillan, 1995.

Zeitlin, Froma I. *Playing the Other: Gender and Society in Classical Greek Literature.* Chicago: U of Chicago P, 1996.

Zunder, William and Zuzanne Trill, eds. *Writing and the English Renaissance.* London: Longman, 1996.

Index